FOR KING
AND
COUNTRY

Dungannon and District in
The Great War

Vol. 1

Sarajevo to the Somme 1914 - 1916

Robert Butler

Derek Gallagher • Trevor McKay

For King and Country

Dungannon and District in The Great War

Vol. 1 - Sarajevo to the Somme 1914 - 1916

Robert Butler

Derek Gallagher • Trevor McKay

ISBN 978-0-9954708-0-4

Published by
KILLYMAN & DISTRICT CULTURAL GROUP
49 Killybracken Road, Dungannon, Co. Tyrone BT70 1NU

June 2016

Printed and Bound in Northern Ireland

Front Cover Image:
Captain Thomas Ucher Caulfield Knox (Lord Northland)
2nd Battalion Coldstream Guards, killed in action on 1 February 1915 at La Bassee
Former Worshipful Master of Killyman District LOL No.1 and Commanding Officer
Dungannon Battalion UVF (1913)

Back Cover Image:
Privates James and John Cumberland
9th Battalion Royal Inniskilling Fusiliers, killed in action on 1 July 1916 at the Somme
Members of Kilnacart LOL 296 and Derrygortreavy UVF (1913) Company

For
Denis Boyd

"Onward Christian Soldiers
Marching as to War"

Contents

Foreword

On the Dungannon and Moy war memorials are inscribed the names of 597 people from the locality who paid the ultimate sacrifice in the Great War, many of them were members of local Orange lodges sadly there are many others who are not remembered on these or other memorials.

As you read through this book you will come across the names of people from both sides of the community you have heard of and in some cases their names appear as wounded only to reappear in another chapter as being "killed in action". Many families had brothers and daughters who enlisted and in some cases fathers and sons. I hope in some way this book paints a picture of the life of those individuals during those dreadful years and maybe help shed some light on their reasons for enlisting.

I have the honour of being the Worshipful District Master of Killyman District Loyal Orange Lodge No. 1, Co. Tyrone and in 1914, when war was declared, my Grandfather, William John Rea, (an army reservist) enlisted with the Royal Inniskilling Fusiliers. He served in France along with his two brothers Bob and Hamilton. Their names are listed on the Roll of honour in St Anne's Church, Dungannon. One story handed down within the family was of my Grandfather being wounded and missing for 2 days before his brothers found him.

Since 1795 when the Orange Order was formed there have been Orange lodges in the Dungannon area. The earliest records dates back to 1798 when A.B. Dawson was installed as the first WDM of Killyman District. In those days there were only seven lodges in the District. By 1914 the District lodge had grown to 23 lodges and 676 brethren and Viscount Northland had been installed as WDM on the untimely death of his predecessor Hunt Chambre. Viscount Northland was also Commanding Officer, Dungannon Battalion of the Tyrone Ulster Volunteer Force in 1913.

On the 5th August 1914 the day after war was declared, Viscount Northland re-joined his former Battalion in the Coldstream Guards and along with many other reservists was despatched to the Western Front. Before leaving Dungannon, Northland encouraged the men under his command in the "Volunteers" and in the Orange Order to enlist. Many of these did so in great numbers with the 9th Batt. Royal Inniskilling Fusiliers, better known as The Tyrones.

The author of this book Bro. Robert Butler, LOL 93, Killyman District No. 1. Many hours of research by Robert and his two assistants Wor. Bro. Trevor McKay, LOL 178 and Wor. Bro. Derek Gallagher, LOL 708 have gone into the production this book. Their painstaking research has uncovered a list of 98 members of the Lodges in Killyman District who served with 42 paying the ultimate sacrifice. The names, numbers and lodges of these Brethren have now been preserved for all time. Of these 98, 4 were awarded Military Medals for their gallantry.

In this period of commemorations, this book, the first in a series of three, is a timely and significant addition to the history of this area. The book conveys the reader from the assassination of the Grand Duke in Sarajevo to the withdrawal of the 36th (Ulster) Division from the Somme area in July 1916 due to the heavy losses and casualties inflicted during the first days of that notorious battle. It also covers other campaign fronts such as Gallipoli, East and South West Africa.

The 2nd and 3rd editions will explore the periods from the Somme to the Armistice and finally from the Armistice to the formation of Northern Ireland.

> *"Young men approaching manhood and young women approaching womanhood should read it and ponder over the example their predecessors have set them. For all who read will realise that in the great struggle which convulsed Europe for more than four years the men of Ulster did not fail"*

These words were penned by Field Marshall, The Lord Plumer in 1922.

I hope that this book and the others to follow, will be read, not only by the relatives of those that served but by all - young and old . . . Lest we forget.

Kenneth D. Montgomery

Worshipful District Master,
Killyman District LOL No. 1, Co. Tyrone

Chairman, Killyman & District Cultural Group

Acknowledgements

I would like to thank everyone who has assisted me with this book.

In particular I want to acknowledge the unfailing commitment of Trevor McKay and Derek Gallagher. I am grateful to Trevor for designing the book and making the arrangements to have it printed. I am deeply indebted to Killyman & District Cultural Group who financed the publication of the book.

I must extend special thanks to fellow Tyrone man, Robert Corbett, for his constant encouragement and support. Quite simply without Robert's assistance this book would never have been completed. Of course it helped that Robert had a personal interest in the project: his grandmother's first husband, Lewis Meenagh, was one of the Dungannon men killed during the First World War.

I also want to express my sincere gratitude to all those who provided information and images for the book, especially the Mid Ulster Branch of the Friends of the Somme.

I am also grateful to my friends who travel on the train with me to work. For the past few years they have not only tolerated my obsession with the First World War, but have been very supportive.

Lastly, but by no means least, I wish to thank my wife, Linda, and my family. They encouraged and supported me throughout this project, despite the fact that it often meant that I spent time working on "the book" when I should have been with them or doing something else. Thank you for your patience and forbearance.

Of course any errors or omissions are my responsibility and if I have prevented any more able person from writing this book, I apologise.

R.B.

Introduction

Although not an historian, I have always had a keen interest in the First World War. This prompted me to begin research to identify the people from Coalisland who served King and Country in this conflict. This encouraged me to find out more about the role played by other local people in the war and, consequently, the scope of my project soon broadened to cover the wider Dungannon area. I also became convinced that the experiences of the local men and women who served should be documented to make them accessible to future generations. I was, therefore, delighted when Killyman and District Cultural Group asked me to write this book.

To obtain information about the men and women from the Dungannon district who served in the war, I trawled the contemporary editions of local newspapers, particularly the Belfast Newsletter. I also consulted the online databases of the Cookstown and Dungannon War Dead compiled by the Mid Ulster Branch of the Friends of the Somme. I was astounded and somewhat overwhelmed by the huge amount of information available and soon realised that it would be necessary to present my findings in two volumes.

This volume covers the period from the outbreak of the war in August 1914 to the early days of the Battle of the Somme in July 1916. It tells the story of the local men who fought and the women who served as nurses. I have attempted to provide details about as many local people as possible, but undoubtedly I will have failed to mention some. This is partly because there are more comprehensive records for the individuals who were killed than those who survived. The period from July 1916 to the signing of Armistice in November 1918 will be covered in a second volume, which will be published in 2018.

Critically what this book illustrates is that men and women from all social backgrounds served King and Country during the First World War. This included both Protestants and Catholics, unionists and nationalists. They were ordinary people who did extraordinary things. For me, they are all heroes who deserve to be remembered.

Robert Butler
2 May 2016

Chapter 1

1914
The Opening Months

Sarajevo and the Countdown to War

THE SPARK in 1914 that lit the fuse which led to the outbreak of the First World War on 4 August was the assassination of Archduke Franz Ferdinard, the heir to the Austro-Hungarian throne, and his pregnant wife, Sophie, in Sarajevo on 28 June 1914. The assassin was a Serbian nationalist, Gavrilo Princip. The murder of the royal couple, in the capital of Bosnia, caused widespread international outrage and it ushered in the so-called July crisis, which culminated with the outbreak of War in August 1914.

The summer of 1914 Europe was a tinder-box waiting to explode. While the assassinations in Sarajevo on 28 June 1914 did not make the First World War inevitable, it did trigger an intricate series of competing alliances involving all the main European empires that ultimately led to the outbreak of the War.

The Austro-Hungarians blamed the Serbian government for the assassinations and issued a ten-point ultimatum. Serbia accepted nine of their conditions, but partly rejected the demand that Austrian officials should be involved in investigating the assassinations on the grounds that it undermined Serbia's sovereignty. With Germany's encouragement, Austria-Hungary declared war on Serbia on 28 July 1914.

Russia, bound by a treaty to Serbia mobilised its huge army to support Serbia. Germany, which had a treaty with Austria-Hungary, viewed the Russian mobilisation as an act of war against its ally and declared war on Russia on 1 August 1914. This prompted France, which had a treaty with Russia, to mobilise its military forces, although France still had grave doubts about whether Britain would come to its aid.

The Germans now faced the prospect of a war on two fronts, against the French in the west and the Russians in the east. To defeat the French quickly, the Germans had a plan to attack France by marching through Belgium. But Belgium was a neutral country and, moreover, both Germany and Britain were long-standing guarantors of its neutrality. On 3 August when the Belgium, government rejected German demands to march unhindered through Belgium, Germany declared war on France and invaded Belgium. When Germany did not respond by 11pm London Time on 4 August to the British ultimatum that German forces withdraw from Belgium, Britain was at war with Germany.

Declaration of War

4 August 1914

At 11.17pm it was announced that a state of war existed between Great Britain and Germany.

Late last night it was reported that the Government had received news of the sinking of a British mine-laying vessel by the German navy. The destroyer Pathfinder was chased, but eluded her pursuers.

Great Britain delivered an ultimatum to Germany yesterday, and demanded a reply by midnight. This action followed Germany's declaration of war on France and Belgium and the receipt of official news during the forenoon of the invasion of Belgian territory.

The Premier, in announcing the Government's momentous action to the House of Commons, stated that early yesterday morning Germany was asked for an assurance that her demand upon Belgium would not be proceeded with, and her neutrality should be respected.

An immediate reply was asked for, and a message was received from the German Foreign Secretary to the effect that no Belgian territory should be annexed but that Germany was compelled to disregard Belgian neutrality owing to fears of a French attack through that country.

News also reached London that the German army was marching into Belgium.

Thereupon the British Government repeated its request for an assurance of Belgian neutrality on the same lines as that given by France, demanding that a satisfactory reply should reach London before midnight.

This grave announcement was received with loud cheers.
Great Britain is prepared for war. The Navy is mobilised and at sea; the army is being mobilised. Men and youths are flocking to the colours, and crowds besiege the recruiting offices. [1]

Mobilisation and Recruitment

When war was declared the British army consisted only of volunteers. Men volunteered for duty, with no compulsory service being imposed. The army was made up of regular soldiers who enlisted for seven to eight years with the colours (active ranks) followed by five or four years in the reserve, the total term being twelve years.

In 1914 on the eve of war the strength of the British regular army in Great Britain and the Colonies was 156,110 officers and men. In addition there were 78,400 troops serving in India. The regular Reserve, all trained men numbered 146,000, with the Special Reserve, partially trained men, numbering 63,000. However in August 1914 the British army was considered to be 12,000 men short of its establishment.

The second line behind the regular army was the Territorial Force. On the outbreak of the War this force numbered 250,000 men, some 63,000 below its proposed strength of 313,000. The Government's apathy towards the army not being at full strength can possibly be explained by its firm belief that a strong Navy would protect Great Britain from any peril.

The Empire could call on men from its Dominions but some were better prepared than others. India for example had a splendid native army with a military strength of 164,000 men and an additional 35,700 in the reserves. On top of this there were 20,000 Imperial Service Troops maintained by the native Indian states and 42,000 European and Eurasian volunteers.

Australia which had a system of compulsory military training from 1911, had a total of 170,000 men who had received some sort of military training.

New Zealand had a Territorial Force of 30,000, but in South Africa despite the Defence Act 1912, which rendered all citizens liable to compulsory service, the South African army was still in the process of organising when war broke out. The Canadian Dominion had a trained force of 3,500 officers and men, with a militia of 73,900.

Despite being fit to call on the Dominions of the Empire, it would take time to move these men and the resources they required to the front line.

So while the Empire was mobilising the German's were on the march through Belgium and heading for France.

Britain did have plans in place for an outbreak of war. The plans allowed for an Expeditionary Force of 160,000 men, mostly regulars to be deployed. The logistics of this call up was in the hands of the War Office and on the outbreak of war, a series of Acts of Parliament was speedily passed in order to meet the requirements of the emergency. Despite these plans, the fact remained that no large army could be placed on the continent immediately.

Scenes of mobilisation in Ulster were reported in the *Belfast Newsletter* on 4 August 1914, including a description of unusual scenes at Larne Harbour on the night of 3 August:

> *The occasion being the departure of local reservists who had been called up for service. The Town, Harbour and Victoria companies of the Ulster Volunteer Force were mobilised with full equipment, and marched to the quay, where a crowd, numbering eight or nine hundred spectators, had assembled. Several of the departing men were members of the Volunteer Force, and their send-off was of a most enthusiastic character. The Volunteers lined up facing the quay and presented arms. The National Anthem was heartily sung, as well as other patriotic songs, and just before the boat sailed "Auld Lang Syne" was feelingly rendered. This was followed by ringing cheers and the discharge of fog signals.*

Imagine the hustle and bustle in the homes, streets, villages, towns and cities of Ireland in those early days. Indeed, Ulster was embroiled in its own political crisis, but despite the Home Rule question being unresolved, Sir Edward Carson was unequivocal in his stance on what should happen if the Empire became involved in a war. Carson's telegram to Mr R. Dawson Bates secretary of the Ulster Unionist Council on the 4 August 1914, shown overleaf, was carried in the *Belfast Newsletter* the next day:

The effects of the Empire going to war were quickly seen in and around Dungannon, with the *Belfast Newsletter* reporting on 6 August that:

> *All the leading officers of the Dungannon Battalion Ulster Volunteer Force have also been called up, including Viscount Northland, Major*

VOLUNTEERS AND THE CRISIS.

MESSAGES FROM SIR E. CARSON.

"First Duty as Loyal Subjects."

HOME RULE CONTROVERSY.

An Unprejudiced Position.

The recent announcement by Sir Edward Carson that if required by the Government a large body of the Ulster Volunteers would be willing and ready to give their services for home defence, while others would be willing to serve anywhere they might be needed, has met with widespread approval throughout the Imperial province, and there is every indication that there will be a prompt and practical response to any call that may be issued. The organisation has attained a remarkably high standard of efficiency, and the aptitude and discipline of the rank and file have won the favourable comments of many military officers of distinction. Yesterday Sir Edward Carson sent the following telegram to Mr. R. Dawson Bates, secretary of the Ulster Unionist Council :—

All officers, non-commissioned officers and men who are enrolled in the Ulster Volunteer Force, and who are liable to be called out by His Majesty for service in the present crisis, are requested to answer IMMEDIATELY His Majesty's call, as our first duty as loyal subjects is to the King.

(Signed) EDWARD CARSON.

2

Alexander, C.M.G.; Major E Milnes-Gaskell, and Mr Percy Mallett, battalion instructor. A large number of Unionist Volunteers assembled on the railway platform to bid farewell to Mr Mallet, battalion instructor, and Mr David Williamson, and Mr Stevenson, second in command, presented Mr Mallet with a purse of sovereigns.

In the same report, the *Belfast Newsletter* described the unprecedented scenes in Dungannon, where a number of army reservists from within the ranks of the Irish National Volunteers had been recalled to the colours. They paraded through the streets to the railway station accompanied by the local nationalist flute band playing the "Marseillaise" and a number of Irish National Volunteers (INV) wearing bandoliers marching behind. On departing the station on the mail train loud cheers were raised and the band gave a rendition of "The girl I left behind me" and "Auld Lang Syne". Similar scenes of reservists belonging to the Cookstown Battalion of the Ulster Volunteer Force (UVF) and Nationalist Volunteers from the town were reported leaving on the same train for regimental headquarters that same day.

Such scenes were being repeated the length and breadth of the country with reservists and those in the special reserve being mobilised. Many men returned to serve the colours in regiments they had previously served without being asked. Men reported to their regimental headquarters all over the British Isles to serve "King and Country" many being cheered off by large crowds from the local railway stations and ports.

In Ireland while unionism was embracing, what it saw as its duty to King and Country, nationalism was somewhat more in a quandary. Certainly nationalists in the army reserve did return to the colours and some others did enlist, but much speculation existed regarding nationalist loyalty and whether it was dependant on the implementation of Home Rule. Proof that all was not well within nationalism in County Tyrone could be seen manifesting itself in Cookstown and Pomeroy with the return of reservists to the colours in early August 1914. The *Belfast Newsletter* reported that in Cookstown when a draft of North Irish Horse and a considerable numbers of reservists were leaving for their regiments chants of "Home Rule" were heard coming from nationalists while Unionists rendered "Rule Britannia." The events that took place in Pomeroy were described as follows:

The army reservists from Pomeroy district had a hearty send-off at the railway station on the evening of the 7th inst, from a large crowd of Unionists. In marked contrast was a large number of Nationalists, who booed the reservists and sang "A nation once again." After the train had departed and until the early hours of the morning the Nationalist Volunteers paraded the village singing "The Boys of Wexford" and other airs. A very similar scene was enacted on the following evening when both forces of Volunteers assembled at the railway station in connection with the departure of the final batch of reservists, and it was with the utmost difficulty that an encounter between the parties was averted.[3]

Mobilisation was being carried out at speed and many reservists and special reserve from the Dungannon area would have made their way to the Omagh Depot. The events from Friday 7 August show how quickly mobilisation was taking place and the logistics of onward movement:

Scenes of popular enthusiasm marked the departure from Omagh on Friday night of the last detachment of the army reserve of the Royal Inniskilling Fusiliers, and the streets were lined with thousands of Loyalists, who joined in wishing them God-speed. About 500 men were conveyed from Omagh by special train. Long before the departure of the troops a company of Ulster Volunteers assembled outside the depot gates, and as the military appeared the Volunteers, with torchlights, formed a triumphal procession to the railway station. Three bands, including the fine band of the Royal Inniskilling Fusiliers, under Sergeant-Drummer Turnbull, were in the procession, and cheers were raised by the assembled crowds on the route. At the railway station a guard of honour of the Ulster Volunteers had been drawn up on the platform, and a pipers band, composed of pipers of L.O.L. 937, and the Omagh Boys' Brigade, played loyal airs as the men entrained. Cheers were given for the Inniskillings, and were heartily responded to by the troops, who joined with the civilians in singing patriotic songs and choruses. "God Save the King" being sung with great enthusiasm just before the departure of the train. On Saturday afternoon the 3rd Battalion of the Royal Inniskillings (special reserve), about 750 strong, under the command of Colonel J. K. McClintock, D.L., left the town.[4]

The Omagh Depot in the early days of mobilisation was used as a rallying point for the men reporting, and from there they were moved quickly to their battalions in preparedness for going to France. Omagh would however become a centre for training recruits in the future. Captain A. St. Q. Ricardo DSO (Adjutant Tyrone Regiment UVF) was placed in command. Captain Ricardo would go on to play a hugely influential role in the war, especially for the people of Dungannon and Tyrone.

The initial mobilisation of the regular army, reservists and special reserve was over by mid August and many of these men landed in France as part of the British Expeditionary Force (BEF). They were about to see action on a scale unimaginable before the commencement of the war.

Kitchener's New army

At the commencement of hostilities between Britain and Germany in August 1914, Ireland had been in the middle of the Third Home Rule crisis. Some would argue that Germany viewed the situation in Ireland as being so grave that it would prevent Britain from engaging in a war.

Lead by Sir Edward Carson, with Sir James Craig at his side Unionism in Ireland had embarked on defending the civil rights of its people and resisting the Third Home Rule Bill. Carson and Craig in conjunction with the Ulster Unionist Council drew up a strategy of protest against the Third Home Rule Bill. The so called Covenant trail, a whistle stop tour of Ulster undertaken by Carson commencing in Enniskillen on 18 September 1912 and culminating with a rally in the Ulster Hall on the night of Friday 27 September, saw unionist men and women prepare for the signing of the Ulster Covenant and Declaration respectively on Saturday 28 September 1912. Almost half a million men and women signed the Covenant and Declaration in total. The Covenant as penned by Thomas Sinclair saw the men of Ulster declare that they would oppose Home Rule by all means necessary. Ulster Day, as it became known was a solemn occasion and a day for religious reflection. The Protestant churches played a leading role on Ulster Day, with services and signings taking place throughout the province.

Unionism militancy was harnessed in January 1913 when the Ulster Unionist Council created the UVF. The UVF grew in strength to approximately 100,000 men. Organised on a County basis, it stretched the length and breadth of Ulster and beyond. In Tyrone a UVF Regiment was raised consisting of five battalions, with an approximate strength of ten thousand men. The Dungannon Battalion was commanded by Lord Northland and numbered approximately 2,400 men at its height.

The UVF initially were nowhere near fully armed, however in late April 1914 this changed. Between 30,000 to 40,000 rifles and over three million rounds of ammunition were landed at Larne, Bangor and Donaghadee, and distributed throughout Ulster.

Prior to this gunrunning incident, an event had occurred at the Curragh Military Barracks, Co. Kildare, during March 1914, that significantly undermined the proposed use of the British army by the Government against the unionists of Ulster. Commonly known as the Curragh Incident or Mutiny, it involved a number of commissioned officers under the command of Sir Hubert Gough indicating that they would be prepared to resign their commissions rather than move against the Ulster unionists. While ultimately no officer either resigned or suffered a court martial, this event undermined the ability of the government to use the army against the unionists. The Dungannon UVF Battalion sent a telegram of congratulations and support to Sir Hubert Gough and his men for their stance they adopted.

While unionism had the UVF, nationalism had followed suit and had formed the Irish Volunteers in November 1913. They also armed themselves by landing guns at Howth on 26 July 1914. With drilling in both organisations taking place cheek by joule, extensive efforts were made by both leaderships to ensure that their paths did not cross or lead to sectarian violence. The UVF leaders issued strict orders advising their men that they had no quarrel with nationalism and their dispute was with the government and the government alone, over the imposition of Home Rule.

With the Third Home Rule Bill passing its final vote in the House of Commons on 25 May 1914, new ground was being broken. Whereas the previous two Home Rule Bills had been defeated in the Houses of Parliament, the situation was now very different. Due to the passing of the Parliament Act of 1911, the House of Lord's could no longer veto the Bill. Following the Bill's third defeat in the Lord's, the Parliament Act was enacted and Home Rule was now ready to be placed on the statute books as law. However, the determination of Ulster Unionist's to resist had not weakened.

As the summer approached, it appeared that Ulster was on the verge of civil war. The Ulster Provisional Government formed by the unionists met for the first time on the 10 July 1914, and the role of the UVF was to enforce its authority. With no solution to the Home Rule question looking likely the King personally intervened and summoned all parties to a conference in Buckingham Palace on the weekend 21-22 July in an attempt to resolve the crisis. The failure of the Buckingham Palace Conference to find a resolution saw Ulster and Ireland hold its breath in anticipation of future events. On the eve of the conference the Dungannon Battalion of the UVF were undertaking field operations in Roxborough Demesne, Moy, where its members were being trained in the use of a Maxim Machine Gun. A week after the Buckingham Palace conference failed to reach agreement, events that would ultimately lead to War in Europe, rather than Ireland, began to dominate affairs in the Palace of Westminster.

At the outbreak of the War and the disembarkation of the BEF to France, the drive to recruit men into Earl Kitchener's New army was stepped up. Kitchener, saw the men in both the UVF and the Irish Volunteers as being a fertile recruiting ground. However, differing opinions between the leaders of Nationalism and Unionism on how and under what conditions these men would be utilised began to appear. John Redmond, the leader of Irish Nationalism seemed to be pushing for full implementation of Home Rule before he would advise the Irish Volunteers to enlist. On the other hand Sir Edward Carson believed, that due to the seriousness of the international situation, the only wise course to take was to drop all controversial matters and for all sections to devote themselves wholeheartedly in support of the Government and the Empire in whatever measures may be thought essential.

It was against this backdrop in Ireland that Kitchener's appeal for men was launched.

With the resignation of Colonel Seely from his position as Secretary of State for War just shortly before hostilities broke out, the duties of the role had been taken over by the Prime Minister, pending a new appointment. The press sought the appointment of Lord Kitchener to the post. Lord Kitchener was viewed as being the military colossus of the day, and was described as "Cromwellian" by the Observer.[5] He was held up as a hero by much of the general public for the role he had played in the latter part of the Boer War where he was Commander-in-Chief of the British Forces. It was felt that Kitchener imbued a feeling of national solidarity. Despite vacillating, the Government finally appointed Kitchener as War Secretary on Wednesday 5 August 1914.

Lord Kitchener did not subscribe to the argument that the war would be over by Christmas. He set to work immediately urging recruitment, and on 6 August an increase in the size of the army by 500,000 men was authorized by Parliament.

On 7 August the recruiting appeal began, and the creation of Lord Kitchener's New Armies started:

YOUR KING AND COUNTRY NEED YOU

A CALL TO ARMS

An addition of 100,000 men to His Majesty's Regular army is immediately necessary in the present grave National Emergency. Lord Kitchener is confident that this appeal will be at once responded to by all who have the safety of our Empire at heart.

TERMS OF SERVICE

General service for a period of three years, or until war is concluded.
Age of enlistment, between 19 and 30.

Recruiting offices were over whelmed by eager volunteers, but given the incapability and confusion that reigned in authority the first 100,000 of this new army were not obtained until 25 August. By 28 August the age limit for enlistment was raised to 35. By 15 September over 500,000 men had volunteered and a further 500, 000 had been authorised by Parliament to be recruited. Further authorisation was given for 1,000,000 men to be recruited in November, and by 21 December a further recruitment of 2,000,000 men had been authorised.

During August 1914 plans were made to form six divisions from the first of these recruits. The First New army or K1's, as they became known were to be mainly formed on a territorial basis. Of these six divisions the 10th was composed of newly formed or "Service" battalions of all the Irish line regiments. The division would be known as the 10th Irish Division for no more reason than it was to be recruited from Irish line Regiments and its geographical location. The10[th] Division would be commanded by, Lieutenant General Sir B. T. Mahon, KCVO, CB, DSO and would have two training centres, Dublin and the Curragh.

The 10th (Irish) Division

Recruiting to the new Division started immediately within the Dungannon area and the men of the locality would not be found wanting in enlisting for King and Country. Examples of this early enlistment could be seen at the evening service on Sunday 23 August 1914 in Moy Parish Church. Under the charge of Mr Alexander Robinson, JP and Mr William Gilmore the Moy Company, Dungannon Battalion UVF paraded to the service, as 23 of the company were leaving the next morning to join the colours in response of Lord Kitcheners appeal. The rector Rev. C. F. Archer BA made special reference to this fact in his sermon. A large congregation was present that night and you can only wonder at what thoughts were going through the minds of those in attendance that summers evening.

In the evening of Monday 24 August public meetings were arranged in both Dungannon and Moy. Addressing these meetings were Major W. F. Hessey DSO, Reserve of Officers and Captain A. Ricardo DSO respectively. Captain Ricardo was in charge of arrangements for raising two new battalions in Tyrone to be known as the 5th and 6th Battalions, Royal Inniskilling Fusiliers, which in turn would form an integral part of the 10th Irish Division. While much focus in and around Dungannon was on recruitment to the 5th and 6th Battalions Royal Inniskilling Fusiliers, the proximity of the surrounding area to Armagh and the recruitment depot of the Royal Irish Fusiliers would see some locals enlist in these regiments also. Recruitment took place to the 5th and 6th Battalions the Royal Irish Fusiliers and along with the 5th and 6th

Inniskillings they would form the 31st Brigade of the 10th Irish Division.

At that meeting in Dungannon on the evening of 24 August three local companies of the local UVF Battalion were on parade with rifles and full equipment. Large crowds of spectators were also in attendance. At this meeting it was arranged that those members of the local UVF who intended to join the new battalions would leave by special train for the regimental depot at Omagh on Wednesday 26 August and receive a public send off. The *Belfast Newsletter* reported these events in its paper dated 27 August as follows:

> *A scene of great enthusiasm was witnessed in Dungannon yesterday afternoon when over 100 members of the local battalion of the Ulster Volunteer Force left by special train for Omagh for the purposes of joining the new 5th and 6th Battalions of the Inniskilling Fusiliers. The men paraded at the Royal School, and, headed by the Dungannon Brass Band, and escorted by a large number of the members of the battalion, wearing full uniform, marched through the principal streets to the railway station. The station premises were besieged by an enormous crowd, and the men had the utmost difficulty in making their way through them. As the train steamed off hearty cheers were raised, the band playing " See the conquering hero comes" and "Auld Lang Syne" and detonators were exploded. A number of the battalion officers had enrolled with the men and accompanied them, including Mr Robt. Stevenson (second in command), Messrs. R. H. Scott, W. T. Dickson, and V. Acheson, company officers, and Mr. W. Porter, half company officer. Viscount Charlemont and Mr. J. S. Crothers, officers of Cookstown Battalion, also accompanied the men.*

In the excitement and fervour of patriotism that was evoked at these meetings and parades some men may have become overwhelmed by the occasion, but the underlying motive for many was a sense of duty. Imagine the scenes of families saying goodbye to sons, as they puffed out their chests and put their best foot forward to do their duty for King and Country. As had been the case during the early days of the UVF, the Unionists of Dungannon and Tyrone generally were amongst the first to enlist into Kitchener's New army. The early enlistment of men from Tyrone is borne out by this report from the *Belfast Newsletter:*

> *On Wednesday evening about 250 men of three battalions of the Tyrone Regiment Ulster Volunteer Force marched into Omagh depot and enlisted*

in Lord Kitchener's new army for the period of the war. In the words of several of them, they had decided to adopt Sir Edward Carson's advice of " the Empire first," and were prepared to serve King George loyally during the present war, and at its termination finish up their own quarrel with regard to Home Rule. They were prepared to drop all question of politics for the present and to show that when the Empire needed help they could be relied upon to come forward and back up the army. One man remarked that their loyalty had been questioned, but they were now prepared to give an example of unconditional loyalty to the King and afterwards back up Sir Edward Carson in his fight against Home Rule. The men were attested and supplied with uniform and equipment. Since the mobilisation of the army and special reserves recruiting has been very brisk in Tyrone. Apart from the men enlisted for special corps or for the special reserve, about 500 men have joined at Omagh Depot for Lord Kitchener's new army, and two new battalions of Royal Inniskilling Fusiliers are being formed. [6]

Calls to enlist came not only from national figures like Earl Kitchener but also from influential local families, such as the Northland's in Dungannon. Viscount Northland lead by example and on the outbreak of war had rejoined his old regiment, the Coldstream Guards. Being Officer Commanding the Dungannon Battalion, UVF, he issued the following appeal to his men in August, prior to the commencement of recruiting to the 36th Ulster Division:

Ulster Volunteer Force. 4th (Dungannon) Battalion. – Your King and country need you now. Enlist at once for the duration of the war at the Inniskilling Fusiliers' depot at Omagh. No one should hesitate. No personal or political consideration should stop you. We will deal with politics later. I personally appeal to all members of the Dungannon Battalion to join at once and prove the loyalty of Ulster. Enlist today: Northland, lieutenant 4th Coldstream Guards. [7]

Viscount Northland was not only the commander of the 4th Battalion (Dungannon) UVF, as on the death of Hunt Chambre J.P. in August he took over the mantle of District Master of Killyman District LOL No. 1 County Tyrone. Viscount Northland's mother lodge was Dungannon Volunteer LOL 178.

The men of the locality responded to Kitchener's call and there was no prevarication. They went for King and Country when called upon. The article below that appeared in the *Belfast Newsletter* on 14 September 1914 illustrates this point:

The officers and men of the Dungannon Battalion of the Tyrone Regiment, Ulster Volunteer Force, have nobly responded to the call to arms; almost two hundred members have already volunteered to recruit the ranks of the two new battalions of the Royal Inniskilling Fusiliers. The men are being trained at the regimental depot at Omagh. A number of the battalion officers and non-commissioned officers enlisted with their men, including Mr Robert Stevenson, second in command; Mr W. T. Dickson officer commanding "C" Company; Mr R. H. Scott, officer commanding "D" Company; Mr Vincent Acheson, officer commanding "G" company; and Mr W. Porter, half company officer, "A" Company. Viscount Northland, officer commanding the Dungannon Battalion, left for the front last Thursday night with the 4th Battalion Coldstream Guards, in which he is a lieutenant; while Major D. Alexander, C.M.G., adjutant of the Dungannon Battalion, and Colonel R. T. G. Lowry, D.L., officer commanding "J" Company, have been appointed to various duties by the War Office. A large number of the non commissioned officers and instructors of the battalion had already gone on service with the North Irish Horse and various line regiments.

By mid September 1914 it was being reported that the 5th and 6th Battalions of the Royal Inniskilling Fusiliers were each at strength of 1,150 men. The new Battalions left Omagh by train to continue with their training in Dublin. The scenes were described as follows:

Scenes of remarkable enthusiasm were witnessed at Omagh yesterday on the occasion of the departure from the depot 1,250 men, forming the 6th Battalion Royal Inniskilling Fusiliers, for Dublin. The men, on marching out of the barrack square, were headed by the Tyrone Pipers' Band, which escorted them to the station, the route to which was lined with cheering spectators. An immense throng had assembled at the railway station, and many ladies and gentlemen who had taken a sympathetic interest in the soldiers while in Omagh obtained admission to the platform and exchanged farewell greetings with the men. The departure of the train was marked by loud cheering and the exploding of detonators.[8]

The appeal by Kitchener for recruits had been answered and the 10th Irish Division was formed. Men of Dungannon both, Nationalists and Unionists were amongst the first to answer the call and help fill the ranks of this new division.

By early December it was reported that Lieutenant Robert Stevenson, Dungannon had been gazetted as a captain in the 6th Battalion Royal Inniskilling Fusiliers. Lieutenant Stevenson had been second in command of the Dungannon Battalion UVF when he enlisted. He was known to many as a former Irish International rugby forward and being the President of the Irish Rugby Football Union in 1912/13. More commissions for the men that left Dungannon in those early days to enlist in the 5th and 6th Royal Inniskilling Fusiliers were to follow, as reported in the *Belfast Newsletter* on 6 January 1915:

> *Messrs. W. Porter and J. F. Hunter, of "A" Company, and Mr Stewart Moore, of "D" Company, Dungannon Battalion Ulster Volunteer Force, have received commissions in the 6th Battalion Royal Inniskilling Fusiliers. The new officers joined the Inniskillings in August last as privates, and worked their way up until they received their commissions. Lieutenant Porter is a brother in law of Mr R. W. Bingham, B.A. headmaster of Dungannon Royal School, and as half company commander of "A" company was very popular with the officers and men. He was in Canada for a number of years, and is well known in Rugby football circles. Lieutenant Hunter is a son of Rev. Dr. Hunter, who is at present engaged in missionary work in China on behalf of the Presbyterian Church. Lieutenant Moore is a well known sportsman, and was a frequent visitor at Elm Lodge, Dungannon, the residence of Captain R. H. Scott, of the 6th Inniskillings, and company officer of "D" Company, Dungannon U.V.F. Mr Ernest M. Harper, Dungannon, has also obtained a commission in the 7th Battalion Royal Munster Fusiliers. He had a distinguished collegiate career, and held the position of senior demonstrator at Queen's University, Belfast which he relinquished on receiving his commission.*

Captain Robert Hamilton Scott was a solicitor prior to enlistment, and played a major role in the anti Home Rule movement in Dungannon. He had close ties with the Bush LOL 163 and after the war the lodge took his name. Although not mentioned in the above newspaper report Robert Hamilton Scott's brother, Victor Scott also enlisted in early

August. Victor prior to the war had been a sub-commander in the Royal Irish Constabulary in Tipperary. He, like his brother, achieved the rank of Captain, but he served in the 5th Royal Inniskilling Fusiliers.

With the formation of the 10th Irish Division under way, focus in Ireland now turned to the formal positions of the UVF and Irish Volunteers. In the midst of the Home Rule crisis in July 1914 the UVF had been assessed by General John Gough VC, who formed the opinion that the Ulster Volunteers, with experienced leaders could become a formidable fighting force. Lord Kitchener arrived at a similar conclusion and by 7 August he had sent for Brigadier-General T. E. Hickman and said "I want the Volunteers". The reply was "You must see Carson and Craig".

From this point it would be fair to say the UVF would be utilised but in what format and when were the questions that still required answers.

The 36th (Ulster) Division

Unionism and Nationalism were still split on the issue of Home Rule. Against this backdrop, unionists, had some reservation about UVF members enlisting, but Carson never faltered from the belief that the men of the UVF would do their duty when requested. He worked with the War Office in order to create a separate Ulster Division, as he wanted the volunteers to serve together collectively. Indeed on the day that Lord Kitchener was meeting Brigadier-General Hickman, at a public meeting convened by the Lord Mayor of Belfast (Mr Crawford McCullagh), Captain James Craig MP gave one of the most important addresses on the position of the UVF. Craig advised that he and Sir Edward Carson were keeping in touch with the War Office to make sure the services of the volunteers would be used in the best possible way.

By early September Sir Edward Carson had persuaded the War Office to create a separate division in which the members of the UVF would enlist. The 36th (Ulster) Division was born and soon became an active symbol of Ulster's loyalty to Britain.

Wasting no time Sir Edward Carson speaking at a special meeting of the Ulster Unionist Council on 3 September 1914 delivered a very impressive and inspiring speech. During the speech he reviewed the situation that has been created by the great European conflict, and urged that in view of the grave menace to the Empire the Volunteers should respond to the call for men to assist in maintaining Britain's prestige against a formidable and ruthless foe. Carson went on to say:

> *Therefore our duty, in my opinion, is clear. Our country, our Empire, is in danger. We have never yet been beaten. We never will. (Cheers) We have got to win and we will win. (Renewed Cheers). And under these circumstances, knowing that the very basis of our political faith is our belief in the greatness of the United Kingdom, and of the Empire to our Volunteers, I say without hesitation, Go and help to save your country. (Loud and prolonged cheering). Go and help to save your country and to save your Empire, go and win honour for Ulster and for Ireland. (Renewed Cheers) To every man that goes, or has gone, and not to them only, but to every Irishman, you and I say from the bottom of our hearts "God bless you and bring you home safe and victorious" (Cheers) And, now gentlemen, we have had considerable communications with the War Office, and it is not necessary to go through these communications in detail, but we have a scheme and proposition which we are able to put before our men, and which can confidently commend to them, and which will keep our men together - (cheers), - that they should go as old comrades accustomed to do their military training together. If we get enough men to go from the Ulster Volunteer Force, they will go under the War Office as a Division of their own. (Cheers).*[9]

The resolution put to the Ulster Unionist Council was as follows:

> *That we deprecate any attempt to interfere with the truce agreed to between our leaders and the Government for suspension of the Home Rule controversy during the acute state of the present international troubles of the Empire: and we strongly urge that the existing political situation should be so dealt with by Parliament as that all parties may be assured that they will be in the same position on the termination of the war so far as passing legislation is concerned as they were before it became imminent.*
>
> *That being of opinion that the first duty at the present time of every loyal citizen is to the Empire, we not only cordially approve of the arrangement made by our leaders with the War Office for the enlistment for active service abroad of one or more Ulster Divisions, but we urge all Loyalists*

who owe allegiance to our cause and who are qualified to enlist at once for service with such Divisions.

That we appeal to Loyalists not already members of the Ulster Volunteer Force and who may be unable to enlist in the army to at once join such Force, on that vacancies caused in its ranks by enlistment in the army may be made good, and render the Force even more effective than it is now is for home defence and protection against trouble from whatever source or cause arising.

That we pledge ourselves to maintain the effectiveness of the U.V.F. during the war not only as a feeder to the Ulster Divisions in the field, but for the purposes for which it was originally formed, so that we may, in such manner as shall be found necessary, continue to resist Home Rule and carry out our Covenant.[10]

With the resolution passed, and agreement reached with the War Office, recruitment to the 36th (Ulster) Division started across the country in earnest. Captain Craig and Brigadier-Colonel Hickman were appointed as Chief Recruiting Officers.

The desire of the UVF command was to ensure the men would be the best equipped corps in the army. Such was this desire, that on Captain Craig's appointment he left the War Office and went straight to a firm of out-fitters and ordered 10,000 complete outfits. The funds for this were provided by Mr. Oliver Locker-Lampson, a staunch supporter of the Ulster unionist's cause, who on speaking to Craig wrote a cheque for £1,000 and promised that £9,000 would follow in a day or two. On enlistment the UVF members would be supplied with 1 great coat, 1 cap, 2 pairs boots and laces, 2 tunics, 2 pairs trousers, 1 pair putties, 1 cardigan waistcoat, 1 pair braces, 2 pair woollen drawers, 2 flannel shirts, 3 pairs woollen socks, 2 towels, 1 holdall, 1 hairbrush, and comb, 1 toothbrush, 1 shaving brush, 1 razor, soap, 1 knife, 1 fork, 1 spoon, 1 housewife (needles, thread &c.), 1 kit bag. The fact that the Ulster Division had a complete kit would ensure it was much better equipped than many other divisions who would commence training with limited resources and drill in civilian clothing.

With agreement in place for the raising of the Ulster Division, advertisements were placed virtually immediately in the newspapers, like this one below that appeared in the *Belfast Newsletter* on 8 September 1914, addressing the members of the UVF specifically, urging them to enlist.

TO THE MEMBERS

OF THE

ULSTER VOLUNTEER FORCE.

I greatly appreciate the action of our Volunteers in rallying so enthusiastically to my call for Defenders of the Empire. To those who have not already responded to that call and are eligible and can go, I say—QUIT YOURSELVES LIKE MEN AND COMPLY WITH YOUR COUNTRY'S DEMAND.

Enlist at once for the Ulster Division in Lord Kitchener's Army for the period of the War.

You were formed to defend our citizenship in the United Kingdom and the Empire, and so preserve our civil and religious liberty. Now the United Kingdom and the Empire are threatened we must fight with our fellow Britishers until victory is assured.

To those Loyalists who are not eligible or cannot go I appeal that they shall fill up the vacancies in the U.V.F. ranks caused by those going to the Front, so that we may maintain in fullest efficiency the Ulster Volunteer Force to protect your homes and hearths—that is a duty we owe to the Volunteers who go abroad to fight the country's battles. Let every Loyalist be faithful to the trust, and by each one doing his duty our country will be saved and our own interests preserved.

NO SURRENDER.

God Save the King.

EDWARD CARSON.

Old Town Hall, Belfast,
7th September, 1914.

A powerful supporting call for enlistment into the 36th (Ulster) Division by the prominent Orangeman the Earl of Erne K.P. appeared in the *Belfast Newsletter*, dated 14 September:

> *Brother Orangemen – The present war has arisen so suddenly that it may be well that I should address to you a few words as to its cause, the dangers which it threatens, and the duties which it imposes upon us all. It is well known that the Germans have been carefully taught that we are unworthy of the great position which the energy of our fathers has obtained for us, and that they are justified in seizing it for themselves. This they mean to do. The cruel blows which are falling upon our Belgian and French Allies are aimed through them at us. If we fail in this struggle we shall lose our Empire, our means of subsistence and even our very homes.*
>
> *Honour, duty and interest all call on us to be up and doing, for in this crisis everyman must serve his country to the utmost of his ability.*
>
> *Our leader, Sir Edward Carson, has made an arrangement with the War Office by which Ulster Volunteers can serve together as distinct divisions.*

I would most strongly urge that all who are able should avail themselves of this opportunity of showing the loyalty of Ulster Protestants. It is true that our own political future is uncertain, but (no matter what happens now) the question of Home Rule itself, and the methods by which men have sought to secure it, must at last be submitted to the judgement of the people, and the best way to secure the support of loyal Englishmen and Scotsmen is to earn it by loyal service in the time of the Empire's danger.

There need be no fears as to the safety of Ulster if her sons rally in defence of their King and country, for, the age limit for Volunteers having been fixed at 35 years, when these have gone there will still remain a large number of men amply sufficient to deal with any local trouble that, may arise.   God Save the King

(Signed) ERNE, I.G.M.

The infantry of the 36th Division was formed on perhaps the most strictly territorial basis of any division of the New Armies, based on the UVF's regimental structure. This had the great advantage that it engendered a natural companionship and spirit of pride in the unit. The company, was a close community, in effect an enlarged family.

By mid-September the success of the Ulster Division within Lord Kitchener's army was assured given the response of the UVF members throughout the province. Recruits were still coming forward in large numbers and on 26 September the *Belfast Newsletter* carried the following report that showed that recruiting to the Ulster Division had been brisk:

Recruiting for the Ulster Volunteer Division of Lord Kitchener's Army is going on briskly throughout the Imperial Province, and already there are about 10,000 members of the Force in camps at Ballykinlar, Donard Lodge demesne, Clandeboye, and Finner. The First Brigade, which is formed by the recruits from the Belfast Division of the Ulster Volunteer Force, is encamped at Ballykinlar and Donard Lodge under Brigadier-General G. H. H. Couchman, D.S.O.; the Second Brigade, established by the men from Antrim, Armagh, and Down, is at Clandeboye under Brigadier-General G. Hackett Pain, C.B.; and the Third Brigade, composed of the Tyrone, Derry, and Fermanagh battalions and the Young Citizen Volunteers is at Finner Camp, where it is expected Colonel T. E. Hickman, C.B., D.S.O., M.P., will be the Brigadier. The following details of the present strength of the Ulster Division will doubtless be read with interest:

THE FIRST BRIGADE
Ballykinlar and Donard Camps

Battalion	Officers	Men
7th R. I. R.	17	1,042
8th R. I. R.	11	992
9th R. I. R.	15	1,011
10th R. I. R.	15	1,050
	58	4,095

THE SECOND BRIGADE
Clandeboye Camp

Battalion	Officers	Men
Central Antrim	20	614
South Antrim	13	653
Armagh	17	910
Down	27	1,165
Medical details	1	8
	78	3,350

THE THIRD BRIGADE
Finner Camp

Battalion	Officers	Men
Tyrone	4	411
Derry	14	648
Fermanagh	3	138
Young Citizen Volunteers	7	1,000
	28	2,197
Total:	164 Officers	9,642 Men

The Third Brigade, which is being formed at Finner, is not yet up to full strength owing to the fact that accommodation has not yet been prepared for the entire number, and that the work of recruiting has not been completed. The other brigades are practically up to full strength.

By mid October the Ulster Division had been granted official permission by the War Office to have its own Divisional cap badge. This was unique to the Ulster Division, as no other division within the army had been given such an honour. The badge took the form of the Red Hand of Ulster and was made from bronze. Every member of the Ulster Division was to wear it to ensure that their comrades in other regiments would be able to recognise the division when it went to the front. The territorial designation "Inniskilling," "RIF." (Royal Irish Fusiliers) and "RIR." (Royal Irish Rifles) would be borne on the shoulder straps. The first reference that the Ulster Division would have this distinctive cap badge was made by Sir Edward Carson at the rally in Ballymena on 18 October 1914. The "Dixie", as it became known was produced and brought into use by the Division in March 1915. However, it was relatively quickly withdrawn and the Division would return to wearing the relevant regimental badges.

Recruitment to the Ulster Division was further enhanced as the War Office now wished to recruit the support battalions of Royal Engineers, army Service Corps and Medical Corps from within Ulster as well. It was also decided to raise a squadron of cavalry in connection with the Ulster Division, which would be an Ulster Squadron of the 6th Inniskilling Dragoons.

Advertisements, like the one below were placed in the *Belfast Newsletter* looking for recruits to the Royal Engineers and Inniskilling Dragoons.

NEW EXPEDITIONARY FORCE.

YOUNG MEN, Come and Join NOW

THE ULSTER DIVISION

Squadron of INNISKILLING DRAGOONS
now being raised at

ENNISKILLEN.

Men accustomed to horses are required for this Squadron.

MEN of the following Trades are also required
for the

DIVISIONAL FIELD COMPANIES OF THE

ROYAL ENGINEERS,

VIZ:—

Ship's Carpenters.   Railway Platelayers,
Farriers.   Scaffolding Men.
Quarrymen (used to   Ship Riggers.
explosives).   Wheelwrights.

ALSO FOR THE

Signal Company, Royal Engineers, Telegraphists, and
Men with a knowledge of Telephone Work.

APPLY, CHIEF RECRUITING OFFICE, CITY HALL.

GOD SAVE THE KING.

2039

11

By mid November recruits to the Army Service Corps were being sought under the heading The Ulster Divisional Train.

ULSTER DIVISION.

VOLUNTEERS·WANTED

FOR SERVICE IN

The ULSTER DIVISIONAL TRAIN

(ARMY SERVICE CORPS).

Which includes Horse Transport and Supply Branch.

RECRUITS REQUIRED FOR THE HORSE TRANSPORT OF THE
FOLLOWING TRADES:—

Carpenters and Wheelers, Coopers, Farriers, Saddlers, Collar
Makers, and Harness Makers, Shoeing and Jobbing Smiths,
Shoemakers and Tailors, Grooms and men accustomed to the
care of Horses.

FOR THE SUPPLY BRANCH:—

Bakers, Confectioners, Butchers, and Clerks.

PERIOD OF ENLISTMENT:— For duration of war.

Every possible arrangement will be made for the comfort of
those enlisting.

Every man enlisting will immediately be fitted out with Uniform.

Promptly have separation allowance paid to his wife and family.

APPLY TO RECRUITING OFFICER, CITY HALL.

GOD SAVE THE KING.

3895

12

The UVF was not only providing recruits for the front, they were also offering up practical help to assist with wounded soldiers and sailors. In an open letter dated 13 November 1914 they advised that they had placed at the disposal of the War Office the whole of their medical organisation, for the purpose of assisting in dealing with British wounded soldiers and sailors. It was proposed to fit out and fully equip the Exhibition Hall,

Belfast as a hospital, together with branch hospitals and convalescent homes in the country. The UVF leadership launched an appeal for funds in order to achieve this goal.

Recruitment for medical staff was also sought with this advertisement appearing in the *Belfast Newsletter* on 17 November 1914.

ULSTER DIVISION.

THERE ARE SEVERAL VACANCIES

FOR

YOUNG AND ENERGETIC

MEDICAL MEN AS OFFICERS,

BOTH FOR ATTACHING TO THE VARIOUS BATTALIONS AND FOR THE FIELD AMBULANCE UNITS.

Full particulars can be obtained from the

ASSISTANT DIRECTOR MEDICAL SERVICES, at the DIVISIONAL

HEADQUARTERS, WELLINGTON PLACE, Belfast.

4179

Recruiting to the Ulster Division continued with more and more specialist companies being formed One of these divisional companies was the army Cyclist Corps, its strength was to be 279 of all ranks and was formed by volunteers from the infantry battalions in the brigades at Ballykinlar (and Newcastle), Clandeboye and Finner and the officers were also to be provided with from within the commissioned ranks of the Division. The cyclists withdrawn from the various battalions were to be replaced by recruits. The rates of pay for non-commissioned officers and men were laid down in the pay warrant for infantry of the line, and the required standard to receive proficiency pay was being a proficient cyclist and having the necessary physical endurance.

36th (Ulster) Division.

A Divisional
Cyclist Company

is now being formed as part of the new Army Cyclist Corps.

What the Army Cyclist Corps is.

The Army Cyclist Corps is a distinct Corps like the Army Service Corps and the Army Flying Corps. It was formed by Royal Warrant in November, 1914, **owing to the valuable work done by Cyclists** in the present war.

While the pay is the same as the pay of Infantry of the line, there are special opportunities in this Corps for smart men to earn higher pay.

Duties.

Patrol work. Scouting and Reconnaissance. More exciting, adventurous, and responsible work than almost any other branch of the Service.

A Corps d'Elite.

For these duties a high standard of individual skill and resourcefulness is required. The Cyclist Company will be composed of picked men, active, young, and of self-reliance and initiative. Good eyesight is essential. Preference will also be given to any Recruits knowing French or German.

Constitution.

250 men are immediately wanted. From the number of inquiries already received, it is evident that there is a large class of men, suitable for the Corps, who have not yet enlisted, but to whom this service will specially appeal. They are now offered a chance of serving their King and Country in a picked Corps under advantageous conditions. They are invited to come forward and show that Cyclists are not behind their fellow-Ulstermen in patriotism.

Details.

First-rate quarters at Bangor. Full Uniform on enlistment. Private machines, if suitable, taken over by the Government at a liberal rate.

Separation allowance to wives and families of married men to begin at once.

Enlistment.

Enlist at any Recruiting station in Ulster. Free Railway Warrants to Bangor given to all Recruits.

All inquiries, whether in person or by letter, should be addressed to

LIEUTENANT WARMEN,
Headquarters, Ulster Division,
Wellington Place,
Belfast.

GOD SAVE THE KING.

6486

13

The establishment of these specialist units meant that the Division had to continue to recruit rank and file volunteers.

In the *Belfast Newsletter* dated 23 December it was being reported that the total strength of the Ulster Division as shown by the latest return issued by the Divisional Headquarters, Wellington Place, Belfast, was now 14,804, which left 1,417 men still to be enlisted to complete the strength. The table below hows the establishment and actual strength of the Division, exclusive of officers, and the units for which recruits were required, as well as the trades that were open in the Royal Engineers and army Service Corps:

	Establishment Men	Strength Men	Still Wanted
Infantry	13,911	13,107	804
Cyclist Company	271	20	251
Cavalry	165	198	--
R. A. M. C.	706	614	92
Royal Engineers			
Bricklayers	48	33	15
Carpenters and Joiners	80	47	33
Clerks	10	10	--
Harness Makers	7	--	7
Coopers	4	3	1
Masons	24	13	11
Draughtsmen	4	4	--
Electricians	4	4	--
Engine Drivers	8	8	--
Fitters/Turners	16	39	--
Blacksmiths	30	18	12
Surveyors	4	1	3
Tailors	8	8	--
Wheelwrights	10	2	8
Labourers	20	20	--
Shoeing and Carriage Smiths	4	2	2
Harness Makers	1	1	1
Telegraphist (Line)	26	1	25
Telegraphist (Office)	18	7	11
Blacksmiths	3	2	1
Signallers	50	37	13
Shoeing and Carriage Smiths	2	--	2
Drivers (Field)	114	72	42
Drivers (Signal)	44	1	43

	Establishment Men	Strength Men	Still Wanted
Army Service Corps			
Wheelers	27	27	--
Saddlers	22	2	20
Farriers	23	3	20
Motor Drivers	4	4	--
Drivers (Horse)	471	471	--
Clerks	20	20	--
Trumpeters	5	5	--
		*14,804	1,417

*Exclusive of officers

By the end of 1914 the Division was again recruiting for a highly specialised squadron. An advertisement appeared in the *Belfast Newsletter* on 28 December 1914 looking recruits for the first armoured motorcar squadron under the Admiralty. The men would hold naval rank, with approved men ranking as petty officers under the Royal Navy. Application was to be made to Lieutenant Wright RN, 19 Ormeau Avenue, Belfast, or to Mr Fred H. Rogers, OC UVF Motor Car Corps.

The armoured car division was the idea of Mr Oliver Locker-Lampson. He purchased the armoured cars in the name of the UVF, meaning that after the war, these would return to Ulster and be directly under the control of the Provisional Government that Craig and Carson had formed.

By the end of 1914 the 36th (Ulster) Division had filled the majority of its ranks but were still recruiting and training for the day they would be called upon to go to the front and fight for King and Country. In those early days it was truly an Ulster Division. The only element which had not been recruited from Ulster was the divisional artillery. It had been decided that it would take too much time to recruit and train the men for the artillery from within the ranks of the UVF.

While the Division was made up of a number of battalions, the one that the majority of men from the Dungannon locality joined was the 9th (Service) Battalion, Royal Inniskilling Fusiliers.

The 9th Battalion Royal Inniskilling Fusiliers (The Tyrones)

In Tyrone recruiting from the UVF was to the 9th Royal Inniskilling Fusiliers or The Tyrones as they were popularly known. Captain Ambrose St. Quentin Ricardo DSO was appointed commanding officer to the Tyrone's. Captain Ricardo had been Adjutant of the Tyrone Regiment UVF and had seen service in the North West Frontier campaign in India and in the Boer War. At commencement of the war Captain Ricardo took over the Inniskillings Depot in Omagh but on the formation of The Tyrones he was promoted to the rank of Lieutenant Colonel.

The Tyrones would train at Finner Camp, near Ballyshannon after it had been granted for exclusive use by the War Office to train the members of the UVF who enlisted. Training commenced on 21 September 1914 and recruits from the UVF from counties Fermanagh, Londonderry, Donegal and the Young Citizen Volunteers from Belfast would join the Tyrones at Finner. Accommodation for 4,000 men was to be made available at the Finner camp and that quiet part of Donegal must have wondered what had happened to it, with the commencement of training.

Concerned at the slowness of recruitment at the beginning, Lieutenant Colonel Ricardo issued a stirring recruitment poster on 21 September 1914 in order to increase the numbers in the ranks. He appealed to the loyalty of the men of Tyrone and was confident they would fill the 1000 men requirement for the Battalion from the County.

The initial officer structure contained many a face that the men would

TYRONE BATTALION
ROYAL INNISKILLING FUSILIERS.

The Tyrone Regiment Ulster Volunteer Force has been given the privilege of raising a Battalion of its own in the Ulster Division.

I have had the honour to be given the command of the Battalion, and I appeal to all Officers, not-commissioned Officers, and Men of the Tyrone Regiment U.V.F. to assist me in obtaining sufficient recruits from the County to fill the ranks of the new Battalion.

The nucleus of the Battalion has proceeded to Finner Camp, and a proportion of the Officers and non-commissioned Officers from the Regular Army are being posted to supplement the Officers and Section Leaders of the U.V.F.

It will need a strong effort by the Tyrone Regiment to furnish a thousand men, but as the Tyrone Regiment has always responded when called upon, I feel confident that the Battalion will be filled without difficulty.

It would greatly hasten the training of the Battalion if the ranks could be filled at once. The sooner we are trained, the sooner we shall be sent to support our comrades at the front.

The crops are now in, and with the winter coming on, there should be a better opportunity for the young men in the County to join their comrades already in training.

A substantial increase has been made to the Separation Allowance. The new rates will start on 1st October, and from that date the money will be paid weekly through the Post Office.

The new rates added to the Soldier's allotment of pay will be:—

FOR A WIFE WITHOUT CHILDREN ... 12/6
     „   „   WITH ONE CHILD ... 15/-
     „   „   „   TWO CHILDREN ... 17/6
     „   „   „   THREE CHILDREN 20/-

With 2/- in addition for each child above three (under 16 years of age).

Special arrangements are being made to see that the WIVES OF MEN OF THIS BATTALION RECEIVE THEIR SEPARATION ALLOWANCE WITHOUT ANY DELAY.

Every married man is recommended to bring with him a copy of his marriage lines and birth or baptismal certificates of his children.

HELP IS ALSO TO BE GIVEN TO MOTHERS, SISTERS, and others depending on unmarried Soldiers. Where a Soldier makes such an allotment to such dependent, the State will add a proportionate amount.

Question—*What is the easiest way for a man to enlist in the Tyrone Battalion ?*

Answer—OBTAIN FROM his U.V.F. COMPANY OFFICER A RAILWAY VOUCHER TO BALLYSHANNON, proceed to Finner Camp, and report himself to me at the first Camp on the right hand side of the road. BRING YOUR CHUMS WITH YOU.

A. RICARDO,
Commanding the Tyrone Battalion of the Royal Inniskilling Fus.

FINNER CAMP, BALLYSHANNON, 21/9/'

14

recognise from their days in the Tyrone Regiment, UVF. Those familiar faces must have helped make the transition from civilian life to army life easier in those early days. The initial Battalion command structure was as follows:

Lieutenant Colonel	A. St. Q. Ricardo DSO
Major	E. H. Llewellyn
Captain	J. G. N. Bomford
Captain	P. Cruickshanks
Captain	C. K. Weldon
Captain	R. L. Auchenleck
Second Lieutenant	L. Gibson
Second Lieutenant	J. Peacocke
Second Lieutenant	T. Robinson
Second Lieutenant	T. Fannon
Second Lieutenant	J. Weir
Second Lieutenant	H McClean
Second Lieutenant	J. H. Verner
Second Lieutenant	A. Coote
Second Lieutenant	R. A. Chambers
Second Lieutenant	R. Law
Second Lieutenant	W. S. Furness
Adjutant Captain	E. H. Bell
Quartermaster Lieutenant	F. Hodhson

By 8 October the *Belfast Newsletter* was reporting that The Tyrones had over 700 men, with recruits still coming forward. The battalion's training at Finner Camp was well under way, with route marches being a weekly occurrence. A favourite march for the battalion was to Rossnowlagh and back. Rifle work, field operations and night operations were continuing under company arrangements. Continued pressure was kept up on the recruitment front and Ricardo used his contacts within the press in order that the ranks would soon be at capacity.

Towards the end of November The Tyrones were nearing full strength of 1,100 men in the ranks and also having their full complement of officers. The ranks of The Tyrones had been supplemented by a contingent of Loyal Dublin Volunteers who had been active UVF supporters and a company of men from Tyneside that had been raised by Lt-Colonel Ricardo supporters in the area. Despite living mainly under canvas it was reported that training was being enthusiastically and energetically carried out and the men were in fine spirits.

As December 1914 progressed, there was much talk that the Tyrones

CARSON SAYS—
"Quit yourselves like men."

KITCHENER'S ARMY.

9th SERVICE BATTALION ROYAL INNISKILLING FUSILIERS (TYRONE VOLUNTEERS).

The TYRONE BATTALION at Finner Camp is now 864 Strong. **300 MORE** are wanted to complete.

COME AND JOIN YOUR COMRADES. If the Ballot Act is put into force you will not be able to choose your Regiment.

Hire this time with your Chums

to fight against your Country's enemies.

£9 for the half-year, with free food and clothing, AND YOUR WIFE AND CHILDREN WILL BE PROVIDED FOR; no delay now in receiving Separation Allowance.

IN THE TYRONES

you will find GALLANT COMRADES and a COMFORTABLE REGIMENT.

SURE PROMOTION FOR SMART MEN.

TRAIN NOW FOR EMPIRE AND ULSTER.

A portion of the Drum and Fife Band of the Battalion will attend all Hiring Fairs with a Recruiting Officer.

GOD SAVE THE KING.

Printed by "Tyrone Constitution," Omagh.

15

44

would be moving camp to Randalstown, with all the other battalions in the brigade with the exception the 10ᵗʰ Inniskillings, The Derrys, before the turn of the year. The camp at Finner had over 4,000 men at that stage, with as many of them as possible billeted in Bundoran. Those that couldn't be billeted in Bundoran were still under canvas and despite their hearty cheer, the appeal of constructed huts in County Antrim must have been hugely appealing given that the weather had been very trying during that autumn and winter. Christmas and the New Year came and went, but the Tyrones remained under canvas at Finner due to the accommodation not being ready at Randalstown.

Response from Dungannon

When the call came for the volunteers to enlist formally into the Tyrones the response within the Dungannon area was again immediate. The *Belfast Newsletter* on 12 September reported that:

> *In Dungannon on Wednesday 9 September 1914. A special parade of the "A" and "C" companies of Dungannon battalion Ulster Volunteer Force, was held in the Drill Hall, Circular Road, on Wednesday evening, when there was a large attendance. Mr D.D. Reid, B.L., Unionist and Candidate for East Tyrone, was present, and on behalf of Mr R. W. Bingham B.A. temporary commander of the battalion read Sir Edward Carson's address to the Ulster Volunteers, and emphasised the fact that the Ulster Unionist Council, the Unionist members of Parliament, and the rank and file of the Volunteers had the most implicit faith in their leader. Since Thursday last the members of the Volunteer Force were, at Sir Edward's request, joining the colours in thousands all over the province. He was aware large numbers of the members of the Dungannon Battalion had already volunteered and were in camp, but he appealed for every man present, who could possibly get away to join Earl Kitchener's army and serve his King and country. The proper way to defend their country was to meet the enemy in the open. (Applause) Arrangements were then made for enrolling a further contingent to join the new army, and the meeting terminated.*

Recruitment continued throughout the autumn. In Dungannon, parades were regularly held and large crowns gathered at the train station to show support for, and extend good wishes to, the men from the local UVF who were departing to enlist. Scenes, like the one described below were commonplace in those early months of the war:

An enthusiastic scene was witnessed at Dungannon Railway Station yesterday morning, when six local members of the Ulster Volunteer Force left for Enniskillen to join the extra Service Squadron of the Inniskilling Dragoons. A large crowd of towns people assembled and gave the departing troopers a very hearty send off. Loud cheers were raised and detonators were exploded as the train moved off. [16]

By the beginning of November, figures for recruitment from the Dungannon Battalion UVF were as follows:

Staff Officers		5
"A" Co'y.	Dungannon	23
"B" Co'y.	Dungannon & Moygashel	23
"C" Co'y.	Dungannon	30
"D" Co'y	Bush, Derrycreevy & Ballynakelly	20
"E" Co'y.	Newmills, Coalisland & Stughan	18
"F" Co'y.	Killyman & Tamnamore	12
"G" Co'y.	Donaghmore, Castlecaulfield Aughintober & Cullion	12
"H" Co'y.	Moy, Derryoghill & Drummond	20
" I " Co'y.	Benburb, Derrycreevy & Derryfubble	5
" J " Co'y.	Pomeroy, Drumballyhugh, Mulnagore & Ballymacall	5
"K" Co'y.	Derrygortreavy, Boland & Greystone	6

Total 179 [17]

Not all of these men were specifically recruited into the Tyrones as some within the UVF had been called up at the commencement of hostilities to their former regiments or were reserves or regular army. It does, however, give an indication of the numbers from the local UVF battalion who answered the call. It should also be noted that these figures relate solely to the Dungannon Battalion UVF and do not take account of any other recruitment.

Recruitment was a prime concern and Lt-Colonel Ricardo wanted to ensure the Tyrones were recruited primarily from the county and he ensured that recruiting campaigns were at the forefront of exercises in November. You can only imagine the excitement and pride in seeing relatives return to the town to encourage further recruitment. An example of such an event was reported in the *Belfast Newsletter* on 6 November 1914:

> *The old custom of "beating up" the fairs and markets for recruits was revived yesterday by the 9th (Service) Battalion Royal Inniskilling Fusiliers (Tyrone Ulster Volunteer Battalion). On Wednesday evening the fife and drum band of the battalion arrived in Dungannon by train from Finner Camp, under the command of Lieutenant Furness. A large crowd assembled at the railway station and lustily cheered the men as they emerged, and the Unionist inhabitants billeted them free of charge. After tea the band headed a route march of the Dungannon Companies Ulster Volunteer Force, Mr R. W. Bingham, B.A., officer commanding the Dungannon Battalion, being in charge. The men marched towards Castlecaulfield, and were met by the Castlecaulfield Company U.V.F., under the command of Mr D.A. Frizelle, commanding officer. Yesterday the band played through the town at intervals, and it being market day, much popular enthusiasm was evoked, and many recruits were made. Later in the evening the band proceeded to Moy to "beat up" the monthly fair to-day.*

The following week after this recruitment drive the *Belfast Newsletter* reported that a further detachment of recruits from the Dungannon Battalion of the UVF left the town to join the Inniskilling Dragoons. As a result, the number of members of the Dungannon Battalion UVF who had volunteered for active service had increased to 225.

One such recruit who left to enlist in the 6th Inniskilling Dragoon (Service) Squadron was Randall McManus from Dungannon. He enlisted in late October or early November. His, brothers, Hubert and David had chosen to enlist with the North Irish Horse on 5 October at Antrim.

The 16th Irish Division

Divisions within nationalism became apparent on the outbreak of war. Splits appeared as some saw "England's difficulty" as "Ireland's opportunity". However others, like John Redmond leader of the Irish Parliamentary Party at Westminster and long time advocate of Home Rule for Ireland argued that Nationalist's should come to Britain's aid in order to advance the Home Rule cause. Unionists viewed Redmond, with suspicion and hostility given his stance on Home Rule and this scepticism around Nationalist support for the war effort was further heightened when he initially only offered the Irish Volunteers for Home Service.

Nationalists by mid September felt that they were losing public support in Britain due to their stance on recruitment. This prompted Redmond to call for the formation of an Irish Brigade. However, it wasn't until Home Rule had been passed into law on 18 September 1914, (although immediately placed in suspension until the end of the war and until Parliament had an opportunity to consider making special provision for Ulster) that Redmond, in a speech at Woodenbridge, County Wicklow on 20 September 1914 told the Irish Volunteers assembled that they had a "two-fold duty" to defend Ireland's shores and also to fight "wherever the firing line extends in the defence of the right of freedom and religion in this war.

Redmond's support for enlistment into the British army caused a split in the ranks of the Irish Volunteers, with Eoin O'Neill and his supporters removing Redmond's nominees from the Volunteer's Provisional Committee. However by mid October Redmond had secured control of the vast majority of the Irish Volunteers, some 170,000 out of approximately 181,000 men. The organisation led by Redmond was renamed the Irish National Volunteers (INV). Many of these men, including nationalists from the Dungannon area volunteered to serve in Kitchener's army.

In September 1914, Kitchener granted Redmond his wish that an Irish Division be formed, that would become known as the 16th (Irish) Division. It was agreed that one of the three brigades in this new division would consist of men from the INV, namely 47th Brigade. Unlike the 36th (Ulster) Division, which sought to recruit all of its men from the UVF, the 16th (Irish) Division sought only to recruit a single brigade from the

INV. The other brigades within the Division would be filled with line battalions of Irish Regiments. In Tyrone after the 5th and 6th battalions of Royal Inniskilling Fusiliers had been formed and assigned to the 10th Division, it was decided to form two further battalions of this historic regiment. Known as namely the 7th and 8th Battalions they would go on to play a major role within the 16th (Irish) Division although they were not part of Redmond's 47th Irish Brigade.

By early October the *Belfast Newsletter* reported the transfer of portions of the 7th and 8th battalions to Tipperary:

> *Yesterday morning at about 5 o'clock troops composing portions of the 7th and 8th Battalions of the Royal Inniskilling Fusiliers left Omagh depot for Tipperary, where they will be quartered for the present. The men were headed by the Tyrone Pipers Band on the route to the station, and were heartily cheered by crowds of spectators. At the railway station a number of ladies and gentlemen who had taken a kindly interest in the men since their arrival in Omagh bade them good-bye and wished them all success. The men expressed themselves very deeply grateful for the kindness they had received from the Omagh people since they had came to the depot, and the train departed amidst loud cheering and the booming detonators. The officers in command were Second-Lieutenant W. Longworth and R. Grier.* [18]

Recruiting for the battalions continued through the autumn and by December it was reported that a large party of recruits who had been in training at the Inniskilling's Depot in Omagh were now to be transferred to Tipperary in order to fill out the ranks of the 7th and 8th Battalions, Royal Inniskilling Fusiliers. The *Belfast Newsletter* reported:

> *On Wednesday morning a large party of recruits who, since their enlistments, have been in training at the depot of the 2nd Battalion Royal Inniskilling Fusiliers, left Omagh for Tipperary, where they are being transferred to the 7th and 8th Battalions of the Royal Inniskilling Fusiliers to augment the strength of those regiments. The men, who were under the command of Lieutenant Hutchinson as far as Dublin numbered 147, of whom 76 are being allotted to the 7th Battalion R. I. F. and 71 to the 8th Battalion. Although many of them were but a short time in Omagh they keenly felt their departure, as they had experienced many kindnesses at the hands of the townspeople, and had been very popular in civilian*

circles. All the public halls including the Y. M. C. A. reading rooms had been thrown open to them, and writing materials and literature placed at their disposal. Their transfer leaves a big gap in the ranks of the 2nd Battalion at the depot, the total strength of which now is 131 men, of whom 20 are recruits, 60 trained soldiers and 5 officers and 32 non-commissioned officers, the remainder being in the band. [19]

The 16th (Irish) Division, like the 36th (Ulster) Division and 10th (Irish) Division, would continue to recruit and train the enlisted men during December. None of the three Divisions would see action in 1914 but all were being prepared to fight as the grim reality of stalemate on the Western Front and a long war was becoming more apparent.

Other Regiments and Divisions

While much of our focus is drawn to the three Irish divisions, it is important to emphasise that Dungannon was also represented in other British army regiments and military services. Indeed, by mid November 1914 the Roll of Honour for Drumglass Boy's National School, Dungannon showed that 36 of its old boys were on active service serving in the Inniskilling Dragoons, North Irish Horse, Royal Garrison Artillery, army Service Corps, army Medical Corps, Inniskilling Fusiliers, Royal Irish Rifles and Royal Irish Fusiliers, while one boy is serving on HMS Jupiter.

Men like Mr Richard A. Lloyd, son of Mr Averill Lloyd, J.P. Tamnamore, Moy, enlisted in Liverpool, and was given a commission in the 10th (Scottish) Battalion King's Liverpool Regiment. Richard or "Dickie" as he was known, was an exceptional Rugby player and had captained the Irish international team by that stage. Indeed while being educated at Portora Royal School, he had achieved great things in schoolboy rugby. The Lloyd's had close links with Tamnamore LOL 513 and the Apprentice Boys of Derry, Parent Club in those days and these links still continue to this day.

Mr Edward Caulfield Dudgeon, son of Mr Anthony Dudgeon, Island House, Coalisland, was gazetted as second lieutenant in the army Service Corps initially at the Curragh Camp, County Kildare. Lieutenant Dudgeon was educated at the Royal School Dungannon and was a member of E Company of the 4th Battalion of the Tyrone Regiment UVF.

A. H. Adderley, the youngest son of the Rev. Thomas Adderley, Killeshil Rectory, received a commission in the 3rd Cheshire Regiment. Adderley received his early education at the Royal School Dungannon and subsequently at Trinity College, Dublin and Durham University.

As already noted, some men enlisted in other Irish regiments, such as Hubert and David McManus who joined the North Irish Horse. The Daniels of Derryvale, Newmills, enlisted in numerous parts of the world like South Africa, Canada and England. The Howards of Annaginny, Newmills, returned to Regiments which they had served in prior to the war the Royal Lancaster's etc.

These are only some examples of the many men who enlisted both at home and throughout the Empire ensuring that the Dungannon area had answered the call of King and Country. They would serve in all theatres of battle in this global conflict.

Nursing

While Kitchener's new army sought men, the women were not to be outdone. The Red Cross Society was seeking nurses and some of the earliest to volunteer were from Tyrone. The structures that had been developed by the UVF to resist Home Rule had latterly included Nursing Corps. The women in these units were eager to help the war effort. In the autumn of 1914, 53 Ulster Volunteer nurses in Mid Tyrone when summoned together by their organiser, Mrs. Macafee, decided to place their services at the disposal of the War Office. They were subsequently augmented by a further 10. All these nurses had at least two certificates for first aid and home nursing. Like their men folk, some had been called upon for duty at the beginning of the war and had already rendered valuable service.

Further evidence of the vital role the Nursing Corps would play came in October 1914 when the North Tyrone Ulster Volunteer Force Hospital was accepted by the French Government for service at Pau, in southern France. The French Government agreed to support the hospital when established, but funds to purchase and transport the staff and equipment had to be found locally. This was achieved, and the *Belfast Newsletter* carried the following letter in its 7 October 1914 paper:

Ulster Volunteer Force Hospital For Pau (South France)

Sir – Your readers may be interested to learn that the above leaves Strabane on October 7th. The surgeon in charge, Dr. Norman Darling, has been appointed by St. John's Ambulance Association, as also the assistant surgeon and matron. The Ulster nurses comprise – Nurse Wright, Strabane; Nurse Patrick, Castlederg; Nurse Sullivan, Dungannon; and Nurse Jamison, Shimmon and Stevens, belonging to the U.V.F. Hospital and Nursing Corps, and Dr Clarke (anaesthetist). Other members of the staff include – Miss Sinclair, Holyhill; Miss Ballentine, Lisdivin; Miss Alexander, Moy; Miss Harkness, Plumbridge; Miss Dickson, Dungannon; Miss C. Moore, Strabane; Miss Thompson, Coolermony; Sergeant Buss, Mr Tom Lowry, Mr A. Downer, and Mr R. Hunter, all members of the U.V.F. Hospital and Nursing Corps. We wish to warmly thank all the volunteers, trained and otherwise, whom we have had reluctantly to refuse owing to the necessity of the majority of the staff understanding French. We would like to take this opportunity of thanking Miss Maud Herdman for her most generous gift of hospital equipment, and for her care in the packing and despatching of the hospital luggage, a very large order. We also wish to tender our best thanks to Mr Thos. Gallaher, Belfast Steamship Company, for the free transport of entire staff and baggage between Belfast and Liverpool. As the scheme has of necessity become larger than was first anticipated, we have to meet an expenditure first to last of about £300, so we trust that the great interest that North West Ulster has shown in the matter will have practical results in donations to meet our claims. We thank all those of every class who have already subscribed, but we earnestly plead for more. It has been suggested that any person or district subscribing £16 would provide for a bed among the 50 we are establishing, and it could be named by the donors. Mr W. B. Smyth, Strathfoyle, Strabane, has kindly consented to act as treasurer, but all donations should be sent to Baronscourt, where they will be thankfully acknowledged – Yours, & c.,

ROSALIND ABERCORN,
President St. John's Ambulance Association, Tyrone.

ROSABELLE SINCLAIR,
Battalion Organiser

October 6

While many think of enlistment in the First World War, in terms of men who went off to fight, it should be remembered that women, including some from the Dungannon area, also volunteered and played an important role in the service of King and Country.

The Western Front

The despatch of the British Expeditionary Force (BEF) in August 1914 was clouded in great secrecy, indeed the first portion of the force had been landed in Boulogne and Le Harve before the public at home were even aware it had left the shores of England. Boulogne was an ideal port to land the BEF as it had room to berth five transporters, which allowed for the disembarking not only of men but also of their guns, wagons, ambulances, horses, motor vans, indeed all the resources that the troops would need. The French Fleet, including submarines protected the BEF, as it made it's way across the channel.

Before leaving for France the commanding officers read to their men the following messages from the King and Lord Kitchener respectively:

You are leaving home to fight for the safety and honour of my Empire. Belgium, which country we are pledged to defend, has been attacked, and France is about to be invaded by the same powerful foe. I have implicit confidence in you my soldiers. Duty is your watchword, and I know your duty will be nobly done. I shall follow your every movement with deepest interest, and mark with eager satisfaction your daily progress. Indeed your welfare will never be absent from my thoughts.

I pray God to bless you and guard you, and bring you back victorious.

GEORGE R. AND I.
August 9th 1914 [20]

You are ordered abroad as a soldier of the King to help our French comrades against the invasion of a common enemy. You have to perform a task which will need your courage, your energy, your patience. Remember that the honour of the British Empire depends on your individual conduct. It will be your duty not only to set an example of discipline and perfect steadiness under fire, but also to maintain the most friendly relations with those whom you are helping in this struggle.

The operations in which you are engaged will for the most part take place in a friendly country, and you can do your country no better service than by showing yourselves in France and Belgium in the true character of a

British soldier. Be invariably courteous, considerate, and kind. Never do anything likely to injure or destroy property, and always look upon looting as a disgraceful act. You are sure to meet with a welcome, and to be trusted. Your conduct must justify that welcome and that trust. Your duty cannot be done unless your health is sound, so be constantly on your guard against any excesses.

In this new experience you may find temptations, both in wine and women. You must entirely resist both temptations and while treating all women with perfect courtesy you should avoid any intimacy.

Do your duty bravely. Fear God. Honour the King.

KITCHENER, Field-Marshal. [21]

On 10 August men of the Argyll and Sutherland Highlanders although few in numbers were the first of the BEF to put their feet on French soil. One can only imagine the sensation in the streets of Boulogne seeing these kilted men marching to the skirl of the pipes. To the French citizens in those streets the British and Empire had arrived. Much preparation was made in and around Boulogne with tented villages appearing for the continued arrival of the main BEF. The major elements of the BEF began arriving in their thousands on 13 August and this great invasion took a full 10 days to complete.

The marching of regiments through the French streets must have been a sight to behold, from the Highland Light Infantry and their pipes to the Connaught Rangers singing, "It's a long way to Tipperary". Regiments such as the Gordons, Royal Scots, Royal Irish, Royal Field Artillery, Royal Horse Artillery and Royal Garrison Artillery all were landed and made their way through the streets. The cream of the British army was there for the French to see. While the BEF arrived, the French in turn were heading for the frontline in order to stop the German advance. The enemy by this time had advanced to Brussels and were still on the move despite valiant Belgian resistance.

The following announcement that appeared in the *Belfast Newsletter* on 18 August 1914 advising the general public of the safe arrival of the BEF in France.

BRITISH EXPEDITIONARY FORCE,

Landed on French Soil.

OFFICIAL ANNOUNCEMENT

The Press Bureau last night issued the following :—

9.45 p.m.

The Expeditionary Force as detailed for foreign service has been safely landed on French soil.

The embarkation, the transportation, and the disembarkation of men and stores were alike carried through with the greatest precision and without a single casualty.

The director of the Official Press Bureau, Mr. F. E. Smith, M.P., stated last night :—" Lord Kitchener wishes me to add that he and the country are under the greatest obligation to the Press for the loyalty with which all reference to the movements of the Expeditionary Force in this country and to their landing have been suppressed. Lord Kitchener is well aware that much anpiety must have been caused to the English Press by the knowledge that these matters were being freely described and discussed in the Continental Press, and he wishes to assure the Press in this country that nothing but his conviction of the military importance to this country of suppressing these movements would have led him to issue instructions which placed the Press of this country under a temporary disadvanatge."

One of the first men from Dungannon to feel the effects of war was a civilian, Mr Thomas Gerald Hoy. The third son of Mr John Hoy, solicitor, Dungannon, Gerald had been teaching in a college in Berlin when war was declared. He had been taken prisoner in Germany on the outbreak of hostilities. During the early months of 1915 influential efforts were made to secure his release and it was being reported in the *Belfast Newsletter* that he had arrived safely in England by the end of March 1915.

Retreat from Mons

The BEF received its baptism of fire on 23 August 1914, at the never to be forgotten engagement at Mons. Commander in Chief Sir John French had ordered the BEF forward to join the French army at Charleroi. However before reaching Charleroi the BEF encountered cavalry patrols of the First German army. French decided that his five divisions should dig in at the Mons Canal and create defensive positions. The commander of the German First army was General von Kluck. Von Kluck was surprised to be engaged by the BEF and having been forbidden to outflank the BEF he launched a frontal attack. The BEF had 70,000 men and 300 guns to von Kluck's 160,000 men and 600 guns. The odds were stacked in favour of von Kluck but, the riflemen of the BEF inflicted heavy losses on the Germans. Indeed the efficiency of their rifle fire led von Kluck to assume they were using machine guns. The BEF suffered upward of 1,600 casualties that day and with the French in retreat Sir John French ordered the strategic retreat from Mons to the British second line of defence.

With the realisation that the Germans forces had superior numbers, the BEF would over the next few days fight a series of rearguard actions. They did make a stand at Le Cateau on 26 August, and again with the efficiency of rifle fire they greatly slowed the German advance allowing a further strategic retreat, despite the absence of flank protection. The stand at Le Cateau did not come without a cost, as the BEF suffered some 8,000 casualties. However the Germans also suffered high casualty rates, and crucially it further delayed the German army's march on Paris.

With the BEF tied up at Le Cateau, the French Fifth army launched an attack at Guise – St Quentin on 29 August. The German army knew the plans of this attack in advance. Despite this the French army did capture Guise but the position could not be held so the French withdrew, taking care to blow the bridges across the River Oise as they retreated. By 6 September the Germans had advanced to within 30 miles of Paris. The French and British armies were exhausted and had by then retreated to the south bank of the River Marne. Many believed Paris would fall, indeed the French Government transferred to Bordeaux given the seriousness of the situation. It was now or never for the Allies and despite their exhaustion they launched a counter offensive that split the German army. By 9 September, despite nearly achieving a breakthrough, the

German army began a retreat as ordered by the Chief of Staff Helmuth von Moltke which saw them fall back some 40 miles. The Germans dug in just north of the River Aisne and the Allies launched frontal attacks on the Germans on 13 September. The Germans had entrenched themselves well and with the aid of artillery pieces and machine guns defended their positions with much success. By 28 September the Germans were well entrenched and the attrition of trench warfare had commenced.

Accounts from Mons

First hand accounts of events at the front were received by people in Dungannon in letters sent from relatives or from injured soldiers returning home. Many of these letters and stories were carried in the *Belfast Newsletter.*

The newspaper report below details a letter home from Trooper Harry Newell, North Irish Horse, describing his experiences in the early days of the war:

> *Mr Joseph Newell, Perry Street, Dungannon has received a letter from his son, Trooper Harry Newell, of the North Irish Horse, under date 2nd inst., in which after stating the whereabouts of a number of other Dungannon men, and mentioning various articles which he was in need of he says – We left our kit bags at Havre, and I could only take with me what I stood in and what I managed to roll up in my great-coat. I can carry more stuff now owing to being in charge of a German saddle belonging to Mr Combe, which has two wallets in it. On arriving in France on the night of Saturday, 22nd August, we camped out until Monday afternoon a few miles outside Havre. After entraining until Tuesday we passed through Rouen and arrived in St. Quentin, remaining there until the following night. We then left for La Fere just in time to escape the Germans, who according to rumour, arrived in St Quentin just a few hours after we had left. We rode down to the south east of Paris and within fifteen miles of it to Tournay, where we joined the Fifth Division. All the luxuries the people possessed they showered on us, but things changed when we turned up north again to follow the retreating German, for he had rid the country very well on his way. We received regular and substantial fare, but when we cannot eat it or change its form*

we have to go hungry. As we follow up the Germans and sometimes thousands of our own troops you can guess how impossible it is to get anything to buy. Our fellows all have plenty of money, yet cannot buy matches. [22]

An account of Dr Robert Elliott's experiences shows that his efforts in the war came to a rather abrupt end soon after hostilities had commenced and how close he came to being executed as a spy:

Dr. Robert A. Elliott, son of the late Rev. Dr. Elliott, M.A., for some years rector of Pomeroy; nephew of Mrs Browne, Northland Row, Dungannon; and grandson of the late Dr. John Wilson Elliott, R.N., Deputy Inspector-General, Grange, Moy, had some unpleasant experiences whilst in the hands of the Germans. He was one of the first British officers to be taken prisoner by the German army, and the tale he tells is a remarkable one in many ways. Under the pretext of being suspected as a spy he was subjected to sundry cross-examination and trials, the issue of which really meant life or death to him, but finally he was able to prove that he was a bona-fide surgeon and not a spy, and henceforth he was treated as a prisoner of war and interned at various places along with other captured officers- British, French, Belgian and Russian. Dr Elliott left England on 16th August of last year as a member of Sir Fredrick Travis's first Belgian unit of the British Red Cross Society. On the 17th they went by motor car to Namur, and on the following day they encountered the pickets of the German army at Havelange, and, running into the head of the German army advancing on Namur, their car was stopped and searched for arms. With the other surgeons he was taken before the commander-in-chief of the German army and solemnly tried by court martial for espionage. He was cross questioned for about an hour and a half, stripped naked, and his clothes were searched for secret pockets. He had to undergo three trials, and to prove that he was a medical doctor was subjected to a professional examination, in which he was interrogated about medicine and about the details of a particular operation. He was sent to Cologne, and marched through the streets under a heavy guard, amid crowds that became extremely violent and obviously wished to lynch the party. He was there subjected to a further examination by three or four officers who constituted the court of inquiry, and until whose judgment was delivered he would have to remain in prison. On about the sixth day of his solitary confinement he was allowed to purchase tobacco, but was never allowed to supplement his dietary. On Friday, 8th January, the ten British Medical officers who were in Waggon House No. 9 at Magdeburg were summoned to the commandant's office, and Dr. Elliott's name, along with that of surgeon L. J. Austin, also of the London Hospital, was read from a large document, so they stood aside. The commandant then asked, "Are any of you gentlemen married?" One man held up his hand, and he was at once told "You can go home." Next the commandant said, "There are two more to go home and the matter must be decided by lots" Seven matches of varying lengths were than placed between his fingers, and Dr Elliott, who was lucky enough to draw one of the shortest matches, was allowed to go. He reached England after many difficulties on 12th January. [23]

The *Belfast Newsletter* dated 19 November 1914 carried an extensive interview with Private John Carberry of the Royal Irish Regiment, who had returned home to Eskragh, Dungannon, to recover from wounds received in the fighting on the banks of the River Aisne:

Private John Carberry, of the Royal Irish Regiment, has returned home to Eskragh, Dungannon, to recover from wounds received in the fighting on the banks of the River Aisne.

Interviewed by our correspondent he stated that he landed in France with the Expeditionary Force on 14th August. They were inspected by General Sir John French on their arrival at Boulogne, and camped there that night. On their arrival at Mons they found the Middlesex Regiment on outpost duty, and Carberry's battalion were served out with rations. These they had commenced to cook when the "assembly" was sounded, and almost immediately they were subjected to a terrific artillery fire from the Germans. One of the battalion's Maxim guns was smashed by a shell and the other was plied so hard that it became red-hot. There was no available water to pour on it, and it had to be abandoned. Corporal Smith tried to carry the gun away with him and got badly burned, and Major Ponsonby Downes succeeded in destroying it, but was mortally wounded in doing so. The enemy still continued advancing in large masses, and the British regiments were forced to retire. The Germans entered Mons in full force, and the British were again compelled to retire, and took up strongly entrenched position. The enemy continued to advance, and when they were within ninety yards Carberry's regiment was ordered to fix bayonets, but although the Germans outnumbered them by ten to one they were afraid to advance. During that time No. 6 Battery Royal Field Artillery became surrounded, but after a desperate fight they managed to get away without losing a man. On the following day they got a few hours' sleep, but in the afternoon German aeroplanes passed over them and signalled the range to the artillery, who opened fire. On 27th August they were still retiring, and he was billeted, with 23 others, in a one-roomed farmhouse, the owner of which had lost a leg in the Franco-Prussian war. The farmer showed them every kindness. On the following morning at an early hour, they were cooking their meals in the house when the enemy's artillery again opened fire. The shells kept dropping round them like hail. One of the "Jack Johnstons" fell between two platoons, but although the concussion knocked the men down, not one of them was injured. In the next village they met with in their retreat they entrenched in a garden and the electric light plant for lighting of the village was smashed to pieces quite close to them. A chapel had been turned into a Red Cross hospital, which was filled with wounded, but although the Red Cross flag was flying from the spire the Germans shelled it, with the result that some of the wounded were killed outright, and Carberry's officer, Lieutenant Cox, who was in the building at the time, was severely wounded before being rescued. Carberry vividly described the further retirement until they were fifteen miles off Paris, and the subsequent advance. At the passage of the Aisne the English force was subjected to very heavy artillery fire, and Carberry saw his chum turn a double somersault as they charged the bridge. He thought the man was blown to pieces by a shell which fell near him, but he was only slightly stunned by the concussion. The bridge was blown up as they were about to cross it, and a pontoon bridge was hastily constructed over which the men passed in single file. On the other side they found over 600 Germans lying dead in heaps. During the subsequent week the Germans relied mainly on their artillery and their "farewell" volleys from four o'clock to six o'clock each evening came as thick as hail showers. It was during that exciting time that Carberry was wounded by a German bullet, which ricochetted off a rock and struck him on the left hand, shattering the middle finger.

Under the title "Dungannon Man's Thrilling Story", Private J. Maguire's graphic description of the war and how he sustained his wounds was recorded:

Private J Maguire Royal Inniskilling Fusiliers, arrived in Dungannon yesterday from a private hospital in England, where he had been treated for severe wounds to the head, necessitating the insertion of a silver plate to replace portion of his skull, which had been shattered at the battle of St Marguerite. He had four ribs smashed, one of which had to be removed in hospital. These latter wounds were caused by Germans jumping on him in the trenches.

Interviewed by our Dungannon correspondent, Private Maguire stated he was a member of the reinforcing battalions which arrived while the struggle at Mons was proceeding. He had only been there half an hour when the enemy's shells commenced to burst among the British forces. His company was ordered to charge, and in the conflict a German caught his bayonet and hugging it, shouted "Gnade! Gnade !" ("Mercy mercy.") Maguire, however, says he gave him a kick which knocked him hors-de-combat. Subsequently, before the general retirement the Inniskillings were getting badly worsted, and an exciting incident took place. A private named Wilson had in his possession a green flag bearing the harp and motto "Erin-go-bragh" and on the order to charge being given Wilson pulled the flag from his pocket and headed the charge waving it. The "boys," with a wild shout rushed at the Germans and hacked their way through.

Maguire vividly described the retirement to Paris and subsequent advance. He states that on 28th October he was on outpost duty at daybreak, when he observed the Germans making trenches. He reported the matter to the corporal in charge, who replied that they couldn't be Germans, and that it could only be piles of tobacco leaf drying. Maguire answered, "You'll find that out in a minute or two." and almost immediately the battalion was subjected to heavy fire. Maguire was struck down by shrapnel, which caused the severe wound already mentioned. Private McCann who was beside him said "Maguire, you are knocked out this time," and proceeded to apply the field dressing. Maguire became unconscious, and on recovering he thought in his dazed condition that water was being given to him, but after a time he discovered that McCann's body was lying over him, and that it was his life-blood which was pouring down his throat. Maguire in his turn then attempted to attend to McCann's wounds, but the latter expired immediately after exclaiming "Good-bye, Maguire. I'll not forget you," Corporal Gibson was at that same time shot through the chest and fell across Maguire, and the Germans advanced and jumped into the trench on top of the bodies, thinking that the men were dead. A German jumping on Maguire broke four of the latter's ribs. To make matters worse Maguire's brother Thomas, who belongs to Stewartstown, County Tyrone *was killed only a few yards distance from him by a shrapnel discharge. It was on the same occasion that Captain Auchinleck, Captain Roe and Lieutenant Roberts, all of the Inniskillings, were killed, and Lieutenant Williams received a shoulder wound. The Germans were subsequently beaten back, and on the trenches being regained Maguire was removed to the base hospital and afterwards sent to a private hospital in Kent.* [24]

Corporal Wingfield Espey, North Irish Horse, from Lowertown, Bush, Dungannon, went to France with the First Expeditionary Force. In a letter home Espey told of how on arriving at Mons the first indications he received of the proximity of the Germans was seeing a number of their aeroplanes, and the British troops opening fire on them. Corporal Espey told of the lucky escape he had in those early days of the war when during the famous retreat from Mons he accompanied an officer and some men in charge of a machine gun which was placed on a little hill:

The Uhlans (German cavalry) could be seen advancing in swarms, and Espey's party signalled by means of a field telephone to the British artillery. They soon found the range, and for the first time in his life Espey saw both horses and men being literally blown into the air. The Uhlans rapidly retreated, but the shell fire followed them accurately and inflicted heavy losses. So interested were Espey and a companion in the scenes that they did not observe the departure of their officer and the other men. They were unable to overtake them, and had given themselves up for lost, as the Germans were rapidly approaching in the rear, when a British staff officer overtook them and on finding that Espey had not got a map of the country, directed him to through a wood which was in front. On entering the wood Espey found that it was intersected with cross roads every hundred yards or so, but taking his direction from the sun he and his companion fortunately debouched on a road filled with retiring British troops. [25]

It was a further two days before they found their squadron in the North Irish Horse. Espey would later serve as a member of Sir John French's bodyguard.

Corporal Wingfield Espey was a prominent member of the Orange, Royal Black and Masonic institutions in the Dungannon area. He was WM of RBP No. 4 at the outbreak of war, a member of Bush, LOL 163 and belonged to Masonic Lodge No. 185 Dungannon. Corporal Espey had also being instrumental in setting up the Bush Flute Band in 1911.

One of the first men from Dungannon to be reported missing and feared dead was Private Thomas Hayes of the Royal Irish Fusiliers. Having been posted as missing by the War Office since the Battle of Mons on 27 August 1914, and with no news of him, the family probably feared the worse. The *Belfast Newsletter* printed the following article on 22 March 1915 detailing that Private Hayes was in fact a prisoner of war. One can only imagine the relief of the family in finding out he was alive:

> The German Government has notified the War Office that Private Thomas Hayes, 2nd Battalion Royal Irish Fusiliers, whose relatives resides in Dungannon, is a prisoner of war at Senne, Germany. Private Hayes has been posted as missing since the battle of Mons on 27th August last, and as nothing had since been heard of him his relatives had feared the worst. His wife, who lives at Brighton, has also received a postcard from him stating that he was wounded at Mons, but has since recovered.

A further account in the *Belfast Newsletter* on 27 January 1916 reported that Private Hayes was by then in a prison lager at Dulmen, Germany, and had written to his relatives at Union Place, Dungannon. The article noted that Private Hayes was the youngest of eight brothers who served throughout the South African War, and that several of them were at present still with the colours.

Captain Robert Jackson Adams who was Adjutant of the 25th Brigade Royal Field Artillery, 1st army Corps, was another local man who was wounded in those early battles, although his wounds were not serious enough to keep him out of action. In a letter home to his sister Miss Adams, Torrent Hill, Newmills, Dungannon under the date 20 September he wrote:

> I am fit and well, and my hand is nearly quite well again. I had an exciting day on which it happened. I had four escapes, and only had my finger hit, and it caused no pain. I did not have to leave duty, and took the adjutancy when Blount was wounded (since dead). We had a lot of casualties. I feel quite safe with all such good people praying for me, and we are doing our work well. I don't think the Germans will forget the British soldiers in a hurry. They won't wait now, but clear out when they see the steel. The cavalry have done wonders, and so have the infantry, and the guns are doing good work as they always do. Every man is worth five Germans, and has accounted for more. I cannot tell you where we are, but all is well with us and the gallant little army.[26]

In mid November, Capt. R.J. Adams was promoted to the rank of Major.

Not all the Dungannon men were as lucky in those early exchanges as Major R. J. Adams. Private Edward Mulgrew, Irish Guards, suffered severe wounds during the retreat from Mons. During this rear guard action on 1 September 1914, Private Mulgrew was wounded in the side by shrapnel, but, worse was to follow. As he crawled to safety, Mulgrew was struck on the head and arm by portions of another shell, resulting in his arm being blown off at the elbow. Private Mulgrew returned to Dungannon on the 10 December 1914 for convalescence.

The Dungannon Fallen at Mons

The first Dungannon man to be reported as killed in action was Private Robert McShane (8751) of the 1st Battalion Royal Irish Fusiliers. Robert was born in Dungannon, and is recorded in 1901 census as being an orphan. He died in France on 27 August 1914. His grave is in Esnes Communal Cemetery, Cambrai. Robert wrote to his sweetheart on the 21 August 1914, saying:

Dear Martha,

Just a few lines in answer to your kind and welcome letter received yesterday (20th August). I expect this will be the last for some time because we have to go to the French Frontier by Monday. You need not write because I would not receive a letter. I will be able to drop you a postcard when I get out there. I am also glad to hear of the great reception you got at Sixmilecross. Do not be uneasy. By God's help I will return to you safe again. I am also glad that you got my watch. Dear Martha, don't fret about me. I want you to take sole possession of all I have. What is mine remember it belongs to you. You can auction all out if you think it foolish keeping the house on.
Remember me to your mother and Susy. Do not worry any more about me. You shall be alright. I will now draw to a close.

By remaining yours only.
Robert. Goodbye. [27]

The last word of Robert's letter is particularly poignant.

Private Armour Weir (8992) of the 1st Battalion Royal Inniskilling Fusiliers, who had been born in the Moy, is the next recorded death. He died of wounds as a prisoner of war on 2 September 1914. His grave is in Porte-de-Paris, Cemetery, Cambrai and his name also appears on the Moy War Memorial.

Private James Devlin (10583), 2nd Battalion Royal Inniskilling Fusiliers, died in a French hospital on 29 October 1914, as a result of wounds he received at Battle of Aisne on 21 October 1914. Private Devlin was a regular soldier having enlisted about twelve months prior to his death and went to France with the BEF on 8 August. The family lived at Railway View in Dungannon. Private Devlin's grave is in Cite Bonjean Military Cemetery, Artmentieres and his name also appears on Dungannon War Memorial. Undeterred by the death of their brother, Edward and Daniel Devlin volunteered and joined the Royal Dublin Fusiliers.

Ypres

By the end of September 1914, a 400 mile long trench line had emerged which ran, from Delle on the Swiss border to Nieuport on the North Sea coast of Belgium. The dilemma for the Germans was whether they could seize French ports such as Calais from the Allies' grasp. If the Germans has seized these ports it would have enabled them to impede the transport of troops and munitions from England to France. Whether it was a tactical error or not, the Germans decided to attack both Calais and Antwerp at the same time splitting their forces. They seized Antwerp, but in doing so allowed a large element of the Belgian army to escape and strengthen the Allies' lines. Calais remained in the hands of the Allied forces. Pushing out from this position the BEF First and Fourth army Corps took up positions along the Ypres Salient. The Third army Corps were centred at Artmentieres, and the Second army Corps at La Bassee.

The locality around Ypres was destined to become one of the most hotly and fiercely contested battle zones over the next four years. The First Battle of Ypres would commence in and around 14 October 1914. The Germans sought desperately to break the BEF and gain the coastal ports. Indeed, the German Emperor issued the extra-ordinary command to his generals to exterminate the BEF. While they did not succeed, it is fair to say that by the end of the year the original battalions of the BEF had suffered heavy loses.

The "contemptible little army", the alleged description the Kaiser had used for the BEF, had stalled the advance of the German war machine and put paid to German plans for a quick and decisive victory.

Accounts from Ypres

As the war progressed men continued to send stories home of their lucky escapes, while others gave brief accounts of the actions they had fought in and what they were witnessing. Very few details were given of the men's exact locations, due to censorship of their letters by senior officers.

One such description of a lucky escape came from Trooper Isaac Carter, North Irish Horse. Trooper Carter resided at Gortin, a small hamlet between Coalisland and Dungannon. In a letter dated 27 October 1914 he describes how during a charge his horse was shot from under him.

Driver Robert Lynn gave a detailed account of his experiences with the 87th Battery, Royal Field Artillery. From Mousetown, Coalisland, he was one of four brothers who were with the colours, and was a member of Coalisland LOL 93. In a letter he wrote to friends in Coalisland on 31 October, Lynn stated:

> *We are having a bit of a rough time here, with plenty of scrapping. I am still dodging the German bullets, though about a week ago we were in one position, and I thought it was all up with us. It started about three o'clock in the morning, and a terrible fire lasted all day; in fact a proper artillery duel. We had twelve casualties in our troop. My two horses got hit just as I was giving them a bit of spur to get out of range; but I dragged them on. I never was so glad to see a day over in my life. We had a few more severe days at the battle of the Aisne, but we never came as near the enemy as to-day. We were sure the guns were gone, as we had to leave them, but we went back with a rush and got them out again. You should have heard the Germans shout as they advanced. The Germans are very cruel, and sometimes it is all up with our chaps when they get into their hands. They have this country ruined, and it is sad to see every town you come to looted and destroyed, and some of the finest buildings you ever saw tumbled to the ground by shell fire, but their own country will suffer by and by.[28]*

With the return of soldiers from the front the people of Dungannon were getting first hand accounts of the war and the level of casualties that were being suffered. One first hand account was given by Private Hamilton Rea, 2nd Battalion Royal Irish Rifles on his return in December 1914. Private Rea who was from Milltown, Dungannon had been on outpost duty at Ypres when a British shrapnel shell struck a tree, and one of the bullets struck him on the back and penetrated his lung, the bullet had still not been extracted. He told how he had gone to France with the First Expeditionary Force, and took part in all the fighting from Mons to Ypres. He described the fighting as "desperate" and said that all the 21 officers of the battalion had been either killed or wounded, and the 1,900 men of the regiment had been reduced to 200.

Private Patrick Mulgrew, of the 2nd Battalion Royal Inniskilling Fusiliers, and his brother Edward (Irish Guards) also arrived home to Dungannon. Both had been wounded. Patrick was struck on 10 November 1914 on the foot by a shrapnel bullet and had to have two of his toes amputated. While the Mulgrew brothers returned home, Sergeant George Noble, Royal Field Artillery, relatives received notification that he was in a Torquay Hospital, suffering from severe injuries caused by shell fire in Belgium.

On 13 November 1914, Lieutenant Knox Patterson, 1st Battalion, Royal Irish Fusiliers, from Belfast wrote from the trenches to a friend in Royal School Dungannon. He gave a brief description of the weather, his health and the devastation:

> I am still in good health; in fact it is my greatest joy that outside the hourly risk which one must run here, my own physical condition is as good as it has ever been. It is raining frightfully now. Everything is mud, mud, mud and in the middle of it all the same picnic goes on – shells, bullets, fires and devastation. You can understand how great the noise and glare are at times when I tell you that two nights ago were repelling an attack in the middle of pouring rain, when a thunder and lighting storm came on. I didn't recognise as such until told afterwards. The noise and light were so customary to us.[29]

In a further letter to his parents, Lieutenant Patterson spoke of the bravery of the chaplains attached to the BEF:

The chaplains are brave fellows. There were two of them – one a Protestant, and the other a Roman Catholic – going up together in the face of death regardless of all except their duty.[30]

The Dungannon Fallen at Ypres

Dungannon men continued to fall at the front. Private John Dunne (7471), 2nd Battalion Royal Irish Regiment was killed in action on 19 October 1914 during the Battle of La Bassee. It is recorded that the 2nd Battalion Royal Irish Regiment were virtually wiped out during that battle. John had been born in Dungannon in 1874, worked as a coalminer in Sunderland and enlisted in Hamilton, Lanarkshire. He has no known grave but is remembered on a panel in Le Touret Memorial Cemetery, Le Touret.

The end of October and beginning of November 1914 saw a number of Dungannon men lose their lives fighting for the colours.

Private James O'Neill (2868), 2nd Battalion Royal Inniskilling Fusiliers, was killed in action on 31 October 1914 during the course of the battle that was ensuing at Ypres. A reservist, O'Neill rejoined the colours on 12 August and left for the front on 16 September 1914. From Wilson's Lane, Dungannon, Private O'Neill left a widow and two children on his death. Private O'Neill has no known grave but is remembered on the Ploegsteert Memorial, Comines-Warneton and his name also appears on the Dungannon War Memorial.

Private John James Ormsby (2050), 1st Battalion Irish Guards was killed in action on 1 November 1914. Born in Ballybunion, County Kerry, his father was in the Royal Irish Constabulary. Before the war John had been a Guardsman in the Irish Guards but left to become a policeman in the Royal Irish Constabulary. Living in Dungannon at the outbreak of war he re-enlisted with the Irish Guards. Private Ormsby was killed in action at Ypres and has no known grave. He is remembered on the Menin Gate Memorial and on the Roll of Honour in St. Anne's, Parish Church, Dungannon.

The family made many efforts to find out what had happened their son, including making repeated inquires to the War Office and Prisoner's

Bureau, but to no avail. In March 1915 they also sought information from any Guardsmen who had returned home from the front. On 30 June 1915 the *Belfast Newsletter* reported that a fellow Guardsman had mentioned in a letter that Private Ormsby had been killed.

> *Mr John K Kavanagh, Queen Street, Newry, having made inquiries as to the fate of a missing Irish Guardsman named John J Ormsby, who belonged to Dungannon, and was a member of the R. I. C., has received a letter from Private J. Cully a Newry man in the Guards stating Ormsby was killed on November 1.*

While this may have been of some relief to the family, it wasn't until April 1916 that the War Office officially confirmed that Private Ormsby had been killed in action 1914:

> *The fate of Private John G. (sic) Ormsby, Irish Guards, who had been reported missing since 6th November, 1914, has been investigated and his parents who reside at 5, Bellevue Terrace, Dungannon, have been notified that he was killed in action. At the outbreak of the war Private Ormsby had been a constable in the R.I.C. at Portarlington. He was then a reservist of the Irish Guards, and on being called up went to the front with the first Expeditionary Force.*[31]

It was, therefore nearly eighteen months after his death before Private Ormsby was confirmed as killed in action by the War Office. This was not unusual given the level of casualties incurred in the battles and the difficulty in obtaining accurate information.

Leading Stoker Frederick Ekin Bradley (302220), Royal Navy, died at sea on 3 November 1914. He was serving as a submariner on HMS Submarine D5 when a British mine sank it off Great Yarmouth. Frederick's father, mother and some of his siblings were living in Charlemont, Moy, at the time of his death. His wife lived in Plymouth. Prior to the First World War, Frederick had seen action in the Boer War and aboard HMS Hyacinth in the Somali Expedition against the Mad Mullah. Frederick was awarded a medal for that campaign.

A number of Frederick's brothers were already serving the colours with Canadian and Irish regiments. His brother Frank, who had volunteered on the outbreak of hostilities, was originally attached to the Canadian Gordon Highlanders. He returned to England on "Blockade Day" 18

February and was now serving with the 15th Battalion Princess Patricia's Canadian Light Infantry. Another brother, Rowland, was at the front with the North Irish Horse and a further brother, John, was a police constable in Belfast. His youngest brother, Harry, was an active member of the UVF and had responded to the call to join the Ulster Division, with a number of other men from Moy. However despite being in training for some time, Harry was rejected on poor eyesight grounds.

Trooper William Sloan (21205), 6th Inniskilling Dragoon Guards was killed in action on 6 November 1914. Trooper Sloan, the son of Robert and Mary Sloan, Donaghmore, was on duty with the 2nd Life Guards when he lost his life in the battle for Ypres. He has no known grave and is remembered on the Menin Gate Memorial, Ypres.

Private Robert J Averall (4247), 2nd Battalion Royal Inniskilling Fusiliers, was killed in action on at Ypres on 7 November 1915. As a reservist he had rejoined the colours on 7 August and left for the Western Front on 5 September along with Lance-Corporal Joseph McIntyre of Dungannon. Private Averall was from Brooke Street, Milltown, Dungannon. He was a member of Holdfast LOL 1620 and is remembered on their Roll of Honour. Private Averall has no known grave and is remembered on Ploegsteert Memorial and Dungannon War Memorial.

Private Daniel Donnelly (8752), 1st Battalion Royal Irish Fusiliers was killed in action on 14 November 1914. Daniel had been born in Dungannon in 1887 but had moved to Belfast and is recorded as living at 12 Getty Street. Private Donnelly is buried in Houplines Communal Cemetery, Armentieres.

The Christmas Truce

A first hand account of the unofficial truce held at Christmas 1914 was given by Lieutenant Davis Williamson, Royal Field Artillery, in a letter home to his father, Mr J. M. Williamson, Forthill, Castlecaulfield. On Christmas Day he wrote:

There was a sort of truce arranged to-day (Christmas Day) between some of our fellows and Germans in front of them. Although the regiments to the right and left kept firing spasmodically all day the others went across and they and the Germans exchanged tobacco and talked and sauntered about between the two lines of trenches. It was the queerest sight in the world to see two lots of men who a few hours before were intent on killing each other (and will be again tomorrow) talking together as if they were the greatest friends in the world. They even arranged a football match, and since I started writing this letter a telephone message has come through to say that the Germans had won by three goals to two. We all had Christmas cards from the King and Queen this morning, and this afternoon each received a little box from Princess Mary, with tobacco and pipe inside. It is very cold here now, but frosty. It is much better however than the rain. Indeed the country has a real Christmas look this morning with the boar-frost covering everything. We got shelled out of a farm we were occupying one day last week. They fired twenty four large "coal brace" at it but only one did any damage. It went through the corner of a stable and exploded inside, wounding three horses, one of which had to be shot. It was the colonel's favourite charger, a very magnificent black animal, and he was very sorry about it. [32]

As 1914 came to a close, the war had already touched many families in the Dungannon area. Some families had lost those closest to them and all had either heard about or witnessed the wounded returning home. It was becoming obvious that the war that many in August 1914 thought would be over by Christmas, had turned into a war of attrition with stalemate along a 400 mile trench line.

Chapter 2

1915
Stalemate in the Trenches

Preparing for Battle

By the beginning of 1915 Britain's small pre-war professional army was virtually decimated by the heavy losses suffered in the opening months of the war. While reserve and teritorial soldiers were taking the strain, it was apparent that it would be necessary to deploy the wartime volunteers recruited into Kitichener's New Army, including the three divisions raised in Ireland. All three divisions would go to the front in 1915.

Being at full battle strength the 10th (Irish) Division was the first of these contingents to go into battle on the Gillipoli Peninsula in August 1915. The role in this often forgotten theatre of war will be discussed later in this chapter.

Throughout most of 1915 recruitment and training for the 36th (Ulster) and the 16th (Irish) Division's would continue, prior to their departure to the Western Front towards the end of the year.

The 36th (Ulster) Division

In January 1915 the 36th (Ulster) Division commenced a new recruitment drive throughout Tyrone to raise a reserve company for the 9th Battalion Royal Inniskilling Fusiliers, the Tyrones. The *Belfast Newsletter* on 6 and 12 January carried the following articles detailing these efforts:

With the object of raising a reserve company for the 9th (Service) Battalion Royal Inniskilling Fusiliers (Tyrone Volunteers), Captain Fannon with Recruiting Sergeant A. M. Steen and 12 men of the battalion and band, set out yesterday on a four week's recruiting expedition in the Clogher Valley and other parts of Tyrone. Aughnacloy fair was visited yesterday and the party will proceed to Ballygawley, Caledon, Tynan and other parts of the county. During their visits they will be the guests of the local U.V.F. companies.

Dungannon cattle fair was visited yesterday by the band of the 9th Battalion Royal Inniskilling Fusiliers (Tyrone Volunteers), in charge of Captain Fannon, and accompanied by Recruiting Sergeant A. M. Steen and a number of men of the battalion. They are carrying out a recruiting campaign with the object of raising a reserve company for the battalion.

The band played selections through the town during the day and were escorted by an admiring crowd, and were successful in securing a number of recruits. A full parade of the Ulster Volunteers was held later in the evening and was addressed by Captain Fannon.

While this recruiting drive was taking place the Tyrones were preparing for a move from Finner Camp, County Donegal, to Shane's Castle in Randalstown, County Antrim. Details of their transfer to Shane's Castle were carried in the 20 January 1915 edition of the *Belfast Newsletter:*

Scenes of great animation were witnessed at an early hour yesterday morning at Bundoran when the full battalion of the Tyrone Volunteers 9th Service Battalion Royal Inniskilling Fusiliers was mobilised for the purpose of moving from Bundoran and Finner, where they have been quartered during the past five months, to Shane's Castle, Randalstown. The men with complete equipment, marched in companies to the railway station. Colonel Ricardo, D.S.O. officer commanding the battalion, being in command. Four special trains were requisitioned to convey the troops, and these were despatched from Bundoran at intervals of about fifteen minutes. The trains ran through to Omagh without a stop. There was much enthusiasm among the assembled crowds as the various contingents arrived at Omagh Station, many of the ladies and gentlemen who had taken a kindly interest in the welfare of the men, and had been most active in providing them with comforts, being present. At the other stations where the train stopped the Volunteers were given a rousing reception. It is pleasing to note that the men never appeared in better health and spirits, and that they have improved considerably in physique as a result of the excellent training received. The battalion is now well above its established strength, the last recruiting tour undertaken by Lieutenant Fannon having added about 70 men to the ranks. At Cookstown arrangements had been made by the ladies of the town to provide tea for the troops, but the wait was not long enough to permit of all being supplied. However buns and other eatables were distributed on a liberal scale, and a large number were supplied with tea. The trains steamed off amid waving of Union Jacks and the singing of "Tipperary".

Recruiting for the Tyrones continued during 1915. The patriotic fervor at these recruitment events was enhanced by the presence of the fife and drum band of the 9th Inniskillings. The *Belfast Newsletter* reported these recruiting drives in detail:

The recruiting detachment of the 9th (Service) Battalion of the Royal Inniskilling Fusiliers, accompanied by their fife and drum band, in charge of Sergeant Steen, visited Coalisland and Newmills on Tuesday evening, and obtained a number of recruits. The Newmills Company of the Dungannon Battalion U.V.F. paraded under the command of Mr Robert Daniel J.P., and addresses were delivered by Mr R. W. Bingham B.A. officer commanding Dungannon Battalion U.V.F., and other gentlemen. The detachment was afterwards entertained at Derryvale by the local Volunteers.[1]

On Friday, on the occasion of the monthly fair, Moy (County Tyrone) was visited by a detachment of the 9th (Service) Battalion Royal Inniskilling Fusiliers (Tyrone Volunteers), under the command of Captain Fannon, and accompanied by a fife and drum band, conducted by Sergeant A. M. Steen. The advent of the troops caused considerable stir. A public meeting, which was addressed by Captain Fannon, was held in the Courthouse, and several recruits were enrolled.[2]

Many members of the Dungannon Flute Band, who had enlisted nearly to a man in 1914, played in the Tyrones band. Moreover, Private James Stewart, who had been Secretary of Newmills LOL 183 prior to his enlistment, played a fife in the band. His fife was presented back to the lodge by his family in January 2015 and is now on display in Newmills Orange Hall.

On the weekend of 12 and 13 February 1915 all the men of the Tyrones were granted leave. It was reported that the vast majority of the men availed themselves of this concession. A special train on the evening of Saturday 12 February conveyed the men from Randalstown to their various destinations in County Tyrone. Having spent a very happy time with their relatives and friends, on the Sunday afternoon a special train left Strabane about four o'clock and picked up contingents of the battalion at the various stations throughout the country. On their departure large numbers of people assembled at the stations to give the volunteers a very hearty send off.

Recruitment was still a major issue for the 36th (Ulster) Division as spring approached and calls were made by a wide variety of people to encouraged further enlistment. The Church of Ireland Primate, Archbishop John Baptist Crozier, wrote in April 1915 to his clergy asking them to do all that was in their power to further the enlistment of men into the Ulster Division. Archbishop Crozier said that this was a matter of terrible urgency and added that he was relying on the help of the clergy 'for the cause of honour and truth, for our Empire and our native land'.

Recruitment into the Ulster Division was also aided in April 1915 when men under the height of 5 feet 3 inches were allowed to join its ranks. The *Belfast Newsletter* on 8 April reported:

> *The War Office has now authorised the enlistment of men under 5ft. 3in. and not below 5ft in height, with a minimum chest measurement of 34in., for the Ulster Division. It is desired that this announcement should be widely known, as this is the first opportunity, which has been afforded men under 5ft. 3in. of joining an Ulster corps. Hitherto they have had to be sent to bantam battalions in England and Scotland, and it was only on Friday evening that a batch, left the city for the 17th Royal Scots in Edinburgh. The Birkenhead Bantams (15th Battalion Cheshire Regiment) have also received a substantial number of recruits from Belfast and district.*

By mid April the Ulster Division was nearing its full strength, but still required men with specialist skills and trades as demonstrated by the following article which appeared in the *Belfast Newsletter* on the 13 April 1915:

> The following are the classes of recruits still required by the Ulster Division:-

(1) Pioneer Battalion		215
(2) Cycle Company		47
(3) Royal Engineers:-		
(a) Field Company:-		
Collar Makers		3
Smiths		6
Wheelwrights		3
Shoemakers		2
Platelayers		9
Electrical Engineers		6
Electricians (special for searchlights)		3

Motor Mechanics	2
Plumbers	4
Cooper	1
Shoeing and Carriage Smiths	2
(b) Army Service Corps:-	
Bakers	33
Butchers	10
Saddlers	6
Wheelers	3
Farriers	5

A major event was on the horizon for the 36th (Ulster) Division, namely a divisional parade through the streets of Belfast on 8 May 1915. In the period leading up to the parade the *Belfast Newsletter* reported:

The Headquarters Staff of the Ulster Division is making rapid progress with the arrangements for the forthcoming Divisional parade in Belfast, and the date of the display has been definitely fixed for Saturday, 8th May, instead of the 1st prox., as was originally contemplated. It will be on a more extensive scale than any previous military parade in Belfast, the proposal being to bring practically the whole of the Division to the city for the occasion, and public interest in the event is naturally enhanced by reason of the fact that it will provide the only opportunity which the public will have of seeing the various units together. The Ulster Division, which is commanded by Major-General C. H. Powell, C.B., is largely composed of members of the Ulster Volunteer Force and other signatories of the Solemn League and Covenant, whose patriotism has been amply demonstrated by the splendid manner in which they have rallied to the call of their King and country, and the citizens of Belfast, as well as Loyalists throughout the Imperial Province, will highly appreciate the arrangement to enable them to witness the men on parade. The outstanding feature of the parade will be a march past in the centre of Belfast, with the front of the City Hall as a saluting base, the three brigades and divisional troops subsequently proceeding by different routes through the city. The march past-always an imposing and impressive spectacle when trained troops are engaged- will probably commence at half-past two o'clock, and it is understood that the division will take from an hour and a half to two hours to pass the saluting base. The Lord Mayor (Mr Crawford McCullagh, J.P.) and the Lady Mayoress will witness the proceedings at this point. With the exception of the 10th Battalion Royal Inniskilling Fusiliers (Derry Volunteers) quartered at Finner, which is precluded from joining in the parade owing to the long journey from that camp to Belfast, and the details which will necessarily be detained in the various camps, the division will muster in the city, and it is estimated between 16,000 and 17,000 men will take part. It is well known that some of the battalions are from 1,200 to 1,300 strong, but it is probable that each battalion will be limited to 1,000 men, the remainder being detailed for duty in the camps. Major-General Powell will be the senior officer on parade, and he will be accompanied by his aide-de-camp. Second Lieutenant R. F. Henry, of the 15th Battalion Royal Irish Rifles, . . . An infantry division at war strength covers 8 miles for its fighting portion. 5 miles for its first line transport, and 1¾ miles for its ambulances and trains. The parade on 8th, will not extend to this length, however, owing to the absence of the artillery, which has not yet joined the division, the battalion at Finner, and details in camp, but it will be seen that the display will form a military spectacle such as has never before been witnessed in the city. It is expected that the parade will have a good effect on recruiting, and arrangements will be made for the enrolment of men either for the Ulster Division, the Irish Division, or any other unit that the applicant may desire.[3]

As the 8 May approached more details of the day's events were made public:

Major-General C. H. Powell, C. B. and the Headquarters Staff of the Ulster Division are making rapid progress with the arrangements for the display in Belfast on Saturday, 8th May. In addition to the march past the City Hall, there will be a review of the division beginning at 1 p.m. on a large stretch of ground between the Malone Road and the River Lagan. The approach to this area is by Deramore Park South, opposite St. John's Church, Malone. As far as is possible in the circumstances, facilities will be offered to the public to witness the review. Subsequently the troops, who will number about 17,000 will march in column to the centre of the city via Malone Road, University Road, Great Victoria Street, Fisherwick Place, and Wellington Place, passing the saluting base at the City Hall. The three brigades will then proceed to different parts of the city, but the length of the route to be traversed will depend upon the time available before the departure of the trains which will convey various units back to the camps.[4]

We understand that an invitation on behalf of the Ulster Division has been extended to Lord Kitchener to attend the divisional review, which, as already announced, will take place in Belfast on Saturday next, 8th May. The presence of the Secretary of State for War would naturally enhance the importance of the occasion, and throughout the Imperial Province the hope will be entertained that his Lordship will be able to accept the invitation. Good progress is being made with the arrangements for the parade. The general plans for the transport of the soldiers have been practically completed. All units in the division except the 10th Battalion Royal Inniskilling Fusiliers (Derry Volunteers), at Finner Camp, will, as already announced, take part in the review and parade. The 107th Infantry Brigade (8th, 9th, 10th and 15th Battalions Royal Irish Rifles) and the 108th Field Ambulance will proceed to Belfast by route march on dates and under arrangements for billeting to be made by the Brigade Commander. The 108th Infantry Brigade (11th, 12th, and 13th Royal Irish Rifles and 9th Royal Irish Fusiliers); from Clandeboye and Newtownards, will come to Belfast by rail on the day of the parade, returning by rail on the same evening. The 9th and 11th Battalion Royal Inniskilling Fusiliers, from Randalstown, will travel to Belfast by train. The 14th Royal Irish Rifles (Young Citizen Volunteers), from Randalstown, will come and return by route march on the dates to be arranged by the Brigade Commander. The 16th Royal Irish Rifles (Pioneers), from Lurgan, will travel to and from Belfast by train. The 17th (Reserve) Battalion Royal Irish Rifles, from Newcastle, will come by train, returning on the same evening. The 121st, 122nd, and 150th Field companies Royal Engineers, from Antrim will come by train (transport by march route). The 109th and 110th Field Ambulance, from Newry, will proceed by march, being billeted en route. The 36th Divisional Signal Company from Downpatrick, will send transport and cyclists by march route, dismounted men coming by rail. The company will be billeted in Belfast on the night of the 8th. The Divisional Cavalry (squadron of 6th Inniskilling Dragoons) and the Divisional Cyclists Company, from Enniskillen, will reach Belfast by road, being billeted en route. The Divisional Train 251st, 252nd, 253rd, 254th, and 255th Companies A. S. C. are stationed in Belfast. Advantage will be taken of the route marches of various units to instruct the men in field cooking. Officers commanding units will make arrangements for billets in conjunction with the R. I. C. authorities. As an evidence of the interest, which the parade is arousing it may be mentioned that a well known firm in the city has already received 800 applications for permission to view the march past from their windows.[5]

While Lord Kitchener did not attend the divisional review parade, Sir Edward Carson and his wife did. The leader of Unionism in Ireland, indeed the man who along with Sir James Craig had negotiated with the War Office to allow the UVF to serve together in the 36th (Ulster) Division, witnessed a truly momentous event. As one soldier put it:

> Here was the "pride of old Ulster" on full display and it seemed the whole country filled Belfast to see them. … It was an exhausting day for all the troops with reveille at 04.00, arriving in Belfast at 07.00, taking part in all the ceremonial and returning to Randalstown at about 20.00 in the evening.[6]

The Review Parade was a huge success, as was reported in the *Belfast Newsletter* on 12 May 1915:

> Major General C.H. Powell, C.B. commanding the Ulster Division, has issued the following order with reference to last Saturday's review and parade –
>
>> The G.O.C. congratulates all ranks in the Division on their fine soldierly appearance at the review on Saturday. He was much impressed with their behaviour on parade, and believes that they will show the same steadiness when they come under the enemy's fire.

During the week leading up to the Review Parade and immediately afterwards the Tyrones undertook a concerted recruitment campaign in the Dungannon area. This was very successful in attracting new recruits and received considerable coverage in the *Belfast Newsletter*:

> On Thursday the fife and drum band of the 9th Battalion Royal Inniskilling Fusiliers (Tyrone Volunteers) arrived in Dungannon to commence a tour of the district for the purpose of obtaining men for the reserve battalion, which is being trained in Enniskillen. The party was in charge of Lieutenant J. B. Anderson, and the band rendered a number of selections in Market Square and afterwards paraded the streets. Later in the day the party marched to Moy, via Killyman and Drummond, to attend the monthly fair. Dungannon district, which has sent some 280 members of the Ulster Volunteer Force to swell the ranks of the 9th battalion, will be the headquarters of the party for the next eight days, the programme of the tour being:- Moy fair yesterday; Divisional Review, Belfast, today;

band parade on lawn of Northland House, Dungannon to-morrow afternoon; route march to Coalisland, Monday; route march to Pomeroy, Tuesday; Stewartstown fair, Wednesday; Dungannon hiring fair, Thursday; route march to Donaghmore and Castlecaulfield, Friday 14th; Cookstown hiring fare, Saturday 15th.[7]

On Wednesday evening the members of the fife and drum band of the 9th Battalion Royal Inniskilling Fusiliers (Tyrone Volunteers), who are recruiting through the district, were with their officers and the recruiting party, entertained in the Methodist Church Schoolhouse, Dungannon. The entertainment had been organised by Mrs Bradley, Mount Royal, and a willing band of helpers and stewards. The building had been tastefully decorated with flags, bunting, and flowers, and the soldiers were served with an abundant meat tea. Later Rev. Henry Frackleton occupied the chair, and addresses were delivered by Rev. T. J. McEndoo, M.A.; Rev. W. Waterworth (a missionary lately returned from the Gold Coast), Pastor M. A. Quigley, Lieut, J. B. Anderson, 9th Inniskillings, and the chairman. At intervals Mrs Clugston sang "A Patriotic Pattern to the World" and "They sang God save the King," and was warmly encored, and Privates Dunwoody, R. Reid and Parry rendered "Genevieve" as a flute trio. Miss Clarke, Park View, acted as accompanist. Cigarettes were also distributed. Later in the evening a concert was held for the soldiers in the Parochial Hall. There was a large attendance of the townspeople, and an excellent programme of songs, dances, and sketches was contributed. Rev. T. J. McEndoo M. A. presided. The soldiers were afterwards entertained to supper.[8]

Principally owing to the efforts of the band and recruiting party of the 9th Inniskillings (Tyrone Volunteers), who toured the district for some eight days, one hundred men have volunteered from Dungannon district since the 2nd inst. On Thursday last, the day of the half yearly hiring fair, 40 men enrolled, most of them farm servants and artisans, and on the following Monday 23 factory workers, shop assistants and shop messengers volunteered. It was noticeable (says our correspondent) that the farmers sons were not responding. At least 400 of them were present at the hiring fair, but none joined the colours. As a result the Dungannon Rural Council, after referring at their last meeting to the slackness of the farmers' sons, unanimously adopted a resolution calling for conscription. Of the 100 men who volunteered two joined the Irish Brigade.[9]

Yesterday the drums and pipes of the 9th Battalion Royal Inniskilling Fusiliers (Tyrone Volunteers) visited Dungannon with a recruiting party, in charge of Captain P. Cruickshank and Lieutenant Chambers. It was market day, and there was a large attendance of country people. Some recruits were enrolled.[10]

The newspaper coverage reflected controversy surrounding the recruitment of nationalists, particularly members of the Irish Volunteers, as illustrated in a letter from Lieutenant J. B. Anderson published in the *Belfast Newsletter* on 21 May 1915:

Sir – In your issue of to-day I notice a paragraph about recruiting in East Tyrone, which says that out of 100 recruits only two joined the Irish Brigade. I was in charge of the recruiting party of the 9th Battalion Royal Inniskilling Fusiliers. We sent 12 men to the Irish Brigade and 17 men to the 3rd Battalion Royal Inniskilling Fusiliers, also one to the Irish Guards. These men were all recruited from the Irish Volunteers, and were all good clean young fellows. We got a large number of recruits for the Ulster Division. I may say that Dungannon did exceptionally well, giving us over 50 men, and will, I am sure send more. I understand that over 400 men have now joined the colours from Dungannon and district.

Yours, &c., J. B. Anderson, Lieutenant,
9th Royal Inniskilling Fusiliers
Shane's Castle Camp,
20th May, 1915.

In preparation for action on the Western Front, the 36th (Ulster) Division was soon on the move again. An advance party left Ulster for the village of Seaford in Sussex, England, where the Division would be based. The advance party arrived on 1 July, and the main body of the Division joined them the following week. However, due to a German measles outbreak, the Tyrones had to be isolated and could not be dispatched to England at this stage. The Tyrones left Shane's Castle and headed for the North Antrim village of Ballycastle, arriving on 9 July. This gave some of them the opportunity to see friends and families. Reports of men cycling to Portrush, after a day's work in the camp, to see family who had arrived by train in the seaside resort were not uncommon. This illustrates the fitness of the men who undertook this 40 to 50 mile return trip.

With the measles outbreak behind them, the Tyrones undertook intensive shooting training on the ranges at Magilligan, County Londonderry. This was to ensure the Tyrones maintained the high standard of rifle skills for which the British Army was renowned.

As August progressed, the Tyrones knew it would soon be time for them to depart the North Coast and join the rest of the Division in Seaford. They left Magilligan by train on the morning of 25 August, arriving in Belfast by mid afternoon. They boarded the steam ship Connaught at 20.00 that evening and set sail for Liverpool, arriving at 05.00 the next morning. The Tyrones continued their journey by train through England to meet up with their comrades in Seaford.

The Division had settled quickly at Seaford. Very shortly after its arrival the men celebrated the Twelfth of July, as reported in the *Belfast Newsletter* on 15 July 1915:

> *The great anniversary was duly celebrated by the troops on Monday. According to a Sussex newspaper, many of them were "gaily bedecked with the sashes and regalia of the Loyal Orange Institution, while it would have been an impossibility to discover a man in uniform without an orange-coloured decoration in hat or buttonhole." During the evening several impromptu processions were organised, and, with banners and colours, the men paraded the town, the streets of which were almost impassable owing to the crowds of khaki. Several members of the English branch of the Order were present at the meeting, among them being the Rev. L. Atherton (Lewes), Br. B. V. Reeves, Br H. Trower, and Br Taylor, of Barcombe Lodge 398; Br A B Weir, D.G.M.; Br W Wheatland and Br Salvage, Brighton Lodge 848; Mrs Salvage, Mrs Wheatland, and Alderman Barron, J.P. (London). Rev D.R. Mitchell, Presbyterian Chaplain to the Forces, presided over the meeting, which was opened by the rendering of the hymn, "Oh God, our Help in ages past." A short prayer by the Rev L. Atherton was followed by an introductory speech by the chairman, and an inspiring address was also given by Alderman Barron. At the conclusion, the soldiers sang the hymn, "Fight the Good Fight" and a collection was taken up on behalf of the Lord Enniskillen Memorial Orphan Fund.*

While at Seaford the men of the Ulster Division took steps to maintain their culture and heritage. To this end, they formed six Orange Lodges under the auspices of the Grand Orange Lodge of England. Some of the lodges were soon over 300 strong and the arrival of the Ulster Division gave a strong fillip to the Orange Order in the South of England.

Religious worship was also important to the men and regular visits of clergy from home were common place. For instance, during August the *Belfast Newsletter* reported:

> *The Right Rev. Dr Hamill, Moderator of the General Assembly, paid a visit to the camp at Seaford, Sussex, at the end of last week, and on Sunday last conducted services for the Presbyterian troops of the Ulster Division. During his visit he was guest of Major-General C. H. Powell, C. B., officer commanding the division.*[11]

In mid September a new commander was appointed to the 36th (Ulster) Division, a sign that it would not be long before it would be sent to the front. The appointment of the new Commanding Officer was reported as follows:

> *An important change in the command of the Ulster Division is announced, Brigadier General Oliver S. W. Nugent, D.S.O., A.D.C. to his Majesty the King, who was gazetted last night to the temporary rank of Major-General, having been appointed General Officer Commanding, replacing Major General Charles H. Powell C.B.*[12]

This development was not surprising given that it was an understood fact, that divisions should only be taken to France by general officers with experience of the conditions of warfare in that country. Major-General Oliver S. W. Nugent, DSO met this criteria having already commanded a Brigade in France with distinction. Major Nugent was an Ulsterman, belonging to an old Irish family that lived on the Cavan and Longford border at Mount Nugent. He had been instrumental in helping organise the Cavan UVF during the Third Home Rule crisis.

On 30 September a highlight for the Division was its review at Aldershot by His Majesty King George the Fifth. Lord Kitchener, who had already reviewed the Division on 27 July, was also in attendance. The King congratulated Major General Nugent, and turned to Sir George Richardson and told him what a fine Division they made. On leaving the review, the King's car overtook some men from the Division returning to camp. Recognising the King, the men burst into wild cheering along the line.

The review had been a great success and the following order was issued by Major-General Nugent:

The G.O.C. has much pleasure in conveying to the troops of the Ulster Division the expression of his Majesty's high appreciation of the bearing and training of all ranks. The King desires that his pleasure at inspecting the Division complete for war shall be conveyed to all the ranks, and his Majesty was pleased to say that he was confident that the troops of the Division would do credit to the country of their birth, and worthily uphold the honour of the empire. The G.O.C. desires to add to his Majesty's gracious remarks his own appreciation of the absolute steadiness of all ranks. The march past reflected great credit on all. Distances were well kept, the dressing was good, and men, horses, guns and transports were well turned out.

Signed N. V. F. Russell
Lieut. Col General Staff [13]

The 36th (Ulster) Division's departure for the front was imminent; indeed an advance party was already in France when the King reviewed the Division on 30 September. The Tyrones set sail for France on the evening of 5 October. Just over a year since their inception, they were entering the fray. Prior to their departure the Division received a message from the King:

Officers, Non Commissioned Officers, and Men -
You are about to join your comrades at the Front in bringing to a successful end this relentless war of over twelve month's duration. Your prompt patriotic answer to the nation's call to arms will never be forgotten. The keen exertions of all ranks during the period of training have brought you to a state of efficiency not unworthy of my Regular Army. I am confident that in the field you will nobly uphold the traditions of the fine regiments whose names you bear. Ever since your enrolment I have closely watched the growth and steady progress of all units. I shall continue to follow with interest the fortunes of your Division. In bidding you farewell, I pray that God may bless you in all your undertakings.

GEORGE R.I.
September 30th, 1915 [14]

The Division landed at Le Havre and Boulogne in France. The Tyrones arrived at the latter port, spending a day in the rest camp at Ostrohove, before embarking by train to their first billets in France. The Tyrones underwent further training to prepare them for the challenges that lay ahead. The following letter from an officer in the 9th Royal Inniskilling Fusiliers, carried in the Belfast Newsletter on 3 November 1915, conveys something of the thoughts and experiences of the men during their early days in France:

> *Our friends in Tyrone can take it for granted that as long as they hear little from us all is well, and we are simply carrying out the duties, dangerous and otherwise imposed on us. We take it all as part of the day's work, and whether we are on the trek or in the trenches the 9th sticks to its motto of "Keep smiling". The health of the battalion is good, and the men are quite cheery, realising that in fighting for their country they cannot lie in a bed of roses. Already the mail bags for home have become capacious, and the post corporal's arrival is always welcome. Of what is going on here we hear little. We are a unit in a big army, and are naturally concerned with our immediate front only for the moment. It is quite enough to think of each unit being responsible for it's own share. Of course we take a great interest in other parts of the line, but our only knowledge is gained by what we read in the newspapers which come over from England.*

The men did, however, have some time for some social activities. It is interesting to note that the Orange Lodges that had been formed within the 36th (Ulster) Division continued to meet in France, as illustrated by the following reports in the *Belfast Newsletter:*

> *The Orange lodges in connection with the Ulster Division – six in number meet regularly in France. There were no Orange lodges in France since 1816, when both the 6th Inniskilling Dragoons and the 7th Inniskillings – now the 1st Battalion Royal Inniskilling Fusiliers- had warrants working in connection with those regiments, both of which formed part of the army of occupation after Waterloo. Private W. A. Greer, a member of Donegall Road Total Abstinence L.O.L. 883, Belfast, in the course of a letter to his parents in Sandhurst Gardens says "We have formed an Orange lodge out here - Y.C.V. L.O.L. 871 - and have taken out a warrant. The first meeting was held in an old barn, and we had quite a crowd, mainly composed of old members, but we had a good number of new members for initiation. We carry out everything as far as we can in*

orthodox fashion. The meeting was quite enjoyable, and the circumstances under which it was held reminded one of the old style meetings at home, so you see we are not thinking about the war all the time." Major C. F. Falls, 11th Battalion Royal Inniskilling Fusiliers (Donegal and Fermanagh Volunteers), in the course of a letter to Mr. Alfred Armstrong, Enniskillen, acknowledging gifts from L.O.L. No. 1539 says – "Please tell the brethren that we have a very flourishing L.O.L. in our battalion, and before we have finished we hope to hold a meeting in Berlin." Major Falls is Grand Master of Lisbellaw District L.O.L.[15]

Writing home, a member of the 11th Battalion Royal Inniskilling Fusiliers (Donegal and Fermanagh) says – "When on their way to the trenches the King, on his recent visit to France, passed by portion of the battalion in his motor car. His majesty was recognised and loyally cheered with enthusiasm. In the trenches the men were very cool and some of the English soldiers who were along with them spoke of their work in the highest terms of praise. The battalion Orange lodge (The Inniskillings True Blues No, 870) met as often as they possibly could. After the transaction of the business a social hour was held, as if they were at home, and at this the officers were present, including Brs. Major C. F. Falls and Lieutenant Gordon and Knight. Br. Halliday is the W. M. of the lodge, and Br. Lewis is the D.W.M. The officers of the battalion are loved by the men. Colonel Hessey is always anxious for their welfare, and when they enter their billets he goes round to see that they are comfortable.[16]

The 16th (Irish) Division

The 16th (Irish) Division continued its training in the south of Ireland, having its headquarters at Fermoy, County Cork. Their training, like that undertaken by their comrades in the Ulster Division, was long and the men were eager to get into battle. Some officers writing to family in March 1915 realised it would be September 1915 at the earliest before they would see action on the Western Front.

Recruiting for the 16th (Irish) Division was a major issue and much time was spent going on route marches and travelling the country in order to encourage enlistment, as reported for example in the *Belfast Newsletter* on 15 March 1915:

Scenes of enthusiasm were witnessed in Omagh on Saturday night when a large recruiting contingent from the 7th Battalion Royal Inniskilling Fusiliers arrived by the last train, from Tipperary, with the object of conducting another recruiting campaign throughout the country to bring the battalion up to its established strength. The recruiting party is under the command of Second Lieutenant D. H. Morton, son of Rev David Morton, Presbyterian minister, Newtownstewart, Second Lieutenant Taggart, a Larne man, is also attached to the party, which is accompanied by its band. There were quite a number of Omagh men with the company, and these met with a hearty reception from their friends and comrades. A large crowd of people assembled at the station precincts to welcome the party, who attracted much attention as they marched through the town, headed with the Tyrone Pipers' Band and the Inniskillings' Band alternatively playing lively airs. The party are being accommodated at the local depot during their stay. Tyrone has already done well in the matter of recruiting, having provided over 1,250 men for the 9th Inniskillings and fully another 1,000 men for different other units of Lord Kitchener's army.

The recruiting party of the 7th Inniskillings (who were attached to the 16th (Irish) Division) had carried out a tour of counties Tyrone, Fermanagh and portion of Donegal for 18 days. On its completion the recruiting party returned to Tipperary having secured some 32 new recruits.

While recruiting for the 16th (Irish) Division was a controversial issue for nationalists, large numbers of Catholic men did enlist. In Belfast 600 men from the Falls Road joined the 6th Battalion Connaught Rangers and many a man from the counties of Tyrone and Londonderry also enlisted to the Division.

The 16th (Irish) Division received a set back when approximately 1,700 men were transferred from its 49th Brigade (usually referred to as the Ulster Brigade) to the 10th (Irish) Division in order to fill up its ranks after fighting at Gallipoli. This was a major blow to the 16th Division and led to some accusations that it was to be used to fill up other divisions.

With summer approaching rumours that the Division was moving to England and then onto France were rife. In late June it was rumoured that the Division was to decant to Seaford in Sussex, but ultimately instead this was the destination of the 36th (Ulster) Division. The

Northern Regiments of the 16th (Irish) Division who had initially been undertaking training in Tipperary were moved for a short period to Enniskillen and Finner Camp just prior to their move to England. The Division was finally given its order to quit Fermoy and move to England on the 22 August 1915. Its destination was to be Larkhill in Wiltshire, South West England, situated near the town of Salisbury and the Salisbury Plains. However, there was a change of plan and instead when they left Ireland on 7 September they were sent to Blackdown Camp in Pirbright and Bordon, Surrey, South East of England. Here they received more training, with particular emphasis on rifle practice. In mid November the *Belfast Newsletter* carried the following article on the 16th (Irish) Division:

The "Daily Chronicle" says – The completion of the 16th Division's training really marks a sort of epoch in the reconciliation of Ireland to the Empire. This division, though no religious or political tests have been imposed on its membership, as is the case with the Ulster Division, is the most direct contribution of Nationalist and Roman Catholic Ireland to the war. It has been recruited mainly from the ranks of the Irish National Volunteers, and it includes among its officers a number of Nationalist members of Parliament, including Mr John Redmond's brother and son. It is not the only division of the new armies recruited mainly from Nationalist Ireland, the 10th Division, which has fought splendidly in the Dardanelles, was drawn from much the same sources, and indeed, its casualties were repaired by volunteers from the 16th. Nor do these two divisions represent anything like the whole contribution made by the Irish race to our army and navy – a contribution which Mr Redmond estimated last week in the House of Commons between 300,000 and 400,000 men. More than any other fighting unit the 16th Division stands for those Irish elements whose fighting prowess was specially shown and whose traditional military glories were won under Sarzfield and at Fonteroy, not on our side, but against us. These elements now take their stand as comrades with Englishmen, Welshmen and Scotsmen under the common flag, the representatives of their ancient and martial race long alienated by the tragedy of its history and now reconciled by the pledge of its restored freedom. It is a marvellous transformation, which only the signal political courage of Mr. Redmond and his colleagues has made possible.[17]

On 28 November the Division was told it was to be posted overseas and in mid December Major-General Hickie replaced General Parsons as the Division's commanding officer.

The 47th and 48th Brigades of the Irish Division moved to France in December 1915, arriving in Le Havre on the 18 December. They then travelled by train to a village called Gosnay, near Bethune, in Northern France, which they reached on 19 December. Major-General Hickie, had hoped to keep his men in billets for as long as possible, but events overtook him and by 23 December 1915 some of the Division were transferred to the front line trenches.

The 49th Brigade would not leave England until January 1916 due to the transfer of so many of its men to the 10th (Irish) Division. It would be February 1916 before the 3 Brigades that made up the 16th (Irish) Division would serve together again.

Local Commissions

During 1915 many men from the Dungannon area or those who had a connection with the locality received commissions in a diverse range of military units performing a variety of roles. These men were expected to lead by example. Lieutenants and 2nd Lieutenants, for instance, tended to be the first out of the trenches with their men. Their roles required courage and valour, and many of them made the ultimate sacrifice. Reports on some of the men who received a commission are listed below:

> *Mr W. E. Reid son of Mr Richard Reid, Shanmoy, Dungannon, has received a commission in the army, and has been detailed for immediate duty at Bradford. He has just returned from Canada with the West Knotenay contingent of the Royal Montreal Infantry. He had been educated at Dungannon Royal School, and left it to take up a position in the Canadian Bank, but on the outbreak of hostilities he volunteered for the war. Lieutenant Reid is a keen sportsman and a good shot, and was very popular in the Royal School, where he captained the Rugby team in 1912-13.*[18]

> *Mr R. N. A. Bailey, son of Rev W. H. Bailey, M.A. Presbyterian minister, Clogher, County Tyrone, who was in the Public Schools and University Brigade at Epsom, has received a commission and will be attached to the 14th Battalion Highland Light Infantry and stationed at Brixton, Devon. Lieutenant Bailey, who is at present home on leave, was a pupil at*

Dungannon Royal School, from which he received an appointment in the Belfast Bank.[19]

Mr. Whiteside Macky, son of the Rev D. T. Macky, Presbyterian minister, Newmills, Dungannon, has received a commission in the 17th Battalion Royal Irish Rifles. Lieutenant Macky was educated at Dungannon Royal School from which he went to the McCrea Magee College, where he held the Fullarton Scholarship for two years. He then went to Trinity College and was preparing for the examination for the B. A. degree when war broke out. He had been a member of the Officers Training Corps at college, and at home he was an enthusiastic member of the U.V.F., and when Lord Kitchener's call came he offered his services. He is at present in training at the Officers School of Instruction at Queen's University, Belfast. (In August 1915 Macky was posted to the 15th Battalion Royal Irish Rifles and met up with the Ulster Division at Seaford Camp).[20, 21]

Mr Richard Simmons, a native of Dungannon, who was admitted a solicitor in 1902 and has in recent years practised in Dublin, has obtained a commission in the Army Service Corps, and is posted for immediate duty at the Curragh. Lieutenant Simmons, who is the only son of Mr John Simmons, a well known Dungannon solicitor, served his legal apprenticeship in that town with the firm of Messrs, Simmons & Meglaughlin, and was an ardent rugby footballer.[22]

Mr J. M. Crowe, M.R.C.V.S., Market Square, Dungannon, has obtained a commission in the Army Veterinary Corps. Mr Crowe has practised in Dungannon for some time past.[23]

Mr William Best, late of Tate's Medical Hall, Royal Avenue, Belfast, and eldest son of Mr. John Best, George's Street, Dungannon, has obtained a commission in the Army Medical Corps, and is detailed for duty in the South of England.[24]

Dr T. F. Wilson, Northland Row, Dungannon who has practised in that town for several years and had considerable previous experience in India, has volunteered for service and obtained a commission in the Army Medical Corps.[25]

Dr. Joseph Marmion, eldest son of Surgeon Marmion J.P., Dungannon, has obtained a commission in the Royal Army Medical Corps, and is on duty in the South of England.[26]

Lieutenant Samuel Howard, second son of Major R. J. Howard, Annaginny, Dungannon who is now in the trenches with the Connaught Rangers has been promoted captain.[27]

Mr William G. Scott, son of Mr John Scott, Elseben House, Belfast, and nephew of Mr W. H. Darragh, J.P. The Villa, Dungannon has received a commission in the Royal Dublin Fusiliers (regular force).[28]

Major and Honorary Lieutenant-Colonel A.S. Cleaver, whose appointment as draft conducting officer was recently announced, is well known in Belfast and the North of Ireland. He served in the Mid Ulster Royal Garrison Artillery (since disbanded) at Dungannon for several years.[29]

Mr John Herbert Watson Troughton, of the Officers Training Corps, Trinity College, Dublin, has received a commission in the 4th Battalion Royal Irish Regiment. Second-Lieutenant Troughton is the eldest son of Mr E. Troughton, headmaster of the Model School, Kilkenny, and grandson of Mrs Watson, Garfield Villa, Dungannon.[30]

Mr Charles Newell, C.E., Dungannon, assistant county surveyor, has received an appointment as lieutenant in the Royal Engineers, and will leave for overseas service immediately. Lieutenant Newell, who has been acting as assistant county surveyor in Tyrone during the past six years, volunteered during the South African war, and was with the colours until its conclusion. He is the eldest son of Mr. Joseph Newell, merchant, Dungannon.[31]

Mr E Lassigan, L.D.S., who has been acting as civil dental surgeon to the forces for the past six months, has been gazetted to a lieutenancy in the Royal Army Medical Corps. Lieutenant Lassigan is well known in Dungannon, where his father Mr Pierce Lassigan, lately postmaster of Kilkenny city, was postmaster for a number of years.[32]

At a meeting of the Tyrone Presbytery, held yesterday in Cookstown, Rev. George Wilson, B. A., Ballygoney, was granted leave of absence for three months in order to go to France as temporary chaplain under the Y. M.C.A.[33]

Temporary Lieutenant Malcolm King Acheson, M.D., R.A.M.C., has been promoted to the rank of temporary captain. He is the third son of the late Mr David Acheson, J.P., linen manufacturer, Castlecaulfield, County

Tyrone, and was educated at Dungannon Royal School and at Trinity College, Dublin, where he obtained his degree. He was in practice in England at the outbreak of the war, and has been on active service in France for a considerable time.[34]

Second-lieutenant (on probation) Francis St. Leger Greer, who has been transferred from the 16th (The Queen's) Lancers to the Irish Guards, is the youngest son of Captain J. H. Greer, The Grange, Moy, County Tyrone, formerly of the Highland Light Infantry. His elder brother Captain E. B. Greer, is adjutant of the 3rd (Reserve) Battalion Irish Guards.[35]

Deaths at Home

Two men with connections to Dungannon who had volunteered for service died at home before their battalions were deployed on active service.

Private Thomas Patterson (5/2807), 5th Battalion Royal Irish Regiment, formerly attached to the Royal Inniskilling Fusiliers (11360), died during training on 8 February 1915. Private Patterson had served his country through the South African Campaign. He was a member of Newmills LOL 183 and is remembered on the Lodge's Roll of Honour. He is buried in Tullanisken Parish Church Newmills. Private Patterson's two brothers also served King and Country, Corporal Fred Patterson 9th Royal Inniskilling Fusiliers and Robert Patterson who was a prisoner of war.

Rev. Richard Usher Greer, Army Chaplains Department, was born around 1868 in County Tyrone. The son of the Rev. William Henry Greer and Charlote Pike, Richard was educated at the Royal Schools in both Armagh and Dungannon, and would later attend Trinity College, Dublin. He entered the ministry and initially served as a curate in Belfast. By 1911 he was Rector of Seapatrick Parish Church, Banbridge, County Down. On the formation of the 36th (Ulster) Division, the Rev. Greer immediately secured a chaplaincy with the 8th Battalion Royal Irish Rifles (East Belfast Battalion Volunteers). During a leave of absence from Ballykinlar Camp in County Down, the Rev. Greer suffered a brain hemorrhage and died on 23 June 1915. The Rev. Greer was Chaplain to Banbridge Bible and Crown Defenders LOL 423 and Mount Nebo RBP 53. Moreover, a ladies lodge was named after him in Banbridge, known as The Greer Memorial WLOL 41, which still exists today. At his funeral the RIC and 8th Battalion Royal Irish Rifles formed the guard of honour. The Rev. Richard Usher Greer is buried in Tullanisken Parish Church, Newmills.

The Western Front

On the Western Front at the beginning of 1915 the Germans occupied almost all of Belgium and a substantial part of France. As the British army at this stage did not have enough trained soldiers or weaponry the French largely dictated how the war against Germany would be fought. The French were wedded to driving the Germans back to their own borders and argued that a series of mass assaults should be launched by the allies to split the German lines. The first of these offensives commenced in the Artois and Champagne regions.

Artois and Champagne Offensive

During late December 1914 initial skirmishes broke out in this region between the allies and Germans. The French under the command of Commander-in-Chief Joffre sought to end the war quickly and launched a major offensive from Nieuport to Verdun which covers the regions of the Artois and Champagne.

The plan was to launch a numerically superior force against the Germans at the northerly and southerly edges, followed up by an advance through the Ardennes. The plan was built on cutting off the German retreat. The French army would lead the attack with the BEF supporting it. Despite being outnumbered the Germans had developed well fortified trenches covered by machine guns and little advancement was made by the allies. Fighting was continuous until mid February. The battle lulled for a few days and then continued through to St Patrick's Day when the offensive came to an end. The allies suffered many casualties, but very little territory was gained.

A major battle during this offensive took place at Neuve Chapelle, fought between 10 and 13 March 1915. The attack was one of the first offensives carried out solely by the BEF since the beginning of the war in 1914. The decision to attack at Neuve Chapelle was taken by the Commander-in-Chief of the BEF, Sir John French, and was lead by Douglas Haig's First Army consisting of 40,000 men. They were initially successful in taking the village of Neuve Chapelle, but a subsequent attack at Aubers on 13 March resulted in the loss of many of the 1,000 troops involved, and brought the battle to an end.

Accounts from Artois and Champagne

Sapper Alfred McGowan of the Royal Engineers who was from Donaghmore, provided some interesting details of the lead up to and the fighting that took place in the Artois and Champagne region during the first quarter of 1915:

> *Private Alfred McGowan, of the Royal Engineers, writing to Rev. H. Egerton, B.A., Donaghmore, County Tyrone, says – I am between La Bassee and Ypres. Lord Northland was killed near where I am. My company has been very lucky, considering everything – three killed and five wounded out of 150. The other company that came out with mine has lost 29 men, including officers and non-commissioned officers. I have had a very exciting time here in action since 16th November, and got a slight wound in the left thigh on 21st December, just the day after I received the sad news about my poor mother. War is an awful thing. My first night in the trenches was to go out between the enemy's line and our own to erect barbed wire entanglements under heavy fire, and as soon as we were finished and crept back to our trenches the German Artillery commenced to shell us, and it seemed like hailstones hitting all round, besides machine guns going all over the show. Our artillery responded with rapid fire, as the Germans were coming to attack. They lost heavily this night, and were driven back to their trenches. We had severe fighting round here – once they made five attacks in succession, only to be driven back with very heavy losses. We picked them down as fast as they tried to get through our barbed wire. They were hanging in our wire dead and wounded in rows, and the ground was covered with them. When things settled down it was a terrible sight to look upon. They have learned what the British Army is long before now. We are all in the best of spirits, still smiling, and sure of a glorious victory.*[36]

> *Writing to his friends at Kilmore, Donaghmore, County Tyrone, Sapper Alfred McGowan Royal Engineers, states – I have been in the battle of Neuve Chapelle, where we had a good victory. I was with the first line of infantry in the charge, and had a desperate time of it. We captured over 700 prisoners, for when we charged the first line of trenches a large number surrendered and the remainder were bayoneted. When we got them on the move we mowed them down in thousands with our artillery, machine guns, and rifle fire, and the trenches were piled six and eight*

feet deep in places with their dead, while the fields and village were strewn with them. Most of the captured were glad to come with us.[37]

Sapper Alfred McGowan, 2nd Field Company Royal Engineers, writing to his relatives at Donaghmore, County Tyrone says: - "We have had it very hot lately, having made a most successful attack on the Germans on 10th March and captured their trenches, afterwards capturing the village of Neuve le Chapelle. We lost thousands of brave men, but it nothing compared with the German losses. When we got to their trenches the dead were lying eight deep in some of them, and for almost a mile the place was covered with dead and wounded, friend and foe alike lying side by side. It was, I believe, the heaviest fire ever any man was under. We bombarded Neuve Chapelle and scarcely left a brick standing. In this place alone we captured 750 prisoners, and when they saw us charging with the bayonets they put up their hands and cried for mercy. It was a murderous fight, and when we got to their trenches we made short work of them, even where they were ten to one. Lots of them were buried in houses blown down by our artillery fire. When we had driven them out of the village I was advancing at the double to a brick house with my section officer on my right and a sapper on my left, when both of them were shot. I got wounded in the shoulder at the same time, and thought it was all up with me but as I lay on the ground I saw two Germans firing at us from behind a tree about seventy yards away. I slipped up my rifle steadily and shot both of them stone dead: so you see I had revenge for my comrades. The Germans afterwards made a counter attack but it proved a failure. They came up in massed formation, but we mowed them down in heaps with rifles and machine guns. The Indian troops were then fighting on our right and did splendid work. After our victory everyone was saying how pleased our people at home would be to hear the result. It should be a good incentive to wake up the young men of Britain who are the right age and can be spared to enlist. They will be prouder men when the war is over.[38]

Corporal W. J. Lemon, 1st Battalion Grenadier Guards, writing to his relatives in Milltown, Dungannon, enclosed the address which Lieutenant-General H. Rawlinson, commander of the 4th Army Corps, issued to each soldier on the morning the battle of Neuve Chappelle commenced:

The attack which we are about to undertake is of the first importance to the Allied cause. The army and the nation are watching the result and Sir John French is confident that every individual in the IV Corps will do his duty and inflict a crushing defeat on the Germans VII Corps which is opposed to us.[39]

Corporal Lemon, who was attached to the King's Company, was in charge of the grenade sections at the Battle of Neuve Chappelle. His letter to his family was published in the *Belfast Newsletter* on 29 March 1915, which recorded that during the battle:

He had ten men with him at the start, but he lost most of them, as they got shot down during the advance. He was with the third line of advance, and becoming somewhat breathless and tired, they slowed down to walk, the German bullets meantime hitting the ground around them. He saw one chap pick up a piece of stick and commence scraping the heavy clay off his boots quite as unconcerned as if he were at home in his potato field. Hundreds of Victoria Crosses were won on that day, but no one had any time to take notice of brave acts. Some of the officers had done deeds meriting the Victoria Cross over and over again, and never knew that they were doing so.

Formerly a prison warder in Belfast and Maryborough, Co. Laois, Corporal W. J. Lemon had been called up as a reservist. He was wounded at the Battle of Neuve Chapelle by a shell which injured him on the left knee and killed one of his companions and wounded five others. He was conveyed to a hospital in Boulogne and afterwards shipped to England, spending time in the East London Hospital. The *Belfast Newsletter* reported on 19 June 1915 that:

Corporal W. J. Lemon, 1st Battalion Grenadier Guards, has returned home to Milltown, Dungannon, suffering from wounds to his knee, received at Neuve Chapelle on 12th March.

Lord Northland

Viscount Northland,
Capt Coldstream Guards

During the offensive in the Artois and Champagne regions, the Germans launched very strong counter attacks along the La Bassee Canal from early January to the first week of February. It was during one of these offensives that Captain Thomas Ucher Caulfield Knox, Viscount Northland was killed in action on 1 February 1915. Lord Northland was hit by a shot to the head which killed him instantly. The Northland's had been linked with the Dungannon region for generations and his death was a major blow for all in the town. The death of Lord Northland was deeply regretted within Unionist and Orange circles. Shortly before his death, great pride had been taken in the announcement that he had been promoted to the rank of captain:

> *Lieutenant Viscount Northland, 2nd Battalion Coldstream Guards, who has participated in very active work in the trenches for a long period has been promoted captain. Lord Northland will be remembered as the commanding officer of the very efficient Dungannon Battalion Ulster Volunteer Force, and his promotion carries the utmost satisfaction in County Tyrone. Lord Northland is the only son and heir of the Earl of Ranfurly, D. C. M. G.*[40]

The death of Lord Northland was announced in the *Belfast Newsletter* on 4 February 1915:

> *News of the death of Viscount Northland while on active service in France was last night received at the London House of his father, the Earl of Ranfurly, at Pont Street, says the "Daily Chronicle". The War Office intimation was brief, but sympathetic, and it was understated that Lord Northland, who was in the 2nd Coldstreams, was wounded in the severe fighting at La Bassee, his death taking place on Monday. The Earl of Ranfurly was in Ireland when word was received that his only son had died in action, and the sorrowful tidings were at once cabled to him across the Channel.*
>
> *Lord Northland, who was 32 years of age, had his first experience of active service in the Boer War, in which he served with the Coldstream Guards, earning the South African medal. The Viscount came of age in*

1903 during the time his father was Governor-General of New Zealand, and his majority was celebrated by a ball at the Wellington Government House, which was the outstanding social event of the season. For a short period he acted as aide-de-camp to his father in New Zealand, and he had travelled extensively. Three years ago Lord Northland married Miss Hilda Cooper, daughter of the late Sir Daniel Cooper, and granddaughter of the first Speaker of the Legislative Assembly of New South Wales. Their son was born the following year. Lord Northland was descended from William Penn, the famous Quaker founder of Pennsylvania.

Lord Northland it may be added took a leading part in the Ulster Volunteer movement in County Tyrone. He was very largely instrumental in the raising of the Dungannon Volunteer Battalion and took a great interest in its training and equipment.

Numerous tributes were paid to Lord Northland and his family received many messages of sympathy from far and wide, which were also reported in the local press:

The "Morning Post" says – The following telegram from the King and Queen has been received by the Earl of Ranfurly in reference to the death of his son, Viscount Northland, while serving in the Coldstream Guards:-
"The King and Queen are profoundly grieved to hear of the sad loss which you and the army have sustained by the death of your only son in the service of his country. Their Majesties deeply regret that this young life, so full of promise, should have been suddenly cut off and they offer you their true sympathy in your great sorrow. [41]

General Lord William F. E. Seymour, K.C.V.O., Honorary Colonel of the Coldstream Guards, in a letter to the Earl of Ranfurly expressing the sympathy of the whole regiment on the death of Viscount Northland, says "It is a big price that you have been called upon to pay, but it must be an everlasting satisfaction both to you and the whole family, that he was spared long enough to prove his mettle in this titanic war. He proved himself a splendid officer from the very first. I had hoped that he was going to get through all right, for he had been out a long time without a scratch, although both his colonel and major had continually reported what splendid work he was doing; but alas, it was not to be, and now the regiment is mourning in him the loss of another officer whose services have been given whole-heartedly, and which have been invaluable and can ill be spared. The losses of one good officer after another are a terrible grief to me. What they must be to parents and wives I can only vaguely imagine, but the courage which these show in their bereavements fills me with wonder and respect, and is to me one of the most convincing tributes to the fact that the nation is determined to give its last penny and the last drop of its blood to ensure the war ending in the triumph of right over might; but it is a terrible price many have to pay. This is one of the last letters written by General Lord William Seymour, whose death was announced in yesterday's issue of this newspaper. [42]

The Earl and Countess of Ranfurly and Viscountess Northland have received many messages of sympathy in connection with the death of Captain Viscount Northland, 2nd Battalion Coldstream Guards, who died on Monday last of wounds received in action at La Bassee. Mr. R. Dawson Bates, secretary of the Ulster Unionist Council, has sent the following telegram:- "On behalf of the Ulster Unionist Council I am desired to express their deep sympathy with you in your bereavement and their sense of the loss which the Unionist cause has suffered in the death of Lord Northland.[43]

In reply to a message of sympathy, Mr R. Dawson Bates, secretary of the Ulster Unionist Council, has received the following telegram from Lord Ranfurly. – Please convey to Ulster Unionist Council my grateful thanks for their sympathy and kindly reference to my son. Had he been spared his life would have been devoted to the Unionist cause. [see 47]

The following resolution has been unanimously adopted by the session and committee of First Dungannon Presbyterian Church: - "The session and committee of First Dungannon Presbyterian Church beg respectfully to tender their heartfelt sympathy to Lord and Lady Ranfurly and to Lady Northland in their present sorrow. Lord Northland died the death of a true patriot, fighting for his King and country, and his noble sacrifice will never be forgotten by the community where, in his few short years of residence, he had come to be regarded universally with admiration and respect.[44]

At a special meeting of Drumglass Church of Ireland Young Men's Society - Mr R. T. Clarke presiding – a resolution of sympathy with the relatives of the late Viscount Northland, who had been a vice president of the association, was adopted.[45]

A similar resolution was adopted at a meeting of Star of the East Temperance R.B.P. No. 523. Dungannon. At the monthly meeting of Dungannon Total Abstinence L.O.L. No. 1229, held on Friday evening:- Br. D. J. Beatty, W. M., presiding – a resolution was proposed by Br W. J. Beatty, D. M. that the members place on record the great loss sustained by the Orange Institution through the death of Br. The Honourable Viscount Northland, who had been Deputy County Grand Master of Tyrone and District Master of the Orangemen of Killyman District. The resolution was adopted in silence, the members standing. It was also decided to forward letters of sympathy to the Earl and Countess of Ranfurly and to Lady Northland.[46]

Reference to the sad event was made on Friday evening at a special meeting of Dungannon Urban Council, of which Lord Ranfurly is the chairman. Mr T. J. Aiken J. P. (vice-chairman) presided and the other members present were – Messrs Robt. Newton, J.P.; Alexander Patterson, John Hardy, John Beatty, Peter McShane, Gabriel Clarke, R. D. Greeves, Joseph Howard, John Douglas, and W. R. Irwin. The chairman said the news of the death of Lord Northland had caused a great shock to the people of Dungannon, and had brought home to all of them the awful horrors of the war. It seemed but a short time since they had the honour of welcoming home Lord and Lady Northland after their marriage, and in the interval his Lordship and his wife had endeared themselves to the people of Dungannon. Indeed the townspeople had been eagerly looking forward to the time when Lord and Lady Northland would settle amongst them, and take a prominent part in the affairs of the town and district. It was hard to realise that a life so young and full of promise should have been cut off especially at a time when the strength and manhood of the nation were so much required. But they had the consolation of knowing that his death was a heroic one, and that he met it fighting nobly for his King and country. It was fitting that the council should meet, and, both in their own name and on behalf of the people of Dungannon, tender to Lord and Lady Ranfurly and to Lady Northland and her children their sincere sympathy in their bereavement. He moved a resolution accordingly. Mr John Beatty said it was his melancholy duty to second the resolution. Lord Northland, whom he had known from infancy, had endeared himself to everyone. Lord Northland had fallen when leading his men to retake a position. He had died on the field of honour, and no man could wish for a nobler death. Mr Alexander Patterson and Mr John Hardy supported the resolution, which was adopted in silence, the members standing. [47]

The members of Dungannon Volunteer LOL 178 at their meeting on 16 March 1915 passed the following resolution:

> *Bro. Greeves referred in feeling to the great loss to the Lodge, the Orange Institution and the Unionist cause had sustained owing to the death of Lord Northland on the field of battle fighting for his King and Country and moved that the following resolution be sent to Lady Northland and Lord Ranfurly – That we the Officers and members of Volunteer 178 Dungannon at this our first meeting since the lamented death on the battlefield of our Bro. Captain The Hon Viscount Northland hereby desire to place the loss which our Country, the Orange Institution and particularly this lodge have sustained through his death and we humbly beg to tender to Lord and Lady Ranfurly and Lady Northland our sincere sympathy in their great bereavement on the death of one who was beloved by all who knew him.*[48]

Lord Northland was remembered at the County Tyrone Grand Orange Lodge meeting on 21 May:

> *The half yearly meeting of the County Tyrone Grand Orange Lodge was held on Friday in the Orange Hall Dungannon. Mr Anketell Moutray, D.L., Grand Master, occupied the chair, and Mr W. R. Henderson, District Master of Stewartstown District Lodge, occupied the vice-chair. There was a very large attendance. The meeting was opened with prayer by Rev. Andrew Leitch, DGC, and a portion of scripture was read by Rev C. A. B. Milligan, DGC Mr C. B. M. Chambre J.P., County Grand Secretary, thanked the Grand Lodge on behalf of himself and the members of his family, for the resolution of sympathy adopted at the last meeting in connection with the death of his father, the late Mr Hunt W. Chambre, J.P., County Grand Master. Colonel R. T. G. Lowry, D.L., proposed the adoption of the following resolutions:- "That the County Grand Lodge of Tyrone, at this its first meeting after the lamented death of its Deputy Grand Master, Lord Northland, desires to place on record its profound sorrow at the same, and to state its admiration for his disinterested devotion to his country as testified by laying down his life for it; and we tender our deep sympathy to Lady Northland, Lord and Lady Ranfurly, and his sorrowing family. Rev. E. F. Campbell, M.A., Grand Chaplain (Ireland), in seconding the resolution, said he could hardly trust himself to speak on the subject. It was a case where their fairest hopes had been*

dashed to the ground. They had looked forward to Lord Northland giving them a number of years' active work as their Deputy Grand Master, and when, in the course of time, he came to be Grand Master, a new chapter of better and more active things would have been opened. But it was not to be. Lord Northland had been so thorough and so devoted in all matters that his loss was a severe blow to Orangeism. The resolution was adopted in silence, the members standing. On the motion of Mr. C. B. M. Chambre, J.P., seconded by W. T. Miller J.P., Colonel R. T. G. Lowry, D.L., Pomeroy House, was unanimously elected Deputy Grand Master in place of the Late Lord Northland.[49]

A memorial service for Lord Northland led by His Grace the Lord Primate of All Ireland, Most Rev. Dr Crozier, was held in Dungannon Parish Church during the week after his death. Colonel Ricardo, DSO, officer commanding the 9th Royal Inniskilling Fusiliers, along with 80 men from the Battalion, many of whom had volunteered from the Dungannon UVF and a half troop of Inniskilling Dragoons attended. Lieutenant W. Porter and Captain R. Stevenson of the 5th and 6th Royal Inniskilling Fusiliers respectively were in attendance, having travelled from Dublin.

The Dungannon UVF Battalion, which Lord Northland had commanded, paraded at the service. The sacred building was tastefully draped with Union Jacks and the beautiful regimental flag of the Dungannon Battalion UVF occupied a commanding position in the chancel. The day was observed as an occasion of public mourning by the people of the town and district.

Despite their sorrow, the family of the late Lord Northland did not forget the importance of the cause for which he fought and died. This is vividly illustrated in the following letter written by his sister, Lady Milnes Gaskell, to Mr R. W. Bingham, BA, Dungannon Royal School:

Dear Mr. Bingham – I feel impelled to write to you, as you are at the present time in command of the Dungannon Battalion of the Ulster Volunteer Force. From the time of its foundation to the day of the outbreak of the war that regiment was my brother's every thought, because the Ulster Volunteer Force stood for the cause of freedom and right, just as England stands today for those principles. While life was his he gave cheerfully his service, his power, with heart and soul, and when the call came he laid down his life ungrudgingly. No man can do more. He has gone to join those who have made England what she is – the greatest power for good in the world, in spite of all her blunders – and England is what she is because generations of men have given their mind, energy, and life for her, asking no reward; whilst the women have made the men, and given what was dearer to them than life. I know that volunteering in Ulster received a check owing to the fact of the passage of the Home Rule Bill into law. Had this not been so, this letter would have been unnecessary. We must remember, however, that the Bill was passed by the Government, and not by the people of England. Their opinion was never asked- there has been no election- therefore England cannot be to blame. If there had been an election the Home Rule Bill would have ceased to exist. I want you to tell those men of the Dungannon Battalion who are young and strong, and able to give their services, but who had not yet volunteered, that he (their colonel) is calling to them to go. If they love and reverence his memory, as I know they do, they will not let his call remain unanswered. As a tribute to his leadership and example, let the Dungannon Battalion stand first on the list of the U.V.F. Regiments in the number of its Volunteers. He was so proud of his battalion. Ask the men to prove themselves, worthy of that pride.

Yours sincerely, Constance Milnes Gaskell.[50]

Lord Northland was held in high esteem by the men he commanded in the Dungannon Battalion UVF, who were now serving at the front. It was reported in the press that two former section leaders in the local UVF, Corporal John Johnston and Private Robert Taylor, both of the 2nd Battalion Royal Inniskilling Fusiliers had sought out Viscount Northland's grave in a cemetery near La Bassee and had planted flowers on it. The following letter gives an account of the visit to his grave by Corporal Johnston, accompanied by Private John Bell:

Writing to his parents in Dungannon, Private John Bell, Irish Guards, (formerly R.I.C., constable at Rostrevor, County Down), mentions that accompanied by Corporal Johnston, 2nd Inniskilling Fusiliers, he had visited the grave of Captain Viscount Northland, Coldstream Guards, at La Bassee. The grave was neatly bordered with boxwood, and had flowers growing on it, which had been previous planted by Corporal Johnston, who had been one of Lord Northland's section leaders in the Dungannon U. V. F. battalion.[51]

Lord Northland is buried in Cuinchy Communal Cemetery, Cuinchy, Pas-de-Calais. He is also remembered on St Anne's Parish Church Roll of Honour and Dungannon War Memorial.

Another Dungannon born man who was killed in action during the Artois and Champagne offensive was Private Patrick Burke (441) of the 1st Battalion Connaught Rangers. Having enlisted at Boyle, Co. Roscommon, he died on St. Patrick's Day 1915. Private Burke is buried in Carbaret Rouge British Cemetery, Souchez, Pas de Calais.

The Second Battle of Ypres

The area round the city of Ypres in Belgium saw constant fighting throughout the duration of the war. Indeed, the only major offensive the Germans launched on the Western Front during 1915 was at Ypres, known as the Second Battle of Ypres, it began on 22 April and lasted until about 25 May 1915. It is chiefly remembered for the first use of gas by the Germans on the Western Front. Gas was a deadly weapon which caused death by asphyxiation, and those that survived were temporarily blinded and coughed heavily. The first use of gas saw 10,000 troops affected, with upwards of fifty percent dying within ten minutes of the gas being released. Despite the use of gas, the Germans failed in their attempts to take the city. Many men from the Dungannon district served on the Ypres Salient.

Accounts from the Ypres Salient

Sergeant W. H. Bennett of the Royal Highlanders, a Canadian Regiment, was wounded near Ypres on 23 April and was transferred to a hospital in Cardiff. In a letter home to his father, an ex RIC Sergeant who resided at Primrose Hill, Dungannon, he wrote:

Our battalion of the Canadians went into the trenches on Wednesday night, 21st April, relieving the 1st battalion, who had taken them over from a French regiment a few days previously. These trenches were in poor condition, and we at once set to work to get them made a little safer. Eighty yards separated us from the German trenches, and the intervening space was strewn with German dead. At dawn we knocked off, and stood to arms. Throughout the day everything was quiet, but at 5p.m., we were subjected to a terrific bombardment, which continued without cessation for several hours. Fortunately, they failed to hit the section of trench held by my platoon, and at 8pm not a man had been wounded; but just when it became dark the evil news filtered through. Groups of Turoos filed through our lines on their way to the rear, and news soon spread that they had to retire, as they had been subjected to heavy shell fire and that sulphuric bombs had been used. We knew we were in for a hot time, because at that particular point the line in formation represented a gigantic horseshoe, so that when the Germans poured through the breach they were right behind us. So fierce was the shell fire that we did not expect reinforcements and we knew that we were expected to hang on; and we did it. The news that came through was anything but encouraging. Major Norsworthy the finest officer in our battalion, had been killed; four of our guns had been captured: sulphuric bombs were being used: and still we hung on-there was nothing else to do. Our left had been swung back a little to prevent the enemy from coming in behind, and at 5a.m. this portion of the line was reinforced by one company of the Buffs, who reached our trenches by a circuitous route. All day on Friday we held on, although the bombardment was much fiercer than on the previous day. Men were being wounded all around, and barbed-wire entanglements and parapets were blown up in the air. Slowly we waited for their infantry to attack: in fact we hoped for it, as fighting at close quarters would have been more in our line. Still the attack was never made, and at nightfall we carried out our wounded. Then we received orders to retire our left flank still further, which necessitated the digging of new trenches, and we commenced work about 11pm. We had finished just as dawn was breaking, and immediately the shelling commenced. Our trench was now at right angles to the German lines – i.e., their first position, but there were many more on our front. We were enfiladed by the shell fire, and at 7am our trench was practically blown to pieces. Then what were left of us were ordered to retire on the Second Brigade, and I got shot in the left thigh.[52]

After Sergeant Bennett had resumed active service, he wrote home questioning the attitude of those who had not enlisted. The letter was carried in the *Belfast Newsletter* on 30 November 1915:

Sergeant Harry Bennett, Royal Highlanders of Canada, who was severely wounded some time ago at Ypres, has again resumed active service and, writing to his father, Mr. W. S. Bennett, Primrose Hill, Castlecaulfield, County Tyrone, says:- "About recruiting, most of us out here fail to understand the attitude of the young men at home with regard to enlistment. Only last week we read of hundreds of young men being refused a passage to the United States because they were running away from serving their country. To those poor fellows, and all like them, we in the trenches extend our sincere and heartfelt sympathy, because they are branding themselves and their descendants as cowards for all time by running away from imaginary dangers. When we look at the sun the shadow is behind us; so with danger it is only when we turn away from it that it is to be feared. I feel certain that the boys at home do not know what life is like out here. They overrate the dangers and hardships, else we would have such a stream of recruits as would tax Lord Kitchener's powers to handle. If you happen to meet any of those people who are hanging back just let them know what our opinions are on the subject. If those poor weak hearted creatures could only realise it, they are missing the time of their lives. Plenty of good warm clothing, lots to eat and to drink, with just sufficient danger thrown in to make life interesting. This soldiering has become the greatest game in the world, and work is provided for every man according to his inclination. The man who is fond of horses can join the artillery, cavalry, or battalion transport; the man with a taste for mechanics can find a place in the mechanical transport; the R.A.M.C. opens up a way for the man with medical inclinations and so on. But a far more interesting work can be found for the man who loves excitement- I mean the sort of man who is fond of attending football meetings, race meetings, &c. If he wants excitement in its highest form all he has to do is to volunteer for patrol work between the two lines of trenches. There it is that a man feels he is doing a man's work. He knows that the Germans are engaged in the same work and that it is up to him to prove the superiority of the Lion over the Eagle".

The first use of gas in warfare must have been a terrible experience for those soldiers who witnessed it. In a letter to his friends in Dungannon, Private John McFarlane, 1st Battalion Royal Irish Fusiliers described this experience:

I am writing this in the first line of trenches, where I have been for some time. It would not take you to be very nervous here, and indeed my chum an Armagh man, was riddled beside me on Monday. I was in the big "rattle up "on May 24th when the Germans used gas. I never experienced anything like it, but our battalion stood well to their guns in the trenches, and when the Germans advanced behind the gas cloud we gave them a good return with lead. They thought they would have found us all suffocated, but they were wrong. I think there should be a lot more of the men at home sent out to help us, as we would then be relieved oftener in our duties.[53]

Another local soldier who experienced gas warfare was Private Patrick Donnelly, 2nd Battalion Royal Dublin Fusiliers. Writing from the Duchess of Westminster's Hospital, Etaples, France, to his mother at Washingford Row, Dungannon,he commented:

You will be sorry to hear I was poisoned by gas on Monday last at Ypres, and was brought down to this hospital next day. I am feeling much better now.[54]

Private John Devlin of the 1st Battalion, Royal Irish Fusiliers, the son of Mr William Devlin, Anne Street, Dungannon was also wounded at the fighting in Ypres. Private Devlin suffered a bullet wound in the right arm on 16 May 1915 and was hospitalised in France.

Private Joseph Vallely, 2nd Battalion Royal Inniskilling Fusiliers, wrote to his friends in Moygashel, Dungannon telling them that he was suffering from severe wounds to his back and left leg, caused by portions of a shell and two rifle bullets. The wounds had been received during the severe fighting at Ypres in March 1915. Private Vallely was sent to hospital in Guildford, Surrey. On 11 October 1915 the *Belfast Newsletter* reported that Private Vallely had returned to Moygashel, the previous Saturday, but was still suffering from the severe wounds that he had sustained in March 1915.

Sapper Alfred McGowan, who had been in action since November 1914, told of his lucky escape from the falling shells:

Sapper Alfred McGowan, Royal Engineers, writing from France to his brother, Mr Isaac McGowan, Kilmore, Donaghmore, states – "I have just come through a great battle here with a whole skin. The fighting was awful, just like that at Neuve Chapelle and the fields and roads were swept with shell-fire for miles. We started to bombard the Germans on

Sunday morning at five o'clock, and shelled them at a terrific rate for upwards of an hour, immediately after which our men charged. I did not take part in the charge as I was acting as cyclist despatch carrier for my commander. But I was in for a hot time and often had to cycle as fast as an express train. Anyhow I never cycled so fast in my life before. Shells were ripping up the road both before and behind, but the nearest shave I had was when a piece of shell hit the toe of my boot and cut it almost through. Fortunately I sustained no harm." [55]

The *Belfast Newsletter* on 19 May 1915 reported that Private Michael Wilson of the 4th Battalion Royal Dublin Fusiliers was another who was wounded. The article said he had wrote to his mother, Mrs Wilson, William Street, Dungannon to tell her that he had been wounded and was recovering in the 2nd Western General Hospital in Manchester.

Lieutenant John O. Newton, Princess Patricia's Canadian Light Infantry, sent a letter from Flanders on the 19 May to his brother, Mr Robert Newton, JP, Killymeal, Dungannon. John was a member of Golden Knights of Dungannon RBP 52 and was Worshipful District Master of Killyman Royal Black District Chapter No.1 from 1905-1906. John described his experiences at the front and the *Belfast Newsletter* on 25 May 1915 relayed this to a wider audience:

He had just returned from the trenches for a rest. The Canadians had a pretty tough time, but he had escaped without a scratch, though how he did not know. The losses had been very heavy, but the men who were left were hearty. He mentions that during the recent severe fighting he had been sent in broad daylight with fifty men to obtain ammunition, and although they had to cross 200 yards of open ground they sustained no injury. A shell exploded within three feet of Lieutenant Newton and covered him with mud and dirt, but no casualties occurred. A bullet perforated the sleeve of his coat, and a Canadian belonging to another company had seven bullet holes in his tunic and escaped uninjured.

The War Office notified Mrs Doyle, Newmills, Dungannon, that her son Lance-Corporal Thomas Seawright, 2nd Battalion Royal Irish Rifles, had been wounded in Belgium. A bomb thrown from an aeroplane exploded, with three fragments entering his thigh. An operation was performed in France and he was subsequently transferred to the 3rd Southern General Hospital in Oxford to recuperate. The *Belfast Newsletter* 23 July 1915 reported that Lance-Corporal Thomas Seawright had arrived home at Newmills to recover from his wounds.

The *Belfast Newsletter* of 4 June 1915 reported that Private Thomas Kirk of the 2nd Battalion, Royal Dublin Fusiliers had sent a postcard to his mother Mrs Kirk, Barrack Street, Dungannon telling her that he had been wounded in recent fighting and was now in hospital in England. Private Kirk had been both wounded and gassed in the engagement. After being hospitalised in England he had returned home to Dungannon by late July 1915.

Private Thomas White, Royal Dublin Fusilier,s of Union Place, Dungannon was gassed on 5 June 1915. The *Belfast Newsletter* on 17 September 1915 reported that he had returned to Dungannon the day before.

Other soldiers with connections to Dungannon who were reported wounded by the *Belfast Newsletter* in June 1915 were Lieutenant B. Bourdekin of the Royal Field Artillery and Lieutenant W. E. S. Howard, 4th Battalion Royal Irish Rifles (who at that time was attached to the 2nd battalion of the regiment). Lieutenant Bourdekin was well known in the Dungannon area as he had formerly served as a 2nd Lieutenant in the disbanded Mid-Ulster Royal Garrison Artillery. Lieutenant Howard was the son of Mr Samuel Howard, Rathgar, Dublin, who had practised as a solicitor in Dungannon. Lieutenant Howard had been in the Army prior to the outbreak of the war and served in France during the later part of 1914. Despite still suffering from the wounds he received in the face from fragments of shrapnel shells on 10 June 1915, the *Belfast Newsletter* on 25 October 1915 reported that he had received promotion to the rank of Captain.

Private William J. Wilson, 2nd Battalion Royal Irish Fusiliers, and Private John McQuade, 2nd Battalion Royal Dublin Fusiliers, were also involved in the fighting around Ypres. Their battalions took part in the battle of Ypres, St Julien, Frezenberg Ridge and Bellewaerde Ridge during the German spring offensive around Ypres. Private Wilson of Railway View, Dungannon, was a reservist and had actually just returned from training in Dunree, Co. Donegal, when called up to serve King and Country shortly after the outbreak of the war. On 5 June the *Belfast Newsletter* reported that Private Wilson, had during the fighting around Ypres, suffered lacerations to his fingers and had his hands fractured. He was subsequently transferred to Highfield Military Hospital, Liverpool. The *Belfast Newsletter* on 9 June 1915 reported that Private John McQuade had written to Mrs Maria Teague, Anne Street, Dungannon telling her that he had been shot through both ankles but was now recovering. McQuade also stated that he was a prisoner of war at Cologne, Germany.

Lance Corporal Adam Harbinson of the 1st Battalion Royal Irish Fusiliers from Beechvalley, Dungannon and Private Albert James Bradley, Princess Patricia's Canadian Light Infantry, originally from Corr Dunrarsvalley, Charlemont, County Armagh were also wounded in the fighting around Ypres in 1915. Lance Corporal Adam Harbinson, together with his brothers William and Thomas, belonged to Dungannon Holdfast LOL 1620 and appear on its Roll of Honour. Private Bradley was wounded in the right hand on 7 May 1915 by a shrapnel bullet and was sent to a London hospital.

On 8 July 1915 the *Belfast Newsletter* reported that a number of soldiers from the Dungannon area had returned home to recuperate from the wounds they had received. The men mentioned in the report were Lance Corporal Adam Harbinson, 1st Battalion Royal Irish Fusiliers, Private William Wilson, 1st Battalion Royal Irish Fusiliers, and Private Donnelly, Royal Dublin Fusiliers. Lance Corporal Harbinson had been treated in hospital at Ashton-on-Mersey, Cheshire. Private Wilson had been in Highfield Hospital, Liverpool receiveing treatment for bullet wounds to his hands and arm, while Private Donnelly had been in hospital suffering from gas poisoning.

Sergeant William Lynn of the 2nd Battalion Royal Irish Fusiliers was another local man who was wounded in the Ypres region. William wrote to his parents in Coalisland telling them that he had sustained a fractured leg on the 18 June and been sent to hospital in Manchester. William had three brothers serving along with him in France.

Private Patrick Sands of the Royal Garrison Artillery was wounded on 4 August 1915. His mother living at Mullaghanagh, Dungannon received official intimation that her son Patrick had been hospitalised back to Manchester as a result of his wounds. Private Patrick Sands was one of three brothers serving the King. Bombardier James Sands, Royal Field Artillery, and Private David Sands, 6th Battalion Royal Inniskilling Fusiliers, were serving in Gallipoli.

Private Robert Morrow VC

The son of Hugh and Margaret Morrow, Robert was born on 7 September 1891 in the townland of Sessia just outside Newmills, Dungannon. He was educated at Carland National School and enlisted into the 1st Battalion Royal Irish Fusiliers (The Faugh-A-Ballaghs) around 1910. By 1911 he was in St Lucia Barracks, Bordon, Hampshire. Army life seemed to suit Robert despite it being portrayed in those days, as being rough and associated with heavy drinking. Private Morrow did

Pte Robert Morrow, V.C.

not fit this mould as he did not drink, which he attributed to his Presbyterian upbringing.

On the outbreak of war, Private Morrow's Regiment went with the BEF to France. Described as not being a conspicuous soldier in peacetime, Private Morrow showed his true colours in battle. From the first time the Battalion was under fire, Private Morrow proved that he had the heart of a lion and there are many stories of his fearlessness.[56]

Private Morrow and his comrades in D Company, 1st Battalion Royal Irish Fusiliers had been in the Douve sector around Messines on 12 April 1915, which was to be their last day in that sector. At 5pm the Germans, who held the elevated positions around Messines, began to bombard the trenches in the Douve sector and systematically shortened their range till they were achieving direct hits. It was against this backdrop that Private Robert Morrow won his Victoria Cross. However, it was not until late May that the news that Robert Morrow had won his VC broke in Dungannon, but was tinged with sadness given that his death was also breaking news at the same time. On 25 May 1915 the *Belfast Newsletter* carried this story:

> *News has just been received in Dungannon of the death of Private Robert Morrow, 1st Battalion Princess Victoria's (Royal Irish Fusiliers), who was awarded the Victoria Cross, as announced in yesterday's issue of this newspaper.*

113

For most conspicuous bravery near Messines on 12th April, 1915, when he rescued and carried successively to places of comparative safety several men who had been buried in the debris of trenches wrecked by shell-fire. Private Morrow carried out this gallant work on his own initiative, and under very heavy fire from the enemy.

Private Morrow, whose mother lives at Sessia, close to the village of Newmills, near Dungannon, did not live to receive personally the coveted distinction, as he was killed in action on the 26th April, just a fortnight after his gallant conduct at Messines . he was born in Sessia twenty-two years ago, his father being Mr Hugh Morrow, a farmer, who died shortly after Private Morrow's birth, leaving a widow and a numerous family in rather struggling circumstances. Private Morrow was taken under the care of the Presbyterian Orphan Society, and was educated at Carland National School. While at school he was of a quiet disposition, and was regarded with the utmost affection by both master and pupils. He was of very steady habits, and on reaching manhood proved of great help to his widowed mother. He enlisted in the Royal Irish Fusiliers five years ago, and on the outbreak of war was despatched to France with the first contingent of the Expeditionary Force. He there acquitted himself with remarkable courage and on being wounded some months ago the captain commanding his company wrote to Mrs Morrow acquainting her of the affair, and stating that her son was "a man absolutely devoid of fear." On recovering from his wounds he went once more on active service and on the 12th April performed the brave deed for which the Victoria Cross has been awarded. Private Morrow then wrote home to his mother, modestly detailing the scenes in which he had been engaged, and stated that his colonel had informed him that he would recommend him for the Victoria Cross. On that day fortnight, however, he was fatally wounded, and died on the field. Immediately on hearing of his brother's death, Mrs Morrow's eldest son, Richard at once joined the 12th Inniskilling Fusiliers. Recently in the Parish Church the rector, Rev. Gordon Scott, referred in moving terms to the deceased and read to the congregation the reference made by his colonel and captain. Our Dungannon correspondent writes – When Private Morrow fell on the 26th April he was again engaged in the heroic task of assisting wounded soldiers who were exposed to the heavy fire of the enemy. For his gallantry on this occasion his captain again recommended him for the Victoria Cross. Private Morrow was the second Ulsterman to win the

Victoria Cross in the present war, the other recipient of the coveted distinction being Sergeant (now Lieutenant) David Nelson of the famous L Battery, Royal Horse Artillery a native of Monaghan.

Many tributes were paid to Robert Morrow VC on his death and the true esteem he was held in by the officers and men of the regiment and by others could be clearly seen. Details of a number of these tributes were published in the *Belfast Newsletter*, as follows:

Mrs Morrow, Sessia, Newmills, mother of the Victoria Cross hero, Private Robert Morrow, 2nd Battalion Royal Irish Fusiliers, has received the following tribute from Lieutenant-Colonel D. W. Churcher, late commanding the 1st Battalion Royal Irish Fusiliers – "It is with the deepest sorrow that I hear your son, Private Robert Morrow, has met a soldier's death, while serving his King and country in France. No words of mine can I fear help you in your grief, but I should like you to know the boy soldiered straight and served me well when I was commanding the regiment, and I always had a soft place in my heart for him. In these days, when the whole Empire is grieving for its young manhood , it may be some consolation to you to feel that your son has fallen in gallant company while upholding the honour of old Ireland, and that his name will be inscribed for all time on the Empire's roll of honour. Life is very short for all of us, and no one can say when his hour may come, but if we are prepared, as I feel sure your son was, it will not be long before we all meet again in a happier world than this. I pray that time may soften your grief and, with all sympathy, remain yours very truly.

D. W. Churcher, lieutenant-colonel.[57]

Captain G V. W. Hill, 2nd Battalion Royal Irish Fusiliers, has written the following letter to Mrs Morrow, Sessia Newmills, with reference to the death of her son, Private Robert Morrow, V.C.:- I have been unable to write to you before this with regard to your son, for I have been too busy. As, of course, you now known, your son has been awarded this V.C., and how thoroughly he deserved it. I have know your son ever since he joined the regiment, as he has always been in my company, and it was during the time I have had the honour to command this company out here that the incident occurred over which he got his V.C. I am myself proud that I was present and able to put his name forward, for his is the first V.C.

ever won by the 87th, and this fact will, I hope, give you some added consolation in your loss. I need hardly tell you that every officer and man of the regiment is proud of your son, and all mourn his death with you, and offer you their deepest sympathies. It was during our attack on St. Julien on 25th April that your son was wounded, but I do not think he suffered much, and I know that on that day he behaved with his usual gallantry.[58]

At the opening of Dungannon quarter sessions yesterday, His Honour Judge Linehan, addressing the Grand Jury said: It is not my custom or inclination to refer to matters not associated with the ordinary business of the Crown Court, but we are living in exceptional times, and all of us are hearing of the deaths of young friends and relatives who have fallen on the battlefield. In the Dungannon district the losses during the past week have been very considerable, and the casualties include eight men killed and six wounded. That is a very large number for one town or district. One of the gallant number killed was a Victoria Cross hero, Private Robert Morrow, of the Royal Irish Fusiliers. He was a native of Newmills, a short distance from Dungannon, and was well known in the district. We are all sorry to hear of his death, which terminates so distinguished a young life. Private Morrow was scarcely 20 years of age, but he did his duty manfully, and the townspeople must be justly proud of having had in their midst one who so distinguished himself as to merit the most coveted honour known in military service. Barely a fortnight had elapsed after Private Morrow had performed the brave deed for which he was awarded the Victoria Cross until he was called upon to offer his life in performing similar deeds Our sympathy goes out to the brave boys relatives. These deeds should inspire young men who have not yet heard their country's call and who still remain at home. I sincerely trust that these deeds will bring home to them the true sense of obligations. County Tyrone has done exceedingly well in responding to the call to the colours, but there are still thousands waiting for the inspiration to go. Surely they will not now stand by when they are the gap to be filled – a gap which should be filled not with one man alone, but with ten, if necessary.[59]

Mrs Margaret Jane Morrow, Sessia, Newmills, County Tyrone, has received the following personal letter from his Majesty the King relative to her son, Private Robert Morrow, 1st Battalion Princess Victoria's (Royal Irish Fusiliers), who won the Victoria Cross while rescuing the wounded at Messines on 12th April, but was killed at St Julien on 25th April while performing similar acts of heroism:-

Buckingham Palace, 15th October, 1915. "It is a matter of sincere regret to me that the death of Private Robert Morrow deprived me of the pride of personally conferring upon him the Victoria Cross, the greatest of all distinctions.

GEORGE R. I.[60]

Private Robert Morrow did not only receive a Victoria Cross. He was also awarded the Medal of St. George, Third Class, posthumously by His Imperial Majesty the Emperor of Russia as a memorial to his distinguished service.

These medals were sent to Private Morrow's mother and she received some tempting financial offers for her son's decorations, but Mrs Morrow said only his Regiment should have them. Mrs Morrow formally handed over the Victoria Cross to the Regiment at a ceremonial parade in August 1919.

Private Robert Morrow VC (10563) is buried in White House Cemetery in the village of St Jan, on the outskirts of Ypres. He is also remembered on plaques in St Anne's Cathedral Belfast, Newmills Parish Church and Carland Presbyterian Church and Dungannon War Memorial. He was also included in a large commemorative painting commissioned by the French Government.

The Dungannon Fallen at Ypres

Private John McLaughlin (9744), 2nd Battalion Royal Irish Fusiliers, was killed in action on 5 February 1915. John was born in Dungannon and enlisted in Armagh. He is remembered on the Menin Gate Memorial, Ypres, Belgium and Dungannon War Memorial. Little is known of the life of Private John McLaughlin in Dungannon, but he is remembered just the same, like all who served.

Lance Corporal Francis Madden (9973), 2nd Battalion Royal Irish Fusiliers, is listed as being born in Dungannon. He was killed in action on 14 March 1915. Francis enlisted in Armagh and served under the surname Campbell (Madden was his mother's former name). Lance Corporal Francis Madden is remembered on the Menin Gate Memorial, Ypres, Belgium.

Private James M. Arthurs (19682), 10th Battalion Royal Canadian Regiment, was born in 1880 in Dungannon. Private Arthurs was killed in action on 26 April 1915. Prior to the war he had served for 8 years in the 39th Battery Royal Field Artillery before moving to Canada where he subsequently re-enlisted on the 26 September 1914 at Valcartier, Quebec. Private Arthurs is remembered on the Menin Gate Memorial, Ypres, Belgium and on the Roll of Honour Plaque of LOL 183 in Newmills Orange Hall. For a number of months after Private Arthurs' death, he was still being posted as missing:

> *The Canadian Record Office announces the following casualties amongst Ulster men serving with the Canadian Expeditionary Force – Private James M. Arthurs (Dungannon) 10th Battalion, reported missing.*[61]

> *The most recent lists issued by the Canadian Record Office show the following casualties amongst the Ulstermen serving in France with the Canadian forces:- Private James M. Arthurs (Dungannon), 10th Battalion, missing.*[62]

Lance Corporal John Henry Rose (3753), 1st Battalion Rifle Brigade, was born in Dungannon around 1891. The family had left the Dungannon area by 1901. Lance Corporal Rose was a regular soldier having enlisted in Eastbourne in 1910. He was killed in action on 2 May 1915 and is remembered on the Menin Gate Memorial, Ypres, Belgium.

Private Charles McAnaw Kelly (3434), 2nd Battalion Royal Inniskilling Fusiliers, was born in County Donegal. Enlisting in Strabane as Charles Kelly he was killed in action on 6 May 1915. Private McAnaw/Kelly is buried in Cuinchy Communal Cemetery, Cuinchy, Pas-de-Calais and remembered on the Dungannon War Memorial as Charles McAnaw. The *Belfast Newsletter* on 2 June 1915 carried the following report of a letter from Charles' brother:

> *Corporal Edward McAnaw, 2nd Battalion Royal Inniskilling Fusiliers, writing from Flanders to his wife at Barrack Street, Dungannon, states that his brother Charles has been killed in action. He saw him buried in the same graveyard as the late Lord Northland.*

Private William John Telford (18140), 1st Battalion York and Lancaster Regiment, was born in Dungannon around 1887. Prior to the war Private Telford had served for seven years in the RIC, making a name for himself as a excellent instrumentalist in the Depot Band. He moved to England in June 1914 taking up a post with the West Riding Police in Yorkshire. Upon the outbreak of war he enlisted immediately with the York and Lancaster Regiment. Private Telford was killed in action on the 8 May 1915, although initially he was posted as missing. He had been an active member of the Dungannon Brass Band. Initial reports back to the family in Dungannon were that Private Telford had been wounded. On 17 August the *Belfast Newsletter* on 17 August 1915 carried the following article about Corporal Telford:

Much anxiety is felt by the relatives in Dungannon of Corporal William John Telford (18140) 1st Battalion York and Lancaster Regiment, who has been missing since 8th May last. The Army Records state that he was wounded in France on that date, and that his whereabouts are unknown. He had been a member of the Royal Irish Constabulary for several years and was a well known and popular instrumentalist in the Depot Band. For a year prior to the outbreak of war he had been a member of the Yorkshire County Police Force, and had volunteered for service with the York and Lancaster's at the commencement of hostilities. His father, Mr Richard Telford, York Street, Dungannon anxiously awaits further information.

The agony of waiting for news of a loved one must have been terrible, fearing the worst and hoping for the best. Private William John Telford is remembered on the Menin Gate Memorial, Ypres, Belgium.

Private Francis Fitzpatrick (9553), 2nd Battalion Royal Dublin Fusiliers, was born in Dungannon around 1893. He was killed in action on 9 May 1915 but unfortunately for the family, official notification of Private Fitzpatrick's death was not received until 12 June 1915 some days after letters began to arrive home to the Dungannon area advising that he had been killed. The following report in the *Belfast Newsletter* dated 9 June 1915 shows that details of Private Fitzpatrick's death were being circulated some days before official notification:

The published list of casualties contains the name of Private Frank Fitzpatrick, 2nd Battalion Royal Dublin Fusiliers, as having been killed

in action. His father, Mr Hugh Fitzpatrick, Donaghmore Road,
Dungannon, has not yet received the usual notification, but it is
understood that some Dungannon men at the Front have written home
stating that they saw him fall.[63]

Private Francis (Frank) Fitzpatrick is buried in the Ypres Town Cemetery
Extension, Belgium. His brother, Private Bernard Fitzpatrick ,was killed
in the Dardanelles in August 1915 while serving with the 1st Battalion
Royal Inniskilling Fusiliers. A third brother James Fitzpatrick also served
with the 1st Battalion Royal Inniskilling Fusiliers.

Private John Toner (9552), 2nd Battalion Royal Dublin Fusiliers, was
killed in action on 24 May 1915. Born around 1875, John lived and
worked in Dungannon for most of his life until the outbreak of war.
John's battalion was heavily involved in the fighting around Ypres
between April and June 1915. Private John Toner is remembered on the
Menin Gate Memorial, Ypres, Belgium.

Private Joseph Donnelly (9563), was serving with the 2nd Battalion Royal
Dublin Fusiliers, when he was killed in action on 24 May 1915. Joseph
was born around 1895 at Annagher, Coalisland and enlisted in
Dungannon. Private Joseph Donnelly has no known grave, but is
remembered on the Menin Gate Memorial, Ypres, Belgium and
Dungannon War Memorial.

Lance Corporal William Andrew Fairbairn (H/6139), 8th (King's Royal
Irish) Hussars, was killed in action on 13 June 1915. William Fairbairn
had been born around 1892 in Kirkoswald, Cumberland, Scotland. The
family had moved to Dungannon by 1901. William was a regular soldier
and had been serving in India at the outbreak of the war. The 8th Hussars
were a Cavalry Regiment and during 1915 they saw action around Ypres.
Reports in the *Belfast Newsletter* at the time of his death illustrates that
some of his family had moved from Dungannon, but his brother John
still living in the town:

Lance Corporal Wm. Fairburn, 8th Hussars who was killed in action in
Flanders on the 13th inst, was 23 years of age, and had six years service.
His mother resides along with his sisters and brothers at Milford Street,
Belfast, another brother, Mr. John Fairburn, living at Dungannon.[64]

Mr. John Fairbairn, Park Road, Dungannon has received an intimation from the Squadron Commander that his brother Corporal William Fairbairn, 8th Hussars was killed by shell fire in Flanders on Sunday 13th inst. The deceased solider was a native of Dungannon, being the second son of Mr Thomas Fairbairn, and was 23 years of age.[65]

Lance Corporal William Andrew Fairbairn is buried in the Perth Cemetery China Wall, Ypres, Belgium. He is also remembered on the St Anne's Parish Church Roll of Honour and Dungannon War Memorial.

Driver Robert Lynn (45206), 87th Battery Royal Field Artillery, was killed in action on 6 August 1915. Born in 1885 in Coalisland Robert was one of four brothers (James, John and William) who fought for King and Country. He was a regular soldier and had gone to France with the First Expeditionary Force in 1914. Robert Lynn wrote this letter shortly before he made the ultimate sacrifice:

I received your kind and welcome parcel alright and I am very thankful to you for remembering the soldiers at the front; indeed things like these are a great comfort to us as many a time we don't have a chance to get anything. We are having some very nice weather here this long time which is very pleasant when you are always in the open. We are all hoping to be home before long. I think this can't last very much longer; the death roll on both sides is terrible. If the Turkish lot was forced, I think it would

L Cpl Hugh John Cairns (left)
and Driver Robert Lynn (right)

put a near end to this; it would allow us to draw forces from there to here. I think all of us do not want to stop another winter out here. I will close, hoping we all come victorious.[66]

Robert Lynn was a member of Coalisland Faith Defenders LOL 93 and with his friend Lance Corporal Hugh John Cairns would forever remain in Flanders fields. Robert is buried in Hop Store Cemetery, Ypres, Belgium. He is also remembered on the Dungannon War Memorial, Portadown War Memorial and the Lynn Memorial Plaque in Brackaville Parish Church, Coalisland.

Rifleman Owen McGill (6860), 1st Battalion Royal Irish Rifles, was killed in action on 25 September 1915. Born in Donaghmore around 1876 he was living in Castlecaulfield by 1911. Prior to the war he had been a drill instructor with the Annaghmakeown Company of the Irish National Volunteers. He enlisted at Holywood County Down and served with "B" Company in the 1st Battalion Royal Irish Rifles. Rifleman Owen McGill has no known grave but is remembered on the Ploegsteert Memorial, Comines-Warneton, Belgium and Dungannon War Memorial.

Lieutenant Richard A. Lloyd

Not all the men that were reported in the press as missing were killed. A classic example of this is the story of Tamnamore man Lieutenant Richard "Dicky" A. Lloyd. The *Belfast Newsletter* on 11 May 1915 reported that he had been killed in action, but the very next day the paper clarified that he was still alive but wounded, and it was another Lieutenant R. A. Lloyd of the same regiment that had been killed:

> *The announcement of the death in action of Lieutenant Richard A. Lloyd, the brilliant Irish international Rugby player, who was serving at the front with the 10th (Scottish) Battalion of the King's Liverpool Regiment, will be received with feelings of profound regret by a wide circle of friends and acquaintances. The only son of Mr. Averell Lloyd, J.P., of Tamnamore, Moy, County Tyrone, Lieutenant Lloyd was educated at Portora Royal School, Enniskillen, and Trinity College, Dublin, and went to Liverpool to join his uncle, who has an extensive business as a cotton broker in the Mersey city. A keen and enthusiastic Rugbeian, he played for Portora's Invincible school team, which a few years ago carried all before it, in the Schools Cup competition. On going to Trinity he was at once given a place in the University fifteen, which he eventually captained with marked success. He received his first cap in 1910, and figured prominently in practically all the Irish international fixtures since that*

year, being captain of the selected team on more than one occasion. The most brilliant outside half who has appeared in the Rugby field for many years past, "Dicky" Lloyd was a wonderfully deft and powerful kick with either foot, and had probably no equal in the art of dropping goals. A fine opportunist, he was gifted with a good turn of speed and possessed dodging powers above the ordinary. He excelled either in combination or as an individualist, and more than once an Irish team owed its success almost solely to his prowess. The hero of many a memorable struggle in Belfast and Dublin, as well as across the Channel, he gained the wholehearted admiration of the spectators by his skilful and scientific play, which was as clean as it was effective. He was singularly free from ostentation on, or off the field, and bore the honours which fell thick upon him with becoming modesty. His sole desire was to "play the game," and his success in this connection may be judged by the affectionate regard in which he was held not only by Rugby men, but by the football public generally. After he had settled in the Mersey city he joined the Liverpool Rugby Club, to whom he proved a tower of strength on numerous occasions. By a remarkable coincidence, Lieutenant Lloyd is the third member of Liverpool's brilliant side of 1913 1914 to be killed in action, the two others being F. H. Turner and R. W. Poulton Palmer. It may be recalled that another member of the Liverpool team, T. W. Lloyd was recently reported killed, but it was subsequently found that the intimation was incorrect. Lieutenant Lloyd was also a magnificent cricketer, his performance with the bat being almost as notable as his achievements on the football field. With Mr H. M. Read he held the record for the highest score of a first wicket partnership, the pair knocking

Lt Richard A. Lloyd
10th Scottish King's Liverpool Regt.

up no fewer than 323 runs for Trinity College against County Meath. The previous record was made by Mr H. A. Moore and Mr A. N. McClinton, of the North of Ireland Cricket Club, whose first wicket partnership realised 315 against Phoenix C.C. A member of the North of Ireland Cricket Club, Lieutenant Lloyd had the honour of representing Ireland against Scotland. Shortly after the outbreak of war he enlisted in the new Army, and afterwards obtained a commission in the Territorial battalion in which he was serving at the time of his death. To his sorrowing father, so tragically bereft of his only son, the deepest sympathy will be extended by all who knew the deceased, and by the thousands of Rugby enthusiasts who have followed his career with more than ordinary interest.

Widespread satisfaction will be felt not only in Rugby circles but by the public generally at the announcement that the War Office notification of the death of Lieutenant R. A. Lloyd, of the 10th (Scottish) Battalion King's Liverpool Regiment, was incorrect. Inquiries made yesterday elicited the information that Second Lieutenant R. A. Lloyd, 4th (Extra Reserve) Battalion King's Liverpool Regiment, who was a native of the Mersey city, had been killed in action, and that the War Department had made the mistake of giving the corps of the deceased officer as the 10th Battalion – the Liverpool Scottish – in which the famous Irish Rugby international holds a commission. With a view to preventing confusion owing to two officers of the regiment, though of different battalions, bearing the same initials and surname, letters and parcels for the Irish Rugby captain have for some time past been addressed "Mr R. Averell Lloyd" it may be added that in response to a telegram from Mr Averell Lloyd J.P. of Tamnamore, Moy, County Tyrone, father of Lieutenant R Averell Lloyd, the War Office replied: Not killed, but wounded.[67]

Lieutenant R.A. Lloyd of the 10th (Scottish) Battalion of the Kings Liverpool Regiment was sent back to hospital in London. While in hospital he wrote home informing his father of his condition. Richard "Dicky" Lloyd has been described as one of the most brilliant rugby footballers that ever played for Ireland, and he also excelled at football and cricket.

The Lloyd family still have strong links with the Tamnamore area, being closely associated with Tamnamore LOL 513 and Apprentice Boys of Derry, Tamnamore Club.

The Battle of Festubert

The Battle of Festubert was fought in the Ypres Salient by British, Canadian and Indian troops. It lasted from 15 May to about 27 May 1915. The battle was launched under the command of Sir Douglas Haig, the BEF having come under sustained pressure from the French military command to launch a major attack. Festubert on 15 May was the chosen spot for the BEF to launch a second major attack in the Artois region.

Despite an artillery bombardment for four days prior to the attack, the German front line defences had not been destroyed. It was not until the renewed attacks that took place between 20 and 24 May that the village of Festubert was captured. By the end of the attack on 27 May, the allies front line had advanced just over half a mile at a cost of some 16,000 casualties.

The 2nd Battalion Royal Inniskilling Fusiliers played a major role in the battle and many Dungannon men saw action in this engagement, with some making the supreme sacrifice. Festubert was an attempt to break the German line using a night attack on 15 May 1915.

The Inniskillings were to lead the attack, which was planned to begin at 11.30pm. The idea was to cross no man's land in deadly silence and go into the German trenches with bomb and gun. It was hoped that the night attack would surprise the Germans. At 8pm the Inniskillings exited their trenches and crawled across no man's land, through the mud and rubbing shoulder's with dead men who had went before. There they would stay until the signal to attack was given.

Unfortunately for the Inniskilling's just two minutes before 11.30pm the Germans sent a stream of flares into the sky, which turned night into day, and raked no man's land with rifle, machine gun and shell fire. The Inniskilling's only option was to go forward into the hail of bullets and shell fire in an attempt to reach the German lines. They reached the German front lines and an account of this advance was given by Lance-Corporal John McIntyre in a letter home to friends in Dungannon:

Lance-Corporal John McIntyre, 2nd Battalion Royal Inniskilling Fusiliers, who was wounded during the heavy fighting in the Festubert district, and is now in hospital in England, writes to his friends in Dungannon as

125

follows:- *"My brother Joseph and I are in hospital, wounded, but we are coming on well. I was wounded in the back and my brother in the ankle, but we are lucky ever to see England again. Our battalion had a bayonet charge on Saturday night, when we took two lines of German trenches at the point of steel. We were under heavy fire from the time we left our trenches until we reached the Germans, but we fixed them up for the men we lost. I cannot say how many we lost, but I know that a number of my own section fell. Young Willie Dickson of Dungannon is killed, and I got a box from his pocket, the only thing I could take as a keepsake. He and I came out here together last September, and went through a lot since. I got wounded and fell beside two of my chums, and we lay under heavy fire until three o'clock on Sunday morning. We were too bad to crawl out of danger. One of my wounded chums got killed by a bullet as he lay there, so we had a close shave. The shell fire was terrible. On Sunday morning when I revived I tried to make my way back to our trenches, with the German bullets cutting the ground around me. I took cover behind a dead comrade and on looking into his face I thought at first, to my horror, that it was my brother, but on creeping into our trenches he was the first man to speak to me as he had reached it before me and had had his wound dressed. I was obliged to stop all that Sunday in the front trench, and German shells nearly did for the lot of us. It was an awful Sunday, and in the evening they tried a counterattack to regain their lost trenches. Our artillery and machine guns and ourselves with rifles went at them and mowed them down like sheep. The enemy thought it better to go back and let the British keep the trenches. We all wore mouth pads to protect us from poisonous gas. When we charged with the bayonet in the dark and got into their trenches we made them hop for the dirty tricks they do and any of them that were left were easily counted. They kill some our wounded and throw vitriol on others and burn them, and then laugh at the poor fellow's agony. I have seen all this and also the vitriol bombs they throw at night, after a battle, to catch the wounded who are unable to get to safety. Corporal John Johnston of the Inniskillings machine gun section also writes to Dungannon confirming the death of Private W. R. Dickson a Dungannon man, whose name had not reached the War Office.*[68]

Lance Corporal John Johnston, Machine-Gun Section, 2nd Battalion, Royal Inniskilling Fusiliers, also took part in the severe fighting at Festubert on 15 and 16 May 1915. He was promoted to the rank of

Corporal for his brave conduct on the battlefield. Corporal Johnston was very humble about his promotion and had written home to his parents at Killymeal, Dungannon telling them that he had received a promotion in the field following the death of many of the officers and men of his section. It was not until Private John Bonar of the same Battalion, who was also from Dungannon wrote to the Dungannon Worker's Union concerning records and photographs of members who had died in service of their country that the full facts surrounding Corporal Johnston's promotion became clear:

> *Br. Johnston (Corporal John Johnston) was delighted to hear that the Union is getting along so well, and I will say this about him; that he is a credit to his native place and to the Union. I will tell you why. In the early part of a recent attack we made half of the officers and all the non-commissioned officers were rendered hors-de-combat, so that the charge of the section devolved on Johnston. He took charge, and did his duty like a man, cheering us up and running from gun to gun amidst a very inferno of shell-fire from the Germans. He has been promoted for his pluck.[69]*

Further details of the battle were sent by Sergeant Le Gear when writing to his friends in Dungannon. He told them about the great charge of the Inniskillings and the taking of several lines of trenches, which had crowned the regiment with glory and how the Germans were beginning to learn about the mettle of the men that made up General French's contemptible little Army.

Not surprisingly during such ferocious fighting many of the Inniskilling's were killed or wounded. In a letter home Lance Corporal John McIntyre explained that out of the thousand men who made the charge on 15 and 16 May there were between 700 and 800 wounded or killed. Lance Corporal John McIntyre and his brother Private Joseph McIntyre were both wounded at Fesubert. John had wounds to his back and Joseph was wounded in his right ankle and back. The *Belfast Newsletter* reported on 24 May 1915 that John was being treated in Cambridge Hospital and Joseph in a London War Hospital. By late July both had returned to Dungannon to recuperate.

Private John Lynn of the 2nd Battalion Royal Inniskilling Fusiliers was wounded in the head and back on the 16 May during the Battle of

Fesubert. Private John Lynn was a member of Coalisland Faith Defenders LOL 93 and fought for King and Country along with his three brothers James, Robert and William. The *Belfast Newsletter* on 17 September reported that John Lynn, along with his brother Sergeant William Lynn of the 2ⁿᵈ Battalion Royal Irish Fusiliers, had returned to Coalisland to recover from wounds they had received while serving the cause. By this stage their brother Robert of the Royal Field Artillery had been killed in action.

A Dungannon man who was wounded in the lead up to the Battle of Festubert was Private Robert Taylor, 2ⁿᵈ Battalion Royal Inniskilling Fusiliers. Private Taylor, who had been a section leader in B Company, Dungannon Battalion, UVF before the war, wrote to his wife at Moygashel, Dungannon, to tell her that he had been wounded on the breast and hand on 13 May 1915. He said that his injuries were caused by a large shell which burst a few yards from him and he was now in a clearing hospital in France. The Belfast Newsletter reported on 22 July 1915 that Private Taylor had returned home to Moygashel, to recover from his wounds. Having recovered from his wounds, he returned to the front line with the 1ˢᵗ Battalion Royal Inniskilling Fusiliers and saw action in Macedonia.

By mid August, Corporal John Johnston had returned to Dungannon. The following article describes how fortunate he was during the Battle of Festubert:

A very hearty welcome was accorded Corporal John Johnston, machine gun section, 2nd Battalion Royal Inniskilling Fusiliers, who arrived home at Killymeal, Dungannon, by the midnight train on Saturday night. A large crowd assembled at the railway station to greet him and loud cheers were repeatedly given as he emerged from the train. Corporal Johnston, who was a skilful section leader in the Dungannon Battalion U.V.F., was called up with the 3rd (Reserve) Battalion on the outbreak of war, and went to France with the first draft from Derry to fill up vacancies in the 2nd Battalion. During the heavy fighting at Festubert, on 16th May, Corporal Johnston, who was then only a lance corporal performed the heroic action for which the townspeople assembled on Saturday night to greet him. His battalion sustained such severe losses during the charge and subsequent retirement, only Captain C. M. Alexander, Carrickmore (since wounded), and himself were left not injured out of all the many local men in the battalion. His own machine-gun officer and all the non-commissioned officers in his section save himself were killed or wounded, and the sole charge then devolved upon him.[70]

Private Thomas John Duke the son of Mr Thomas Duke, Tamnamore, Moy was wounded on 13 August 1915. Private Duke had joined the London Irish Regiment during the Easter holidays while being in London on business. His wounds required him to be sent back to No. 3 War Hospital, London.

The Dungannon Fallen at Festubert

Corporal Henry Victor Sidney Donaldson (10699), 2nd Battalion Royal Inniskilling Fusiliers, was killed in action on 16 May 1915. He was born in Moville, County Donegal. Corporal Donaldson's father was a Sergeant in the RIC and lived in Mark Street, Milltown, Dungannon. Corporal Donaldson was serving in the same battalion as his uncle Sergeant Philip Le Gear. He had been posted as missing on the casualty list after the fighting at Festubert and his uncle, Sergeant Le Gear, made every effort to trace him. Many families tried to find out information about their relatives last sightings, often placing short messages in the press. Corporal Donaldson's father placed the following message:

> *Sergeant Nixon Donaldson, R.I.C., Dungannon, is anxious to ascertain information regarding his son, Corporal Henry Victor Sydney Donaldson (10699), 2nd Battalion Royal Inniskilling Fusiliers, who took part in the heavy fighting at Festubert, on 16th May, and was posted as missing on that date.*[71]

It was nearly a full year before the family received official notification that Corporal Henry Victor Sidney Donaldson had been killed:

> *A notification from the War Office was received yesterday by sergeant N. Donaldson, R.I.C., Dungannon, intimating that his eldest son, corporal H. V. S. Donaldson, 2nd battalion Royal Inniskilling fusiliers, who has been previously reported missing, was killed in action during the Inniskillings famous charge at Festubert on 15th May last. Corporal Donaldson, who was only 18 years of age, was a nephew of Captain John T. O'Neill 12th Battalion Royal Irish Rifles, now at Ballykinlar, and of*

> *Quartermaster Sergeant Philip Le Gear, 2nd Battalion Royal Inniskilling Fusiliers, who were present at the battle of Festubert.*[72]

Corporal Henry Victor Sidney Donaldson has no known grave but is remembered on the Le Touret Memorial, Le Touret, Pas-de-Calais. He is also remembered on the St. Anne's Parish Church Roll of Honour and Dungannon War Memorial.

Private William Richard Dickson (4077), 2nd Battalion Royal Inniskilling Fusiliers, was born in Dungannon around 1889. Private Dickson had been a reservist and had gone to the front shortly after the outbreak of the war. His brother Corporal Robert Dickson served with the 9th Battalion Royal Inniskilling Fusiliers. Private William Dickson was killed in action on 16 May 1915 at the Battle of Festubert. By coincidence just two days before his death a letter he had written appealing for the men of Dungannon to enlist appeared in the *Belfast Newsletter* on 14 May 1915:

> *Private William Dickson, 2nd Battalion Royal Inniskilling Fusiliers, writing from the Front to friends in Dungannon says – Men of Dungannon, take advice from me and for God's sake wake up and enlist or you will have the Huns in the Market Square soon. It is better to beat the Germans here than have them coming over to Ireland to destroy everything as they have done in Belgium, which is in ruins. Northern France and Belgium look like some wild country, not like a civilised place at all. We have a few Dungannon chaps here, and they are a credit to the gallant City of the Volunteers. I hope, therefore, that all the boys at home will join the colours and help our gallant fellows out here to smash the Germans.*

Private Dickson's father, Richard Dickson, was another to find out that his son had fallen prior to receiving official War Office confirmation. Private William Richard Dickson has no known grave, but is remembered on the Le Touret Memorial, Le Touret, Pas-de-Calais. He is also remembered on the St. Anne's Parish Church Roll of Honour and Dungannon War Memorial.

Corporal Donaldson and Private Dickson were both remembered at a service in St Anne's Parish Church on 30 May 1915:

> *The Dead March in "Saul" was rendered on the organ in St Ann's Parish Church, Dungannon, at the conclusion of the Sunday morning service as*

a mark of respect for the memory of two members of the congregation belonging to the 2nd Battalion Royal Inniskilling Fusiliers who had laid down their lives for the Empire in France on the 15th and 16th ult, Rev. T. J. McEndoo, M.A., before entering upon his sermon, referred to the death in action of Corporal H.V.S. Donaldson, son of Sergeant N. Donaldson, R.I.C., Dungannon, and said that on the previous Sunday they had mourned for the death of Private W.R. Dickson, Lisnahull.[73]

Private Joseph Henry (2354), 2nd Battalion Royal Inniskilling Fusiliers, was killed in action on 16 May 1915. Joseph had been born in Dungannon and the family lived at Ballysaggart, Derrygortreavy. He enlisted in Belfast. Private Joseph Henry has no known grave but is remembered on the Le Touret Memorial, Le Touret, Pas-de-Calais.

Lance Corporal Hugh John Cairns (4354), 2nd Battalion Royal Inniskilling Fusiliers, was born in Coalisland around 1886. Hugh John Cairns was killed in action on 16 May 1915 at the Battle of Festubert. Hugh was a member of Coalisland Faith Defenders LOL 93. Reported missing, Hugh's sister Miss Minnie Cairns sought information regarding her brother through the papers in July 1915:

Every effort to trace Private Hugh John Cairns (4354), 2nd Battalion Royal Inniskilling Fusiliers, who has been missing since the engagement at Festubert on 16th May, has failed. His sister, Miss Minnie Cairns, Sandy Row, Coalisland, is very anxious for news of him.[74]

Lance Corporal Hugh John Cairns has no known grave, but is remembered on the Le Touret Memorial, Le Touret, Pas-de-Calais. He is also remembered in Brackaville Parish Church, Coalisland, along with his brother Thomas who served with the American Army during the First World War. Hugh's name appears on the Dungannon War Memorial. Interestingly, his name is spelt as Kearns rather than Cairns on all Commonwealth War Graves records.

Private John Arbuthnot (8172), 2nd Battalion Royal Inniskilling Fusiliers, was killed in action on 16 May 1915 at the Battle of Festubert. The son of William Arbuthnot, Creamery Row, Newmills he has no known grave and is remembered on the Le Touret Memorial, Le Touret, Pas-de-Calais.

Private John Gray (1812), 1st Battalion Irish Guards, was killed in action on 18 May 1915. John was born about 1888 in Clonfeacle and lived for a time at Doneydade, Bernagh. Private John Gray's brother James served with the 9th Battalion Royal Inniskilling Fusiliers and had been an active member of the Dungannon Battalion UVF. Private John Gray enlisted in Dungannon and was killed in the fighting following the main Battle of Festubert. Having no known grave, he is remembered on the Le Touret Memorial, Le Touret, Pas-de-Calais and Moy War Memorial.

Private John O'Farrell (4418), 2nd Battalion Royal Inniskilling Fusiliers, died of wounds he received during the Battle of Festubert on 25 May 1915. John was born about 1897 and lived at Gortgonis, Coalisland. Private O'Farrell enlisted some six weeks prior to the outbreak of war with the 2nd Battalion Royal Inniskilling Fusiliers in Dungannon and was despatched to France in September 1914. John is buried in Le Touquet - Paris Cemetery, Etaples, Pas-de-Calais and is also remembered on Dungannon War Memorial.

Although the Battle of Festubert was over by late May, fighting in the Pas-de-Calais region continued. By mid June it was the turn of the Scottish Rifles to launch an attack. The 15 June saw the 6th Cameronians go into battle. The Germans seemed to know the attack was coming and on that day were heard to call across "Come along, Jocks; we are waiting for you." Despite high hopes for the attack, the Cameronians ran into a hail of machine gun fire. The attack was costly and unsuccessful. Two men with Dungannon connections took part in the attack, and both made the ultimate sacrifice.

Private William Simpson (1396), 6th Cameronians (Scottish Rifles), was killed in action on 16 June 1915. William Simpson had been born in Dungannon, but moved to Scotland where he got married. He enlisted in Hamilton and is buried in Woburn Abbey Cemetery, Cuinchy, Pas-de-Calais. Private Simpson is also remembered on High Blantyre War Memorial in Glasgow.

2nd Lieutenant Gilbert McClelland Kennedy, 6th Cameronians (Scottish Rifles), was killed in action on 16 June 1915. He was the son of Rev. Gilbert A. Kennedy MA formerly minister of Carland Presbyterian Church, County Tyrone and then minister at Wishaw Parish Church, Glasgow. Gilbert was born in Aghadowey, County Londonderry during his father's ministry in that area. Lieutenant Kennedy was a nephew of Mr John Bryars, Scotch Street, Dungannon, Mr Thomas Bryars, Cromwell Road, Belfast and Dr Kennedy, Portstewart. His sister Miss Kennedy, was for two years commander of a Voluntary Aid Detachment of the British Red Cross Society and was one of the first nurses to be called up by the War Office. 2nd Lieutenant Gilbert McClelland Kennedy was a lineal descendent of Colonel Gilbert Kennedy of Ardmillan, Ayrshire, nephew of John, sixth Earl of Cassilis, one of the Scottish nobles appointed to act as lay assessors at the famous Westminster Assembly. The father of the deceased officer received telegrams of sympathy from the King and Lord Kitchener. 2nd Lieutenant Gilbert McClelland Kennedy has no known grave but is remembered on the Le Touret Memorial, Le Touret, Pas-de-Calais.

The North Irish Horse

A number of Dungannon men served with the North Irish Horse in France. While danger was never far away, life in France seemed to suit some of them, as a letter written by Corporal James Davis in March 1915 appears to indicate:

> *Corporal James Davis of the "A" Squadron North Irish Horse, writing from the front to his parents in Dungannon states that he has been, over head and ears in work, and is in the "pink of condition." He had been recently on duty at a bridge which was in progress of erection over a canal by the Royal Engineers, when one of the bridge builders, who was the possessor of a long black beard, accosted him and after some time he recognised him as a fellow Dungannon man, Patrick McCouey of the Royal Engineers. Corporal Davis was also sporting a beard, so that the difficulty of identification was mutual. The bridge which was being built had an untimely fate, for it had no sooner been completed than the Germans destroyed it by shell fire. Numerous dead bodies of German soldiers floated down the canal with the current. He mentions that twenty troopers of the North Irish Horse were recently made prisoners, but managed to escape, and during their return to the British outposts they captured fourteen Germans, aged between 17 and 21 years.*[75]

However Corporal Davis' circumstances soon changed. By the end of May he had written to his father Mr James Davis, Dungannon, to tell him that he had been invalided with an attack of fever, and was now in Moorfield Military Hospital, Glossop. Trooper Davis arrived home to Dungannon in late June 1915.

Another Dungannon man who was with the North Irish Horse and had gone to France with the BEF at the beginning of the war was Trooper Harry Newell. He was the son of Mr Joseph Newell, Perry Street, Dungannon. Trooper Newell suffered leg injuries while on active service at the front, as reported in the *Belfast Newsletter* on 24 March 1915, and was transferred to one of the base hospitals in France. Having recovered by early June he was serving with Headquarters Staff of the Second Army Corps. In a letter home he was forthright in his views regarding shirkers:

> *Trooper Harry Newell, North Irish Horse, who is at present attached to the Headquarters Staff of the Second Army Corps now operating in France, in writing to his father, Mr Joseph Newell, Perry Street, Dungannon, says – The local papers sent me are very illuminating in the petty sessions news and otherwise as to men eligible for active service who have quite made up their minds to "live" for their country. I wonder that eligible men are not ashamed to parade themselves in the limelight of the public Press. I am informed that about Dungannon the eligible are receiving scant respect, and I can assure you that men who have been here only since Easter have no respect for such shirkers, while those who have endured the campaign since last August know that they have done not only their own bit but are doing the shirkers work into the bargain.*[76]

By the autumn of 1915 Trooper Harry Newell was in hospital at Cassel, France suffering from the effects of recent trying experiences. While in hospital he was medically attended by another Dungannon man, Lieutenant Harold Sugars, RAMC. Trooper Newell had two brothers Lieutenant Charles Newell and Sergeant John Newell also at the front with the 6th Inniskilling Dragoons. By the end of December 1915 Trooper Harry Newell had returned home on leave owing to illness contracted in France.

The *Belfast Newsletter* of 15 June 1915 reported that Trooper Wingfield Espey of the North Irish Horse who went to France in the First Expeditionary Force had been permitted to return home to Lowertown, Bush, Dungannon for a few days on urgent private business.

Artois, Champagne and Loos Offensive

At the end of summer 1915 the Artois region, which had been the scene of the allies offensives earlier that year, was again to become the focus of attention. By late September the allied forces were ready to launch further attacks in the region around Loos, Champagne and Vimy Ridge at Arras. The plans for the allied attacks relied upon numerical supremacy over the Germans, with the French forces being three to one greater in the Champagne region while in some parts of the Loos front the British held a seven to one advantage. The attacks were to be pre-empted with an artillery bombardment that would last four days.

The bombardment at Loos commenced on 21 September and the troops in the frontline trenches would commence their attack on the 25 September. Sir Douglas Haig presided over the attack, although he had serious misgivings. Haig was concerned about the terrain and the fatigued state of the British troops. In addition, shells for the bombardment were in short supply, a point that became more evident as 1915 progressed.

Part of the British battle plan was to use chlorine gas and approximately 5,000 canisters were released. Unfortunately in some parts of the line the wind blew the gas straight back towards the British lines knocking out some of their own troops. The attack would cover the region from the La Bassee Canal, to the Loos Valley. Good progress was made on the first day in the southerly region with Loos being captured, however the attack stalled due to lack of supplies and delays with reserves. In the northerly sector around Hulloch and Vermelles progress was slower. German defences were exceptionally strong and on the second day of attack in this region the British forces were decimated. The attack to the surprises of the Germans was made without any covering fire. By the 28 September it was called off in failure. The attack recommenced on 13 October but was no more successful. British casualties numbered upwards of 50,000 and many believe the failure at Loos led to Sir John French being replaced by Sir Douglas Haig as Commander in Chief. The French, while having a little more success in the Champagne and Vimy regions, could not consolidate their initial success and the frontline moved relatively little.

Dungannon man, Battery Sergeant Major George Noble of the Royal Field Artillery was severely injured during this offensive. His injuries occurred on the 28 September when he was returning to the rear with ammunition wagons to obtain a fresh supply. He was passing a French Battery which had been firing, causing him to be pushed off the wagon he was in. On falling to the ground a wagon passed over his leg and crushed his knee. Sergeant Major Noble had been at the front since the beginning of hostilities and had been badly wounded in the back in December 1914 near Ypres, but had recovered and returned to Flanders in the summer months of 1915. The *Belfast Newsletter* reported on 4 January 1916 that Battery Sergeant Major George Noble had returned home to Church Street, Dungannon, to recuperate from the effects of a severe accident sustained in Flanders.

The newspapers carried reports of others with connections to Dungannon who were wounded during the autumn offensive:

Corporal Eric Bradshaw, Royal Engineers, eldest son of Mr James Bradshaw, District Inspector of National Schools, of Glendaragh, Ballymena, has been wounded, and is now in one of the base hospitals in France. Corporal Bradshaw received his early education in Brussels, and prior to joining the colours in August last, was at the Royal School, Dungannon.[77]

Mr John Reilly, J.P. Bowling Green, Strabane, has received official notification that his brother Dr Joseph Reilly, R.A.M.C., has been wounded in the present severe fighting in Flanders and that is at present in hospital in London. Dr Reilly is a son in law of Mr James Cullen, Park Road, Dungannon and brother-in-law of Mr Maurice P. Cullen, J.P. Dungannon.[78]

2nd Lieutenant Thomas Aiken Wilson, 7th Battalion East Lancashire Regiment was wounded in France on the 22 October 1915, he was the son of Mr Samuel Wilson, Dungannon, and Chief Engineering inspector to the Estate Commissioners. The family received letters from Rev. H. S. Broadbent, Church of England Chaplain at the clearing station, and Sergeant Darres advising them that Thomas had been wounded by a rifle wound to the back. Lieutenant Wilson was educated at Dungannon Royal School where he was captain of the Rugby team which won the Schools Cup in 1907. He had been an enthusiastic member of the UVF and enlisted with a Dungannon contingent during October 1914. He subsequently received a commission. He was also a well known golfer.

2nd Lieutenant Thomas Wilson was hospitalised to the 14th General Hospital, Boulogne.

Major R. J. Adams who commanded the 113th Battery Royal Field Artillery also took part in the Loos offensive. Major Adams had been out with the 1st Division since the beginning of the war and by October 1915 had returned home to Torrent Hill, Newmills, Dungannon for a few days leave. While at home Major Adams did not rest, he instead it was reported that he was at the forefront of raising funds for the comforts of the men of the 113th Battery:

> For the purposes of providing comforts for the men of the 113th Battery Royal Field Artillery, now in Flanders, of which Major R. J. Adams, Torrent Hill, Coalisland, is in command, and also for all local soldiers, irrespective of creed, a sale of fancy goods, jumble and country produce was held in Coalisland on Friday and Saturday in the Canal Stores, kindly lent by Messrs. John Stevenson & Co., Ltd. A sum of £25 was realised. As a result of a house to house collection, a concert and a "Flag Day" the sum of £90 has been raised in the Coalisland district on behalf of the British Red Cross Society and the Order of St John of Jerusalem. A substantial sum on behalf of the British Red Cross Society and the Order of St John of Jerusalem Joint Committee was realised in Moy, County Tyrone, on Friday, by means of a Flag Day. The matter was carried through by an energetic local committee, of which Miss Greer (Grange Park) and Mr W. E. Stevenson (Grange Lodge) were moving spirits.[79]

> The working class district of Coalisland, County Tyrone has now contributed the substantial sum of £100 to the funds of the British Red Cross Society and the Order of St John of Jerusalem (Joint War Committee), the balance necessary to make up that sum being provided by a cinematograph entertainment given by Mr Daniels in St Patrick's Hall, Coalisland, on Thursday evening, and organised by Messrs John Corr, solicitor and C Beatty. A sum of £42 2s 6d has also been raised by a sale of work and farm produce to provide comforts for the men of the 113th Battery Royal Field Artillery, of which Major R. J. Adams, Torrent Hill, Coalisland, is commander, and for all local soldiers on active service.[80]

While the infantry fought, the men of the Royal Army Medical Corps tried to save the lives and limbs of the wounded. One of these men was

Lieutenant Bernard S. Browne, MB who was attached to the 2nd Battalion Cheshire Regiment. The second son of Colonel Abraham W. Browne, St Kilda, Clooney, Londonderry, he was a nephew of Colonel William Browne JP, Northland House, Dungannon. Lieutenant Bernard S. Browne, M.B. was awarded the Military Cross:

> *For conspicuous gallantry and devotion to duty near Vermelles. He spent the whole night of 2nd 3rd October searching for and carrying back wounded who were lying between our own and the enemy's lines, which were only 200 yards apart. The enemy were firing and the ground was lit up by flares. After daybreak he carried back three men under a very heavy fire At one time he tended the wounded within 15 yards of the enemy's trenches. By his courage and ceaseless work all the wounded in this area were brought in.*[81]

Lieutenant Bernard S. Browne, MB was a relation of the Browne family of Killymaddy, Dungannon many of whom served during the First World War:

> *The names of no fewer than four members of the Browne family, of Killymaddy, Dungannon, appear in the list. Colonel Edward George Browne, of the Headquarters Staff, is the youngest son of the late Mr William Browne, Killymaddy House, Dungannon, and brother of Colonel William Browne, J.P., Dungannon, late commanding officer of the Mid-Ulster Royal Garrison Artillery: Colonel A W Browne, St Kilda, Londonderry, P.M.O. of the North Irish Coast Defences; Major James Browne, Belfast: Dr T .D. Browne, Benburb, Moy and Dr T .D . Browne, Dublin, Chief Medical Inspector, Local Government Board. He had had considerable service in India, and went out to France with the First Expeditionary Force, being attached to the Third Cavalry Brigade and afterwards to the First Brigade. He was appointed Assistant Deputy Director General of Medical Services in France, and is now the Deputy Director General. Major James Glendinning Browne, Army Service Corps, is the eldest son of Major James Browne, who was second in command of the 1st Devons, and retired under the age clause. He went out to France with the First expeditionary Force, and has been previously mentioned in despatches. Major William Theodore Redmond Browne, Army Service Corps, is the younger brother of Major James Glendinning Browne. He was stationed in Belfast at the outbreak of the war and then*

held rank of captain. He went to France with the first Expeditionary Force, where owing to his meritorious work, he obtained the D.S.O. and was promoted major for his services in the field. He also has been previously mentioned in despatches. Temporary Lieutenant Bernard Scott Browne, R.A.M.C., attached to the 2nd Cheshire is the second son of Colonel A. W. Browne. He was formerly a medical missionary in China and volunteered at the outbreak of the war. He has recently been the recipient of the Military Cross for tending in the wounded under fire.[82]

2nd Lieutenant H. F. M. Reid of the 12th Battalion Northumberland Fusiliers was wounded in France on 24 November 1915. He was the son of Mr W. O. Reid, Castle Hill, Dungannon. 2nd Lieutenant Reid wrote home to his father telling him that while he had been on patrol duty in front of the trenches he was fired on and received a gunshot wound above the right ankle. He was treated in the General Hospital, Boulogne where he had been operated upon and was recovering as well as possible. Afterwards he was sent to Mrs Mitcheson's Hospital, Chelsea. Prior to the war Lieutenant Reid had been a teacher in St. Enoch's School, Belfast. At the outbreak of the war he was a member of the Officer Training Corps and obtained a commission in the 15th Northumberland Fusiliers, being subsequently posted to the 12th battalion. The *Belfast Newsletter* reported on 18 January 1916 that 2nd Lieutenant Reid had returned home to Castle Hill, Dungannon, to recuperate.

The *Belfast Newsletter* on 21 December 1915 reported that Mr James Abernethy, Palm Lodge, The Bush, Dungannon had received news from his eldest son, Private James Abernethy, 2nd Infantry Brigade, 1st Canadian Division that he had been wounded in France and was in hospital. James told his father that he had lost some teeth and had also been wounded in the back and knee. Prior to the war Private Abernethy had been in Canada for five and half years and was in the timber trade at Saskatoon. Private Abernethy's sister, Miss Maud Abernethy had volunteered for nursing duty and served in Netley Hospital, Hampshire on the south coast of England.

The Dungannon Fallen at Artois and Loos

Major Henry Newton Kelly, 33rd Punjabs, Indian Army was killed in action on 25 September 1915. Henry was born in Killymeal, Dungannon around 1870. Major Kelly had been a professional soldier receiving a commission with the Royal Irish Regiment in 1890 at age 20. He rose through the ranks and was appointed Major on 3 May 1908. Kelly had spent a considerable part of his life in India. The 33rd Punjabs like many in the Loos offensive suffered heavy casualties and Major Kelly was killed in action near Moulin-du-Pierre. Major Kelly's brother Colonel C. R. Kelly of the 133th Battery Royal Field Artillery was also heavily involved in the First World War. Henry's death was reported in the *Belfast Newsletter* on 27 December 1915:

> *Henry Newton Kelly, Major 33rd Punjabis Indian Army, eldest son of the late Mr Henry Russell Kelly of Dungannon, and son-in-law of the late Sir Stanley Isray K.C.S.I. Killed in France on 25th September 1915.*

Major Henry Newton Kelly is buried in the Pont-du-Hem, Military Cemetery, La Gorgue, France. He is also remembered on St Anne's Parish Church Roll of Honour and Dungannon War Memorial.

Private Patrick McGee (7876), 9th Battalion Cameronians (Scottish Rifles), was killed in action on 25 September 1915. Born in Dungannon about 1884, little is know of Patrick's life in Dungannon, but his father and mother are listed as living at 47 Churchill Street, Belfast and his wife as 58 High Street, Kilkenny. Private Patrick McGee has no known grave and is remembered on the Loos Memorial, Loos-en-Gohelle, Pas-de-Calais.

Private John Lavelle (12874), 10th Battalion Highland Light Infantry, was killed in action on 25 September 1915. John was born around 1890 in Coalisland and again little is known of his life before the war. In his will made at the front, John left his property and effects to his sister Sarah Lavelle. Official notification of John's death was recorded in the *Belfast Newsletter* on 15 October 1915:

> *The relatives of Private John Lavelle (Annagher, Coalisland), 2nd Battalion The Queen's (Royal West Surrey) Regiment, have been officially notified that he was killed in action in France during the recent advance.*

Private John Lavelle has no known grave but is remembered on Loos Memorial, Loos-en-Gohelle, Pas-de-Calais and Dungannon War Memorial.

Private Edger Reid (7111), 2nd Battalion Irish Guards, was killed in action on 8 October 1915. Private Reid was the nephew of Mr W. O. Reid, Castle Hill, Dungannon. Edgar was born in Mullingar, County Westmeath and had just left school in County Wexford when the war broke out. He volunteered in June 1915 and had been in France for just two months. Private Edgar Reid is buried in Vermelles British Cemetery, Vermelles, Pas-de-Calais.

Private John Connolly (911), 2nd Battalion Royal Munster Fusiliers, died of wounds on the 20 October 1915. John is listed as being born in Dungannon although little is known of his life in the town. He is buried in Netley Military Cemetery, Southampton, Hampshire.

Conditions at the Front

A letter sent home in early November1915 by Driver Godfrey Duncan Daniel provides an insight into the tough conditions the men at the front were experiencing:

Driver Godfrey Duncan Daniel, of the Royal Canadian Horse Artillery, 1st Contingent, now in Belgium, sixth and youngest son of Mr Robert Daniel J.P., of Derryvale, Dungannon, writing to his mother on the 6th inst., says The weather here has been terribly wet, and the mud is thick all over. It has cleared up now and is foggy at night. We have been very busy making gun pits, and go into action again tomorrow night. I think we shall be a long time in action in the new position. The little town we are behind has been blown to atoms, and we have secured quite a lot of German fuses. We are under canvas just at present, and sleep ten in a tent, and are quite warm at night. I will have a lot of news to tell you when I get home on leave. Everything we do has to be done at night, such as supplying the guns with ammunition, and it is very dark. The enemy has a hard time to find the position of our batteries, which is a good job. I am very happy, so there is no need to worry about me. Our horses are all in good condition and fit for the winter. We got some new clothing issued to us the other day: it does not last long here. Tell father to do all he can to get the men about to join the colours; we shall need them all.[83]

Godfrey, the son of Mr Robert Daniel, JP of Derryvale, Dungannon, (Officer Commanding E Company of the 4th Battalion of the Tyrone UVF who himself was unable to serve in the new Army owing to the age limit), was one of five brothers serving the colours around the globe.

His eldest brother Robert was in business in South Africa and enlisted at the outbreak of the war with the Kaiffrarian Rifles. Shortly afterwards he saw action with his the regiment in German South-West Africa. Another brother Frank, who was in the Transval joined the City Guard of Pretoria while Alfred an electrical engineer enlisted in the 17th Canadian Cavalry Field Ambulance Corps at Calgary. His youngest brother Ernest had been at home assisting his father in their dyeing and finishing business at Derryvale Mill. Ernest had been an enthusiastic member of the UVF, being a half company commander in his father's company. Ernest responded to Sir Edward Carson's call and enlisted with the 1st Battalion Royal Irish Fusiliers, subsequently receiving a commission in the 4th Battalion Royal Irish Rifles. Godfrey's other brother, who was Robert's twin and also lived in South Africa, was not allowed by his employer to join the forces because he was married. In recognition of his family's service, Robert Daniel received the following letter from Buckingham Palace:

Mr Robert Daniel, J.P., of Derryvale, Dungannon, has received the following letter, dated Buckingham Palace, 25th February:-

Sir – I have the honour to inform you that the King has heard with much interest that you have at the present five sons in the army. I am commanded to express to you the King's congratulations, and to assure you that his Majesty much appreciates the spirit of patriotism which prompted this example, in one family, of loyalty and devotion to their Sovereign and Empire, - I have the honour to be, sir your obedient servant,

F Ponsonby,

Keeper of the Privy Purse.[84]

Another letter sent from France by George Burleigh in mid November 1915 gives further details of life at the front:

> *Mr R. W. Burleigh, Bellevue, Dungannon, has received the following letter from his brother, Mr George Burleigh, who is serving at the front with the Royal Garrison Artillery:- I am trying to write to you under altered circumstances and surroundings. My domicile is a barn; my midnight couch is of straw. The couch is here at midnight: sometimes I'm not. The lighting arrangements are of wax in single candelabra; the light is what is sometimes called 'dimly religious'. I am not complaining, as we are indeed glad to have a roof to cover our heads and to be able to preserve a sound skin. Now, as regards the souvenirs, I am afraid you are doomed to disappointment. Collecting these is not the work of artillery, but of infantry, which are very considerably in advance of us, and therefore get the first selection. However, I may be able to pick you up something, when I can do it legitimately. Souvenir collecting is called by a very ugly name here (i.e. looting), therefore it behoves me to be careful. Anyhow, I have got a couple of curios, which I will send the first chance. I note your remarks re the little wooden cross, and I expect you infer by this time that I have not made acquaintance with it yet. Thank goodness for that. I have a presentiment that neither French nor Belgian soil will cover my casket with a bit of luck. The weather here had been very wet and cold lately, and as a result of the rain a beautiful coating of glutinous mud has been left, which is not altogether pleasant when one has to spend the greatest part of the twenty-four hours in it. In spite of this however to use an official expression, the morale of the troops is excellent. I am writing this during my break-off duty in the very bowels of the earth. When you see Andy McClay, give him my kindest regards. Tell him I'm as happy as a duke, if not as a king. You and he may think of me sometimes when you are having your three and four course commercial dinners. You may have a better dinner than I have, but you certainly have not a better appetite.*[85]

Life at the front was hard and comforts at times were difficult to find. However, there was cheeriness in letters sent home by the men at the front, reassuring those at home that they were safe and making the best of the situation.

Home on Leave

By the beginning of winter 1915 a number of men were now starting to return home to the Dungannon area on leave. The *Belfast Newsletter* carried reports concerning some of those who had returned on leave:

> Sergeant John Reginald Hamilton, motor machine gun section, has returned to Dungannon for a visit after seven months' active service in France. He is the younger brother of Mr J. O. Hamilton, solicitor, and town clerk of Dungannon, and was educated at Dungannon Royal School. On the outbreak of the present war he volunteered with a contingent of Dungannon U. V. F. men, and joined the 6th Battalion Royal Inniskilling Fusiliers. He was rapidly promoted sergeant, and afterwards transferred to the motor machine gun section.[86]

> Rifleman Wm. A. Roulston, London Rifle Brigade (Territorial Force), son of a deceased Methodist minister, returned home on leave to Dungannon yesterday, having been on active service in France since October last.[87]

> Gunner John Gervan, Royal Field Artillery, also returned home to Dungannon on leave yesterday. He has been in France since the outbreak of the war.[88]

The *Belfast Newsletter* on 29 November 1915 also carried reports of two local soldiers who had been in France since the beginning of the war, but had now completed their term of service:

> A largely attended meeting was held in Stangmore Schoolhouse, Dungannon, on Friday evening in honour of two local soldiers – Drivers Daniel Kerr and David McMullan, Royal Field Artillery – who had been on active service in France since the beginning of the war, but whose term of service has now expired. Captain Robert Stevenson, 6th Battalion Royal Inniskilling Fusiliers, who has been invalided from Gallipoli, occupied the chair, and expressed his pleasure at coming into touch with men who had borne the struggle and hardships of the opening of the campaign. He hoped they would enjoy their well earned rest. Mr Barry Meglaughlin, solicitor, made an earnest appeal to the farming class in favour of recruiting, and said that all the young men who had volunteered from the district had acquitted themselves nobly. Mr H. S. Rose-Cleland,

Redford House, said he was sure he was expressing the feelings of every person present when he said that they were truly glad to see the men amongst them again, and wished them long life and happiness to enjoy the peace and rest in which they were so well entitled. Mrs Rose-Cleland then made a presentation to the soldiers and Gunner Kerr suitably replied. Mr L. C. Tottenham, Grange Park, proposed a vote of thanks to Mrs Rose-Cleland, which was seconded by Mr W. E. Stevenson, Grange Lodge, and heartily passed. At intervals musical items were contributed by Miss Mcmenemy (Moy), Messrs H.S. Rose-Cleland, Bertie Charles, and H. Beatty.

The 36th (Ulster) Division

As already noted, the 36th (Ulster) Division arrived in France during early October 1915. Letters written by two men, who had attended Dungannon Royal School, to their fathers describe in considerable detail what they experienced during the first two months on French soil:

Two Dungannon Royal School old boys serving in France with an Irish regiment have written home to their fathers as follows:- "Here we are properly settled after our journey, which was not fatiguing. The boat crossing was very calm and we got a pretty good sleep, although there was a fair crowd. On landing we went to a rest camp for a few hours. Then we had a train journey for a good long time. We were in goods vans about 20 or 30 each, and it was really more comfortable than a carriage, as one could be at full length and sleep well. The country looked very pretty and orchards were plentiful. We exchanged greetings with the sentries here and there. We got out near a town of considerable size, marched through the streets, in which there did not seem to be much business doing, and then out into the country, a long march, at least it seemed so, as we were fagged out. However, we got comfortably bedded in barns, with plenty of clean straw. The people were exceedingly friendly and anxious to do all they can for us. O. and I get plenty of talking, and anywhere we go they ask us in for a chat. When they speak in dialect it is not easy to understand: in fact, they say that a Parisian would not understand them. They have a very good opinion of the English, and consider them fine fellows, and are very much surprised that we should volunteer to come out. They are also tickled by our love of fruit. There is any quantity of apples: they use them largely for making cider. The feeding is very plentiful, and hard biscuits are what we get instead of bread. The boys, however, prefer bread, and go through the whole place to try and buy it. It is rather scarce, as you know they only bake from day to day. Weather is fairly mild, with some rain: today is fine. It's rather a nuisance having to write in such restrained manner, but you may be sure we are all in the best of health and spirits and in no danger. The arrangement of the house here is as follows – There is a courtyard, surrounded on three sides by outhouses and on the remaining side by the dwelling house. As a rule the latter is on the side away from the road, which gives the streets of the villages rather an uninteresting look, though ours is broad and has trees along it. The owners of our billet, indeed all the people here, are most hospitable and make us very welcome. They invited L and me in for breakfast on our first morning here, and were very pleased to find we knew French. I have got a job of interpreter, which, of course is very interesting. I am now living at the officers mess with the sergeant and the men who are employed there. The officers are lodging with the doctor's mother, the doctor being away to the war. The old lady was very pleased when I came, and she is fond of talking to me, besides which, of course, she had difficulty in making herself understood. She calls me 'Le petit' or 'Mon petit Francais'. Everyone is keen on learning all the French they can. There are quite a lot of our chaps who have learnt some at school, and they are beginning to make themselves understood. The chaplain, Captain Robinson, is attached to our ambulance, and he has held two little meetings, which were most helpful. I like the life here very much, its so much more interesting than at home. We hear no news here of the war except the official communiqué, and you can't buy the papers. The children are very nice, bright, and companionable; they are fond of asking for souvenirs, but they don't pester you for them like some of the "gamins" in places we have passed through. You can tell what regiments have been here by looking at the buttons on the boy's caps.[89]

The interpreting job is not such a good thing as it was, as they have got an official interpreter, a Frenchman. I still seem to get a good deal to do, about half the interpreter's work, but it is not the interesting half. Still it gets me out of a good many parades and fatigues. We shifted our quarters a few days back: it was only a very short distance. There we had a very good billet in a big barn. The buildings were of brick, not like most of this district of a wooden framework, plastered with mud; and our billet was up a ladder, and had a brick floor and skylights, with plenty of straw to sleep on, and room to walkabout without tripping over one another. We expected to stay here a good while – some even said a couple of months – but in reality we stayed a number of nights! The place was better provided with water than the village, for there was a pump in our farmyard for the three farms. This well is very deep: it took two or three men five minutes to wind up the little barrel which brings up the water, and nine seconds for a stone to fall to the bottom. We were just settling down when we got orders to move and marched about twelve miles. The weather was not too warm or too cold, and the pace was all right, so that we were not very tired when we arrived at the village where we billeted last night. The first part of the journey was through rather flat and uninteresting country, but afterwards we dipped down into a valley which was well wooded and very pretty. Any hilly country about here seems always to be on a lower level than the flat country, which is a sort of plateau. The village where we stopped is in a valley, and there is a running stream through it – a rarity in this country. Indeed I think it was the first I saw since I landed. We left that place next morning, and after walking up a hill were out on a level country again. The march was quite a short one, and we got to the town where we are now about noon. We ate our rations which we had brought with us from our previous halting place, and I got some hot water from a house to make tea. The lady whom I asked for it was very pleasant, and asked me in till she would boil some for me. Her little girl came in with a tiny puppy, which had attached himself to us at the last halt, and which our chaps had given to the children. They decided to call it "Souvenir." The scarcity of water is one of the chief inconveniencies in this country. We can generally get enough to wash in, but when it comes to watering the horses the difficulty arises. The French people are very much struck with how young most of our boys are, and of course there are a lot who are only officially 19, another thing which surprises them is to hear we are volunteers. They think we have conscription in England. A thousand thanks for the beautiful parcel, which came in perfect condition. Its packing was truly artistic, and the contents beyond praise. The soda bread was certainly quite edible; to judge by the way it disappeared. A course of army biscuit diet renders of less sensitive to staleness. It came to hand in four days. Letters are always a very popular event of the day, and the postman is fairly carried by storm when he arrives. People who get parcels are naturally very popular. We are in a new village now, which is a bit larger though not much cleaner.

These places don't seem to have any drainage systems, and the water of the streets runs into ponds, where they water the horses. It seems as though we were to be in this district for a while. At the last village where we stopped we saw a lot of Indian troops pass. They are a fine looking lot, and smiled and shouted at us, "The weather for the past few days has been very wet, and the roads are deep in mud and slime. We have had big waterproof capes issued to us, so that we did not suffer much. Today, however, the sun has come out and the things are drying a little. We have been mostly occupied in making paths paved with bricks from an old house which was long ago level with the ground and covered with grass. But no sooner had we started to remove them than an indignant lady came along claiming ownership. She said she was saving them up for building purposes as soon as the war was over! Everything in this country has a use and is jealously guarded. However, the good woman had to resign herself, as the material was required in the service of his Britannic Majesty. I was on guard last night: not a very formidable business. When at home we used to get an allowance for cocoa &c, for supper, but this is stopped now. However we managed to collect a few "souvenirs" here and there. The menu contained tea, cake, jam, fried bread and beef. The cookery was on an oil stove, which smoked profusely, so that the whole place was thick with soot, and the cooks were soon as black as sweeps, but everyone was satisfied, and thought the entertainment a great success. Some others have got parcels from home containing apples for Halloween, but this is "carrying coals to Newcastle" as they are as common as stones here. Some of the infantry battalions have been to the trenches for training.[90]

The Tyrones in France

By 7 October the 9th Royal Inniskilling Fusiliers - the Tyrones - had been pushed forward to the village of Bertangles where they billeted for a period of time before moving to Mailly-Maillet on 26 October 1915. During October Private Henry Cullen became a casualty, as reported in the *Belfast Newsletter* on 28 October 1915:

Mrs Orr, Moygashel, Dungannon, received intimation yesterday that her son, Private Henry Cullen, 9th Battalion Royal Inniskilling Fusiliers (County Tyrone Volunteers), had his leg accidentally fractured and was in hospital in Rouen.

The Tyrones were now attached to the 10th Infantry Brigade for instruction in trench work and they entered the trenches for the first time on 26 October. The trench system was based on three lines, first or front line, second and third, and the soldiers would rotate through them over a period of days before going back out of the line. During October the Tyrones would only carry out work in the 2nd and 3rd trench lines. The Tyrones were in the trenches from 26 October to 30 October and then from 31 October to 3 November 1915.

The first member of the Tyrones to loose his life in France was killed on 1 November 1915. However he was not from the county, but was a Derryman. The *Belfast Newsletter* of the 6 November 1915 reported the incident, as follows:

> *Private Samuel Donnell, 9th Inniskilling Fusiliers (Tyrone Volunteers), is the first Derryman of the Ulster Division to fall. Lieutenant Colonel A. St. Q. Ricardo, D. S. O., the commanding officer, writing to the dead soldier's sister in Londonderry says – "Private Donnell was in the trenches close to the German trenches, for instruction with his company, when he just put his head over the parapet to observe what the Germans were doing, and was shot by a sniper, dying instantaneously. It is our first casualty, and we are all much grieved about it, as your brother was a good soldier and comrade" Deceased was only 17 years of age*

Other casualties that were reported during those initial forays into the trenches were:

> *Private John Latimer, 9th Royal Inniskilling Fusiliers (County Tyrone Volunteers) is the second son of Mr William Latimer, Glencon, Newmills. He joined the 12th (Reserve) Battalion of the Inniskillings six months ago, and was subsequently drafted to the 9th Battalion, which he accompanied to the front. On his first day in the trenches he was struck on the head and arm with shell fragments, and was treated at the St John Ambulance British Hospital at Etaples. He was afterwards transferred to the De Walden Court Hospital at Eastbourne.[91]*

> *Mr Thomas Gallery, Castlecaulfield (County Tyrone) received intimation on Saturday that his son, Corporal Richard Gallery, 9th Battalion Royal Inniskilling Fusiliers (County Tyrone Volunteers), has been wounded in action in France. Private Gallery was a mechanic in Messrs. Stevenson's*

149

factory at Moygashel, Dungannon, before enlisting, and volunteered with a large contingent of U.V.F. men shortly after the outbreak of hostilities.[92]

November was a quiet month for the Tyrones in terms of trench work. They spent time route marching and changing billets, ending up in Domqueur and Le Plouy on 27 November. Two local men who were casualties around this time were:

Mr William J. Cumberland, Kilnacart, Dungannon, has received official notification that his youngest son, Private James Cumberland, 9th Battalion Royal Inniskilling Fusiliers (Tyrone Volunteers), is in hospital at the Western front suffering from frostbite. Mr Cumberland's three sons are at the front with the 9th Inniskillings.[93]

Sergeant James Cochrane, 9th Battalion Royal Inniskilling Fusiliers (Tyrone Volunteers) has intimated to his relatives at Moygashel, Dungannon, that he has been accidentally wounded. It appears that he was placing coke on the fire when a cartridge which had by some means been concealed in the coke exploded, and he was struck in the face by the bullet.[94]

During the month of December the Tyrones remained in billets at Domqueur and Le Plouy. Around this time Private William Smith, Union Place, Dungannon wrote home to his friends stating that he was in hospital in France. Private Smith provided an interesting account of spending Christmas in Hospital:

Private William Smith, 9th Battalion Royal Inniskilling Fusiliers (Tyrone Volunteers), who is a patient in a French hospital, writing to his friends in Dungannon says – I spent a very happy Christmas in hospital. All the patients fit to go about gave a helping hand to decorate the wards. As you know, the wards out here are not so well fitted up as those at home, and you would smile at our idea of decorations. We got some blankets and fastened them to the walls and made our mottoes with wadding. These were: "Success to the Ulster Division," "A bright and merry Christmas to all our troops and a Happy New Year," Best wishes to our loyal comrades, the R. A. M. C.," and last, but not least, "Success to our comrades at sea." We had a splendid dinner, consisting of Irish roast turkey, and oranges, nuts, and many other things dear to the hearts of the boys in khaki. The doctors and officers did everything possible to make us happy, and we

*had plenty of good old Irish songs and gramophone selections. There is
a good lot of patients in the hospital, but they all hope to have another
slap at the Germans.*[95]

The Tyrones celebrated Christmas with the usual festivities and Monday
27 December was designated a Sports Day. Music was provided by the
battalion's pipe band and the fife and drum band. Some claim this was
the first public appearance in France of the Dungannon Flute Band, who
had been said to have virtually enlisted en masse at the beginning of the
war. Not all of the Dungannon men in the 36th (Ulster) Division
belonged to the 9th Battalion Royal Inniskilling Fusiliers. For instance,
Rifleman William Hobson was serving with 16th Battalion Royal Irish
Rifles (Pioneers). In a letter home William detailed that he was at the
front with a variety of family members:

> *Rifleman William Hobson, 16th Battalion Royal Irish Rifles (Pioneers),
> writing from France to his relatives at Killylack, Dungannon mentions
> that he has just returned from a spell of duty in the trenches, and that his
> brother Harry, his three nephews (Robert, William and Ben Mitchell), and
> his two brothers-in-law (Jim Brown and Harry Adams) are all at the front.
> Having referred to his brother Hugh having died in China while serving
> with the Royal Inniskilling Fusiliers he adds – "We are surely a great
> fighting family, and have answered our King and country's call, for I am
> sure my brother Joe wanted to come, too; but someone must stay at
> home".*[96]

Another Dungannon man who was serving in the 36th (Ulster) Division
but not with the Tyrones was Private William Lawson, 10th Battalion
Royal Irish Rifles (South Belfast Volunteers). The fourth son of Mr
William Lawson, Milltown, Dungannon, William junior was
hospitalised suffering from rheumatism contracted in the trenches. This
was reported in the *Belfast Newsletter* on 14 December 1915.

Mr William J. Lawson, Milltown, Dungannon had four other sons
serving the colours. His eldest son Samuel and fourth son Joseph had
volunteered for the Ulster Division and were serving with the 12th
Company Royal Engineers. His third son George, who was in Toronto,
had enlisted with the 9th Royal Canadian Horse. His fifth son Thomas
was a lance-corporal in the 1st Battalion Royal Inniskilling Fusiliers, and
had been wounded at the Dardanelles. Mr Lawson's sixth son Albert

had also volunteered on receipt of the news that his brother Thomas had been wounded, but he was under age and could not be accepted at this time.

A further man with Dungannon connections serving in the 36th (Ulster) Division was Lance Corporal Robert Somerville, 10th Battalion Royal Inniskilling Fusiliers (The Derry's). It was reported in the *Belfast Newsletter* in early January 1916 that Robert had written to his brother Mr J Somerville, Dungannon indicating that he was in No. 9, Stationary Hospital, Le Havre, suffering from shrapnel wounds. Prior to the outbreak of war, Robert was employed by Miss Lyle, Laurel Hill, and he was also a member of the local UVF unit.

Despite the appalling losses the allies endured on the Western Front during 1915, they had not managed to make a significant breakthrough against the Germans. However, the allies remained committed to breaking the deadlock of trench warfare. In December 1915 they decided that the next major offensive would take place at the River Somme during the summer of 1916. Dungannon men in the 36th (Ulster) Division and the 16th (Irish) Division would take part in the Somme offensive.

Gallipoli

At the end of October 1914 Turkey entered the war on the side of the Germans and Austro-Hungarians. The Turks immediately launched an attack on Russia, an ally of Britain and France. The allies wanted to send supplies to Russia to strengthen its ill-equipped army and bring back much needed food supplies from the Ukraine. However, the only sea route possible was the difficult North Sea – Arctic passage to ports such as Murmanask and Archangel because the Turks controlled the Dardanelles Straits blocking the easier sea route via the Mediterranean to the Black Sea

Winston Churchill, First Lord of the Admiralty championed the idea of an Anglo – French naval assault on Turkey to take control of the narrow Dardanelles Straits. It was also hoped that this would knock Turkey out of the war and significantly weaken the Germans. Churchill won approval for this scheme and a British and French naval task force was assembled.

On 19 February 1915 the allies began a long-range naval bombardment of the Turkish coastal forts and artillery positions, but it was ineffective. On 25 February the allies renewed their offensive with the ships moving in closer in an attempt to complete the attack. Despite some early success, their progress was thwarted by Turkish sea mines and mobile howitzers.

Frustrated by these setbacks, Churchill urged his naval commanders to launch a major new attack. It was launched on the 18 March, but was an unmitigated disaster for the allies resulting in the loss of five British and French battleships. In face of these losses, the naval offensive was called off.

Following the abject failure of the naval attack, it was decided to launch an overland army offensive. The plan involved an amphibious landing of mainly British troops, but with some French support, along the coast of the Gallipoli Peninsula. The invading allied troops would seize the Turkish forts, which would enable the sea mines to be cleared, and then the navy could move rapidly and safely northwards to capture the Turkish capital, Constantinople (Istanbul).

On 25 April British and French soldiers, along with troops from the

Australian and New Zealand Army Corps (ANZAC) landed at various points on the Gallipoli Peninsula. The British troops were landed on five beaches along Cape Helles, on the southern tip of the peninsula. The Australian and New Zealand Corps landed at Gaba Tepe, which became known as Anzac Cove, on the western side of the peninsula. By the end of the day, with the exception of the French diversionary attack at Kum Kale, none of the allied landings had achieved their objectives. The allied troops faced many problems: the weather was bad; the terrain was difficult; and the Turkish forces were stronger than anticipated and well positioned. During the next three months the line at Helles advanced no more than two miles from the landing beaches, while the front held by the Anzacs was confined to a radius of little more than 1,000 yards at Anzac Cove. The campaign degenerated into the bitterest form of trench warfare.

Helles and Anzac Cove

Most of the British troops who took part in the initial landing and insuing campaign in the Helles area had been regular, professional soldiers before the outbreak of the Great War. Among them were some Dungannon men, the majority of whom served with the 1st Battalion Royal Inniskilling Fusiliers.

One of the local men who landed at Helles in April 1915 was Lance Corporal Thomas Lawson. Thomas was serving with the 1st Battalion Royal Inniskilling Fusiliers when he was wounded in the early stages of the fighting on the Gallipoli Peninsula. Contradictory reports of his wounding appeared in the *Belfast Newsletter* on 21 and 22 May 1915:

Lance Corporal Thomas Lawson, 1st Battalion Royal Inniskilling Fusiliers, a young Dungannon soldier, has written to his brother, Sapper Joseph Lawson. R.E., Antrim, stating that he was shot in the stomach on 26th ult. during the advance in the Gallipoli peninsula, and is now in the Kaarel-Ainy Hospital, Cairo, Egypt.

Official intimation has been received that Lance-Corporal Thomas Lawson 1st Battalion Royal Inniskilling Fusiliers, was dangerously wounded at Gallipoli on the 4th inst., and is now in hospital at Cairo. Lawson has three years' service, and is one of five brothers serving with the colours. His parents reside at Dungannon and a sixth brother resides at 36 Ashbourne Street, Belfast.

Private Robert Bell, 1ˢᵗ Battalion Royal Inniskilling Fusiliers, was another local man who was injured in the early part of the Gallipoli campaign. The son of Mr Ross Bell, Brooke Street, Milltown, Dungannon, he suffered severe wounds to his lower leg on 14 May 1915. Reports in the *Belfast Newsletter* state the following:

> *Mr Ross Bell, Brooke Street, Dungannon, has received a letter from his eldest son, Private Robert Bell, 1st Battalion, Royal Inniskilling Fusiliers, stating that he is severely wounded at the Dardanelles and is now in hospital in Alexandria. Three bullets had entered his right leg below the knee and had shattered the bone.*[97]

On 18 August the *Belfast Newsletter* reported that Private Robert Bell had been transferred to hospital in England and his condition was progressing favourably. Private Robert Bell's brother, Private John Bell, served with the 1ˢᵗ Battalion Irish Guards.

Private James Hutchinson, 1ˢᵗ Battalion Royal Inniskilling Fusiliers, son of Mr Hugh Hutchinson, Sherrygroom, Dungannon, was wounded at Gallipoli on 14 July 1915.

Private Peter Donnelly of the Royal Dublin Fusiliers was wounded during the fighting in the Helles area. From Shambles Lane, Dungannon, Private Donnelly was wounded on 3 August 1915. He was transferred to hospital in Malta, and by late September 1915 he had returned to Dungannon to recover from his wounds. Private Donnelly's younger brother was a Lance Corporal in the Army Service Corps.

In early August Gunner James Neill, Royal Horse Artillery, wrote to his brother in Coalisland, telling him that he was in hospital at Eastleigh, Southampton suffering from wounds he had received in his leg during the Dardanelles operations. James was a member of Coalisland Faith Defenders LOL 93.

Warrant Officer Alexander McCrea of Glenadush, Dungannon also served on the Gallipoli Peninsula. The McCrea family had a strong military tradition, as the following report indicates:

Mr Alexander McCrea, Glenadush, Dungannon, has given all his sons five in number, to the British Army. His eldest son, Warrant Officer Alexander McCrea has received a commission in the Royal Garrison Artillery, and is at the Dardanelles. The second son, James, served throughout the South African war, and was afterwards killed in India by a native. Thomas also served in India and South Africa, and died in the latter country. Trooper John McCrea 5th (Royal Irish) Lancers, is with his regiment in France, and the youngest son, Robert, has just been promoted a master gunner (warrant –officer) at Pembroke Dock.[98]

Colonel Theophilus Percy Jones CMG, CB of the Royal Army Medical Corps. played a major role during the Gallipoli campaign. Born in 1866 in Ardtrea, he was the son of the Rev. Josiah Jones of Tullynisken Parish in Newmills. Colonel Jones was a career soldier and had seen action in a variety of conflicts throughout the Empire prior to World War One. During the Gallipoli campaign he achieved the rank of Lieutenant Colonel and served as the Assistant Director of Medical Services with the Mediterranean Expeditionary Force. For his service in the Dardanelles, Jones was appointed a Companion of the Order of St Michael and St George (CMG) by the King. He was made a Companion of the Bath (CB) for his role in the Sinai Peninsula campaign.

The Dungannon Fallen at Helles

Some Dungannon men made the ultimate sacrifice during the conflict in the Helles area.

Private John Whitley (12122), from the Moy, died on 1 July 1915 as a result of wounds he sustained during the Dardanelles campaign. John had volunteered for service in Dungannon in August 1914 and was serving with the 1st Battalion Royal Inniskilling Fusiliers when he was severely wounded on 27 June 1915. He died in hospital in England. Private Whitley is buried in Over Peover Cemetery, Knutsford, Cheshire, England. The following articles were printed in the *Tyrone Courier* on 24 June 1915 and *Belfast Newsletter* on 2 July 1915 respectively:

Mr Eugene Whitley, courthousekeeper, Moy, has received a letter from the chaplain of the military hospital, Alexandria, notifying that his son, Private John Whitley, 1st Battalion Inniskilling Fusiliers has been seriously wounded at the Dardanelles operations, having been shot through the left jaw, the bullet coming out through the right side of the neck. Private Whitley volunteered for service in August last, and is barely 17 years of age.

Mr Eugene Whitley, Courthouse-keeper, Moy, has received intimation that his son, Private John Whitley, 1st Battalion Royal Inniskilling Fusiliers, had died in hospital in England from wounds received during the operations at the Dardanelles. Private Whitley received a shrapnel wound in the head, the bullet entering the cheek and emerging through the neck.

Another Moy man killed during the Dardanelles campaign was Lance Corporal Charles Heron (10404). He died on 2 July 1915 as a result of wounds. Lance Corporal Heron had been called up with the reserve upon the outbreak of war. He had been wounded at Mons in August 1914 and had been invalided home. On his return to service he went with the 3rd Inniskilling Fusiliers to Gallipoli. News of his death was published in the *Belfast Newsletter:*

Intimation has been received by his relatives at Gorestown, Moy, that Private Charles Heron, 2nd Battalion Inniskilling Fusiliers, has been killed at the Dardanelles. Private Heron was a postman in Moy, and being called up on the reserve at the outbreak of hostilities had been wounded in the second day's fighting during the retreat from Mons. He had been invalided home, and had gone to the Dardanelles four months ago.[99]

Lance Corporal Heron is buried in the Lancashire Landing Cemetery, in the Cape Helles region of Gallipoli.

Private Francis (Frank) Eccles (9949) died on 3 August 1915 in hospital in Malta from wounds he received during the Dardanelles offensive. From Carland, outside Dungannon, he enlisted in Cookstown and served with the 1st Battalion Royal Inniskilling Fusiliers. Private Eccles had six years service in the battalion. He is buried in Addolorata Cemetery, Paola, Valetta, Malta.

2nd Lieutenant Edwin Samuel Frizelle, 5th Battalion Lancashire Fusiliers was born in Dungannon in 1894. Edwin grew up in Belfast and was educated at Antrim Road Baptist School, Methodist College and

Queen's University. Seeking to enter the medical profession he moved to Bury, but on the outbreak of war he volunteered for active service and received a commission in the Lancashire Fusiliers in August 1914. 2nd Lieutenant Frizelle was shot in the arm on 4 June 1915 and spent a period of time in hospital. Returning to the trenches, he was killed in action on 3 August 1915. 2nd Lieutenant Frizelle is buried in Lancashire Landing Cemetery, in the Cape Helles region of Gallipoli.

Suvla Bay

The allied campaign in both the Helles and the Anzac sectors stalled during the summer of 1915 and there had been no breakthrough. Instead the static trench warfare of the Western Front was reproduced. Withdrawal from Gallipoli at that stage may have been the best option, but the opposite course of action was taken.

It was decided to reinforce the Mediterranean Expeditionary Force with a further three divisions from England. Between 6 and 10 August these fresh troops were landed at Suvla Bay in the north of the peninsula, adjacent to where the Anzacs had landed in April. This marked the beginning of a new phase of fighting throughout the peninsula.

One of the divisions that took part in the Suvla Bay landings were the 10th (Irish) Division. By the dawn of 7 August the division had landed on the Gallipoli Peninsula and were soon in the midst of battle. The 10th (Irish) Division fought with great courage and skill on the steep slopes of Kirtech Teppe, but suffered many casualties.

A number of men from Dungannon served with the 10th (Irish) Division at Gallipoli. In a letter home to friends in Moygashel, Private T Gallagher gave an excellent account of the landing at Suvla Bay and the first day that the 10th (Irish) Division spent on the Gallipoli Peninsula:

Private T. Gallagher, 6th Battalion Royal Inniskilling Fusiliers, writing to his friends at Moygashel, Dungannon says: - "We sailed from Mitylene, and on 6th August were put on a smaller boat and set off. At daybreak on the following morning we came to our landing place. The naval guns kept up a terrific bombardment and we landed at about six o'clock a.m. The Turks sent the shells thick and heavy about us as we advanced all day through an open plain. In the evening we got under rifle fire from a small hill where the Turks were entrenched. Our naval guns gave the hill "socks" and so did our artillery. Anyhow, we got to the bottom of the hill after crossing a plain where shells and bullets fell around us like a shower of hail. We made a bayonet charge up the hill, but the Turks did not wait till we got to their trenches. They bolted off, so we hold the hill, which is now known as "Inniskilling Hill". The regulars are with us now, and our 1st Battalion is here. Other larger hills were captured, and now we have a good footing, which we mean to retain, and get as much more as we can. The trenches are fine, just as good as a house. The enemy are very quiet now, except for a few snipers and an odd shell going over our heads. The heat and flies are the only thing which trouble us very much here.[100]

One of the first Dungannon men wounded during the attack on 7 August was Captain (later Major) Robert Stevenson, 6th Battalion Royal Inniskilling Fusiliers. The *Belfast Newsletter* carried the following report:

A telegram from the War Office was received in Dungannon yesterday stating that Captain Robert Stevenson, 6th (Service) Battalion Royal Inniskilling Fusiliers, was wounded at the Dardanelles on the night of the 7th inst. Captain Stevenson is a member of the firm of Stevenson & Son, Ltd, linen manufacturers, Moygashel Mills, Dungannon, and is well known in Belfast. For many years he has been a prominent and popular figure in Irish Rugby football circles. He played for Ireland against England in 1887, and in the ensuing six years he represented his country on no fewer than thirteen occasions, including the match against the Maoris played in Dublin in 1889. In 1892 he was a member of the first Irish team which defeated Wales. After his retirement from active participation in the game, he was for several years on the Irish Five, and was president of the Irish Union in 1913. He was at one time a member of the now defunct Lisburn club, and was subsequently identified with the North of Ireland Club. It is well known that he has been for many years the mainstay of the Dungannon Club, and it is worthy to note that a member of the Stevenson family figured in every match played by the Dungannon Club for a period of twenty-six years. Amongst his colleagues on his first Irish team was" J. Chambers, now Mr James Chambers, K.C. M.P. for South Belfast. Captain Stevenson took a keen and practical interest in the Ulster Volunteer Force, being second in command of the Dungannon Battalion, of which the late Captain Viscount Northland, of

> *the Coldstream Guards, was the commanding officer. As is well-known the Dungannon Battalion was one of the most efficient units of the Ulster Volunteer Force, and on the outbreak of war Captain Stevenson promptly enlisted in the 6th Royal Inniskilling Fusiliers, taking with him 100 members of the Volunteer Battalion with which he was so actively associated. This took place before the formation of the Ulster Division. Shortly after his enrolment as a private, Captain Stevenson received a commission and was gazetted to company rank on 18th November last. Only a few weeks have elapsed since he left England with his regiment for the Dardanelles. It may be recalled that an invention by Captain Stevenson for the protection of men engaged with machine guns was recently the subject of favourable comment.[101]*

Captain Stevenson suffered a bullet and shrapnel wound to his arm and was sent to hospital in Alexandria, before being transferred to the Isle of Wight for treatment. By September 1915 it was reported that Captain Stevenson had been given the opportunity to return home to Dungannon to recover from his wounds. By the end of October 1915 he had returned home and received further treatment in Belfast.

Private Joseph Rainey, who resided at Killylack, Dungannon, was one of the Dungannon UVF contingent who volunteered on the outbreak of war. Serving with the 6th Battalion Royal Inniskilling Fusiliers, he intimated in a letter sent to his friends in Dungannon in August 1915 that he had been wounded in the trenches in the recent fighting in the Gallipoli Peninsula, and was in the same hospital as his company officer, Captain R Stevenson, in Alexandria.

Lieutenant T. W. E. Brogden serving with the 6th Battalion Royal Irish Rifles sent his mother Mrs Neill, Victoria Villas, Dungannon, a telegram on 17 August 1915, intimating that he had been shot during the recent operations in the Dardanelles. He advised her that he had sustained a broken arm as a result of being hit by rifle fire, and was being treated in hospital in Alexandria. Prior to the war Lieutenant Brogden had been training as a manager in the Boyne Weaving Factory, Drogheda. At the commencement of the war he threw up his position, and enlisted in Belfast, Brogden soon obtained his commission as an lieutenant. His battalion, part of the 10th (Irish) Division, had left Basingstoke for the Dardanelles on 6 July 1915. By December Lieutenant Brogden had returned home to Victoria Villas, Dungannon for convalescence.

Second-Lieutenant J. F. Hunter the son of Rev. W. Hunter, an Irish Presbyterian Missionary in Manchuria, China, was wounded between 7 and 10 August 1915. He was serving with the 6th Battalion Royal Inniskilling Fusiliers. J. F. Hunter had been travelling with Dungannon Royal School pupils at Geneva when the war broke out. On returning to Dungannon, he enlisted as a private in the 6th Battalion Royal Inniskilling Fusiliers. Having been involved with the UVF in Belfast and being a member of the Queen's University Officer Training Corps (OTC.), he soon obtained a commission. 2nd Lieutenant Hunter returned to Dungannon at the end of August 1915 to recover from the wounds he had suffered in the right leg during the Gallipoli operations.

The *Belfast Newsletter* on 26 August brought news that:

> *Captain Victor Harry Scott, 5th Battalion Royal Inniskilling Fusiliers, has been wounded in action in the Gallipoli Peninsula. Captain Scott, who is an old Dungannon Royal School boy, is the second son of the late Mr Robert Scott, Howard Terrace, Dungannon, and a younger brother of Captain R. H. Scott, 6th Battalion Royal Inniskilling Fusiliers, who is also at the Dardanelles. The wounded officer obtained a commission in the 5th Battalion Royal Inniskilling Fusiliers in January 1905, but afterwards joined the Royal Irish Constabulary, and was appointed district inspector on 1st April 1910. When the present war broke out Captain Scott was in charge of the police district at Cappawhite, South, County Tipperary, but he threw up his appointment and volunteered for active service. He was attached to the 5th Inniskillings, and in November last was placed in charge of a company. The extent of his wounds is not stated in the official notification.*

Private Patrick Tohall, 5th Battalion Connaught Rangers the son of Mr Henry Tohall, JP Moy, received a bullet wound through the thigh on the Gallipoli Peninsula on 21 August 1915. Private Tohall was educated at Queen's University, Belfast where he obtained his BA and BE (with honours) degrees. He subsequently received an appointment with the Congested District Board, and on the outbreak of the war was stationed at Castlebar, County Mayo. Three days after Private Tohall was wounded he was gazetted to a commission in the 6th Battalion Royal Irish Fusiliers. Private Tohall returned to England for treatment in a military hospital.

Mr James Field, Cranebrook, Ballynakelly, Coalisland, received intimation in mid September 1915 that his son Private James Field, 6th

Battalion Royal Inniskilling Fusiliers was wounded in action at the Gallipoli Peninsula on 30 August, and was in hospital. Prior to volunteering James Field had been an efficient member of the Dungannon Battalion UVF.

Second Lieutenant William Porter, 6th Battalion Royal Inniskilling Fusiliers, was wounded in the chest during the action on the Gallipoli Peninsula. He was the brother-in-law of Mr R. W. Bingham, BA, Headmaster of Dungannon Royal School. (R. W. Bingham at this time was the commander of the Dungannon UVF Battalion). Porter had come to Dungannon on a visit about 1913 when the UVF was in full swing, and at once threw himself into the movement. He was exceedingly popular and was soon appointed half-company officer of A Company Dungannon Battalion, of which his brother-in-law, Mr Bingham, was company commander. On the outbreak of war he volunteered with a Dungannon contingent of UVF men and enlisted as a private in the 6th Battalion Royal Inniskilling Fusiliers, subsequently being granted a commission. 2nd Lieutenant Porter was the youngest son of Mr William Porter, Beechview, Balmoral Avenue, Belfast and was formerly in business in Winnipeg, Canada. Following his wounding in Gallipoli, 2nd Lieutenant Porter was sent to hospital on one of the islands in the Aegean Sea. By the end of September 1915 he had spent a period of convalescence at home in Dungannon and was almost restored to full health.

In mid September the *Belfast Newsletter* carried the following stories about the wounding of Private Spurgeon Jordan and Lieutenant Charles Loraine Carlos Clarke, the son-in-law of the Earl of Ranfurly:

> *Intimation has been received by his friend at Glencon, Newmills, Dungannon, that Private Spurgeon Jordan, 1st Battalion Royal Inniskilling Fusiliers, has been wounded in action at the Gallipoli Peninsula, having been shot in the eye. Private Jordan was a reservist in the 3rd Battalion, and had been called up at the outbreak of the war.*[102]

> *Lieutenant Charles Loraine Carlos Clarke, Buckinghamshire Yeomanry, wounded at the Dardanelles, is a son-in-law of the Earl of Ranfurly, of Northland House, Dungannon, having married last year his Lordship's youngest daughter, Lady Eileen Maud Juliana, who was a trainbearer to Queen Mary at the Coronation in 1911. It is understood that Lieutenant Clarke is returning to England.*[103]

Private William Donaghy, 6th Battalion Royal Irish Rifles, was wounded in action on the Gallipoli Peninsula after participating in six days fighting. His leg was broken above the knee by a rifle bullet and he was sent to hospital in Malta. Private Donaghy was from Curran, Dungannon, the eldest son of Mr William Donaghy.

Second-Lieutenant, John Leslie Bennett, 5th Battalion Royal Irish Fusiliers, Manor House, Antrim Road, Belfast and 25 Fitzwilliam Square, Dublin was wounded at the Dardanelles on 11 September 1915 and was transferred to a hospital in Egypt. 2nd Lieutenant Bennett was intimately connected with Dungannon, having been some time prior to the war engaged as chemist with the firm of Stevenson & Son Ltd, Moygashel Mills, Dungannon. He was married to Miss Norah Greer, daughter of the late Mr F. H. Greer, Bernagh, Dungannon. He took an active interest in the workings of the Dungannon Battalion UVF, and attended the Baronscourt camp of instruction as a representative from B Company. 2nd Lieutenant Bennett returned to Rhonehill, Dungannon, the residence of his wife's uncle Mr George Greer, to recover from his wounds.

Some Dungannon men who had emigrated to Australia were wounded serving with the ANZACS at Gallipoli. One of these men was Edwin Vere Proctor the son of Mrs Proctor, Tullydoey, Moy. Like many families at this time, a number of members of the Proctor family had enlisted to serve King and Country. This is illustrated in the following newspaper report:

> *Information has been received that Mr Edwin Vere Proctor, 21st Brigade, 6th Infantry Battalion, Australian Imperial Force, youngest son of the late Mr Jas E. Proctor, solicitor, Limavady, and Mrs Proctor, Tullydoey, Moy, has been wounded, but is now convalescent. He was in Egypt, and volunteered for special service of a hazardous nature with the signals in the Dardanelles. On the third day he was struck by shrapnel, a fragment wounding him in the right shoulder, and another ripping the sheath of his bayonet. Mr E. V. Proctor's two brothers are also in the army – Lieutenant G. Norman Proctor, Cashmir Rifles, serving in German East Africa, and Captain J. G. B. Proctor, LL. D, M.A., B.L. 10th (Service) Inniskillings at Seaford. Miss E Proctor, who volunteered for nursing service, is at North Evington Military Hospital, Leicester.*[104]

Another man originally from Dungannon and who served in Gallipoli with the Australian contingent was Sergeant William McKay 3rd Battalion New South Wales Regiment. He was the brother of Miss F. McKay, Thomas Street, Dungannon. Sergeant McKay, was the eldest son of the late Sergeant William McKay, Royal Garrison Artillery, and was in his earlier days a boy trumpeter in the Mid-Ulster Royal Garrison Artillery. Later he joined the RIC, and afterwards he emigrated to Brisbane, and joined the police force. On the outbreak of war he volunteered for active service. Sergeant McKay was severely wounded in the left leg by an explosive bullet during the fighting at Gallipoli and was hospitalised. Sergeant McKay returned to Dungannon to recover from his wounds. He was a member of Masonic Lodge 122, Dungannon.

Conditions for the allies troops in the trenches in Gallipoli were awful. Dead bodies were left lying where they fell and the stench of decaying flesh prevailed. There were flies everywhere, and after crawling over the dead bodies they landed on the men's food. The diet of the soldiers was bad and there was a shortage of clean water. Soon diarrhoea, dysentery, typhoid and malaria were claiming as many lives as Turkish bullets and shells. Stories of some of the Dungannon men who suffered illness were reported in the *Belfast Newsletter*:

> *Lieutenant Wm T. Dickson, 6th Battalion Royal Inniskilling Fusiliers, has returned home to Dungannon, invalided owing to an attack of illness contracted at the Gallipoli Peninsula. He took part in the famous landing at Suvla Bay and in the subsequent fighting, but on the fourth day he developed symptoms of illness, and was removed on board ship and sent to England. Lieutenant Dickson, who is the eldest son of Mr. James Dickson, J. P. Milltown House, Dungannon, and grandson of the late Right Honourable T. A. Dickson. commanded C Company of the Dungannon Battalion U.V.F., and was one of the first members of that battalion to volunteer for active service at the outbreak of the war. He enlisted as a private in the 6th Inniskilling Fusiliers, and afterwards received a commission.[105]*

While serving in the Dardanelles, Bombardier James Sands, Royal Field Artillery wrote home to his parents at Mullaghanagh, Dungannon telling them of his narrow escape on 15 September when a shell struck the ground beside him, but did not explode. He also explained that his brother Private David Sands, who was serving with the 6th Battalion Royal Inniskilling Fusiliers in Gallipoli, had contracted dysentery and was in hospital. Private David Sands returned home to Mullaghanagh, Dungannon, to recover.

Captain Robert Hamilton Scott, 6th Battalion Royal Inniskilling Fusiliers, took part in the landings at Suvla Bay and subsequent operations. However he contracted dysentery and was sent to hospital in Malta. Robert Hamilton Scott by this time had been promoted to the rank of Major. Bush Orange Lodge renamed itself 'Scott Memorial LOL 163' after the war.

Maj Robert Hamilton Scott

A further Dungannon man that suffered illness while serving in the near East was Private Adam Hayes. On 16 November 1915 the *Belfast Newsletter* reported:

> *Intimation has been received in Dungannon that Private Adam Hayes, 5th Battalion Royal Inniskilling Fusiliers, now serving in the Near East, has contracted dysentery and is in hospital. Private Hayes is one of eight brothers who were on active service during the South African war, and their mother was at the time the recipient of a congratulatory letter from Queen Victoria. Two of his brothers are serving at present, and a third is a prisoner of war in Germany.*

A further article in the newspaper on 2 March 1916 reported that Private Adam Hayes had returned home to Dungannon to recuperate.

Another local man who returned home by late December 1915 to recover from the effects of dysentery contracted at Gallipoli was Sergeant Bernard Kelly, Royal Irish Fusiliers. He was the oldest son of Mr. Bernard Kelly, Market Square, Dungannon.

Lieutenant Joseph Marmion, who served with the Royal Army Medical Corps., also contracted illness in Gallipoli. The *Belfast Newsletter* on 20

January 1916 carried the following report:

> *Surgeon Marmion, J.P., Dungannon, has received intimation from the War Office that his eldest son, Lieut. Joseph Marmion, R.A.M.C., is in hospital in Alexandria, suffering from a severe attack of dysentery. Lieutenant Marmion, who volunteered for service at the outbreak of the war, was attached to the Mediterranean Expeditionary Force, and accompanied a division which landed at Suvla Bay. He contracted dysentery there, and was sent to hospital at Uxor on the Nile. Since then he suffered a relapse, and was admitted to the 21st General Hospital, Alexandria on the 6th inst.*

The following letter from an unknown soldier writing to his friends in Dungannon, which was published in the *Belfast Newsletter* at the end of September 1915, vividly summarises the awful conditions endured by the British soldiers in Gallipoli:

> *I am afraid after twelve months soldiering and four months fighting, we will all require to be re-civilised when we get away from this God forsaken country. We will likely forget to take off our boots, and will use powerful language &c; but there are a few things I am going to do when I return home. The very first thing I will do will be to turn on a water tap and watch the water running to waste for a whole day; then I will go to my aunt's and feed on new laid eggs till I burst; then to the pub, about every hour for a Guinness stout, and finally, buy some of the papers and gloat over the death struggles of each fly as it is caught. I could go on filling pages with my ardent desire, but I will spare you.*[106]

The Dungannon Fallen at Suvla Bay

Many Dungannon men lost their lives at Gallipoli during the Suvla Bay landings and subsequent campaign on the peninsula.

Major Hugh Price Travers of the 8th Battalion Duke of Wellington's (West Riding Regiment) was killed in action at the Dardanelles. Posted as missing initially he was later confirmed as being killed in action on 7 August 1915. Major Travers formerly resided at Grange Park, Moy, with his father the late Colonel Henry Travers. Major Travers was a noted rugby player, and gave his services to Dungannon Rugby Football Club for several years. His brother Arthur Stewart Travers was also serving in Gallipoli at the same time and witnessed the fall of his brother. Major Hugh Price Travers grave is in Hill 10 Cemetery, North Anzac, Gallipoli.

Lieutenant Ernest Magowan Harper, 7th Battalion Royal Munster Fusiliers was killed in action on 9 August 1915. Reports of his death appeared in the *Belfast Newsletter* on 14 August 1915:

> *Mr Henry M. Harper, Northland Place, Dungannon, received an official intimation yesterday evening that his youngest son, Lieutenant Ernest M. Harper, 7th Battalion Royal Munster Fusiliers, has been killed in action at the Dardanelles on Monday last. In the message the deep sympathy of Lord Kitchener was expressed with the bereaved parent. Lieutenant Harper had just been appointed a demonstrator in chemistry in Queen's University, Belfast, at the outbreak of the war, but relinquished that position to volunteer in the service of his country. He obtained a commission in the 7th Munster's and was soon promoted lieutenant. He was educated at Dungannon Royal School, and afterwards secured a scholarship in the Royal University, being the first science scholar of his year. He also obtained a scholarship in Mathematical and Physical Science, and gained the Andrew's studentship in June 1913. In the following year he obtained the degree of Bachelor of Science with honours. He was always an energetic sportsman, and was a member of Dungannon Royal School Rugby Football team in 1906, when they won the Ulster Schools Cup, and he captained that team two years later. He was subsequently a member of Queen's University Rugby Club, and played for a couple of seasons in their senior fixtures. He also lent a helping hand to the Rugby team of his native town. Lieutenant Harper had attained the age of twenty-five years just two months ago.*

The death of Lieutenant Harper was marked by both Dungannon Urban Council and Second Dungannon Presbyterian Church. The *Belfast Newsletter* reported:

> *In Second Dungannon Presbyterian Church on Sunday, at the conclusion of the sermon, Rev. John Watson, B.A. made an appropriate reference to the death of Lieutenant Ernest M. Harper, 7th Batt. Munster Fusiliers, who was killed at the Dardanelles on 9th inst. He said it was fitting that in the name of the congregation he should tender to Mr Harper and his family*

their sincere sympathy with them on their bereavement. Lieutenant Harper was a very distinguished student, and would no doubt have risen soon to a high position in the world of learning and science. When, however, the call of King and country came to him he gave up all those bright prospects, not counting things dear unto him, and now he has given up his life and had made the supreme sacrifice in what they believed to be a sacred cause.- the cause of righteousness and freedom. To Lieutenant Harper and men like him the nation was greatly indebted for their self sacrificing love, and they prayed that their friends might be comforted by the thought that such sacrifices would not be made in vain.[107]

Lieutenant Ernest Magowan Harper showed tremendous courage in Gallipoli as illustrated in the following letter written by a fellow officer:

Lieutenant F. G. Fitzmaurice, 7th Royal Munster Fusiliers, who was wounded at the Dardanelles on 9th inst., and is now in hospital at Osborne, Isle of Wight, in a letter written to his mother, Mrs Fitzmaurice, The National Bank, Clonakilty, County Cork, pays the following tribute to the late Lieutenant E. M. Harper, of Dungannon: - Every officer in our company is wounded. Every officer in C Company is killed, and one of them, Lieutenant Harper should have got the Victoria Cross if he had pulled through. On Saturday he succeeded in collecting 100 men of his company who had got within 200 yards of the enemy and extricated them from a fearful position after lying out in the open for twenty-four hours. On his way back with this lot he picked up any amount of wounded, and spent two hours looking for me, because he had heard that I was bowled over (wrongly of course, as I wasn't hit until Monday). On Monday he was hit in the head, but insisted on going on with the attack, and continued leading his men until he was killed by another bullet in the head. The late Lieutenant Harper was a well-known Queensman, and had just been appointed a demonstrator in chemistry in Belfast University when war broke out. He relinquished the position to take a commission in the Munster Fusiliers.[108]

The full extent of Lieutenant Harper's gallantry was described in a letter from Major G. Drage to his father:

Mr Henry M Harper, Northland Place, Dungannon, has received the following letter from Major G. Drage, officer commanding C Company

7th Battalion Royal Munster Fusiliers, with regard to the death of his son, Lieutenant E. M. Harper, of the same battalion, who was killed in action in the Gallipoli Peninsula on 9th August. "I have the painful duty of telling you if you have not already heard of the death of your son, who was the most gallant officer I have ever been with on active service. On 9th August C Company had to make a second attack. Your son and Lieutenant Good were in the second line with me advancing under heavy fire, when he was killed instantaneously by a shot from our rear. I had seen five men behind us and heard shots, and I believe they were Turkish snipers who stayed behind, dressed in our men's uniform. On 7th August, during our first attack, your son was near me, under heavy fire. He volunteered at dusk to go and examine Captain Cullman's body, and, with the help of a few men, he brought in to us Lieutenant Bennett, who had been shot through the chest and died later. Early on the following morning (Sunday) when your son and Good had to withdraw their men, your son most gallantly and unselfishly exposed himself while urging the men to leave the Turkish trench they had taken shelter in and he was the last to leave the trench. He had some very narrow escapes himself, while his men had several casualties. On Sunday night he volunteered with one man to go with a stretcher and look for some of his wounded, but lost his direction. He was beloved by the men of his platoon especially, who as long ago as last Christmas wanted to give him presents. I had the greatest faith in your son, but I did not know he could rise to the height of gallantry and unselfishness, which he did. At the Curragh I often said if they took away your son, my oldest subaltern and support, I would resign and I think in his quiet way he knew how I appreciated him. Good wept when he heard the news" Lieutenant W. H. Good, above mentioned, has since been killed.[109]

Ernest's elder brother Henry M. Harper also served with the 7th Battalion Munster Fusiliers, with whom he had received a commission as notified in the *Belfast Newsletter* on 7 May 1915. A former student at Trinity College, Dublin, Lieutenant Henry Harper would subsequently serve with the 8th Battalion South Staffordshire Regiment and was killed in action on 10 July 1916.

Lieutenant Ernest Magowan Harper has no known grave, but is remembered on the Helles Memorial, Gallipoli and on Dungannon War Memorial.

Lieutenant Hewitt Huggard was born in Dungannon about 1889. His father the Rev. Richard Huggard was formerly a curate of St. Anne's Parish Church, Dungannon. On leaving Dungannon the Rev. Huggard became vicar of St John's Barnsley, Yorkshire. Lieutenant Hewitt Huggard was serving with the 6th Battalion East Yorkshire Regiment when he was killed in action on 9 August 1915 in Gallipoli. For a period of time it was hoped that Lieutenant Huggard had been taken prisoner. The engagement in which Lieutenant Huggard was killed was a severe one, as two of his brother officers were also killed, two wounded and five reported missing. Lieutenant Huggard's father, who was a captain in the 14th Battalion of the Yorkshire and Lancaster Regiment, threw himself heartily into the war effort and the work of recruiting in Barnsley. A rugby family to the core, Lieutenant Huggard's father was one of the most enthusiastic rugby officials in Ulster, and was president of the Northern Branch of the Irish Rugby Football Union, 1897-98. He was, subsequently appointed a vice-president of the Yorkshire Union. He refereed a match between England and Ireland in 1903 and was secretary of Barnsley Rugby Club. Lieutenant Huggard's brother Lewis was a Second Lieutenant in the 13th Battalion East Yorkshire Regiment. Like their father both had a keen interest in rugby and played for Barnsley Rugby Club.

It was reported in the *Belfast Newsletter* on 6 October 1915 that Miss Hale, Fairview, Dungannon, had presented a wheeled ambulance stretcher to the 6th Battalion East Yorkshire Regiment, who were fighting at the Dardanelles, in memory of the late Lieutenant Hewitt Huggard. Miss Hale also presented a similar stretcher to the 2nd Battalion Royal Inniskilling Fusiliers serving in Flanders. Both the stretchers were obtained from and despatched by the St John Ambulance Association.

Lieutenant Hewitt Huggard has no known grave, but is remembered on the Helles Memorial, Gallipoli and on Dungannon War Memorial.

Rifleman William Campbell (11159), 6th Battalion Royal Irish Rifles, was born in Dungannon about 1895. The family subsequently moved to Belfast where William worked as a barman. He enlisted in Belfast and was killed in action on 13 August 1915 in Gallipoli. Rifleman William Campbell has no known grave but is remembered on the Helles Memorial, Gallipoli.

Corporal Robert McReynolds (1134), Black Watch, died of wounds received at the Dardanelles on 14 August 1915. Corporal McReynolds was a brother of Mrs Clayton, The Park, Dungannon and was the son of the late Mr John McReynolds. A native of Dungannon, he served ten years in the Territorials and on the outbreak of war enlisted in Glasgow with the Black Watch. Corporal Robert McReynolds' grave is in the Lancashire Landing Cemetery, in the Cape Helles region of Gallipoli and he is also remembered on the Roll of Honour of Holdfast Dungannon LOL 1620.

Lieutenant Lee Tolerton, 6th Battalion Royal Irish Fusiliers, was killed in action on 15 August 1915. He has no known grave but is remembered on the Helles Memorial, Gallipoli.

Private Richard McCourt (11947), 5th Battalion Royal Inniskilling Fusiliers, was born in Dungannon about 1890. By the outbreak of war the family had moved to the Shankill area of Belfast. Enlisting in Belfast he served with C Company of the 5th Battalion Royal Inniskilling Fusiliers in Gallipoli. Richard was killed in action on 15 August 1915. Private Richard McCourt has no known grave, but is remembered on the Helles Memorial, Gallipoli. He is also remembered on the Roll of Honour in Agnes Street, Presbyterian Church, Belfast.

Corporal Frederick James Dunn (3114), 5th Battalion Royal Irish Regiment (Pioneers), was killed in action on the Gallipoli Peninsula on 16 August 1915. Born in Windsor, England, he had previous military experience with the 1st (Volunteer) Battalion Royal Berkshire Regiment. Private Dunn had at the outbreak of war been living in Dungannon with his wife for approximately three years. The estate carpenter on the Earl of Ranfurly's estate, he had played an active role in the Dungannon Battalion UVF prior to the war. Corporal Dunn's wife received the following correspondence on his death:

> Lieutenant T. E. N. Byrne, 5th Battalion Royal Irish Regiment (Pioneers), has written to Mrs. Dunn, The Park, Dungannon informing her that her husband, Corporal Frederick J Dunn of that Battalion, has been killed in action at the Gallipoli Peninsula and stating that he was killed instantaneously. He had carried on his work cheerily to the last, and had behaved as all would have wished him to do. Corporal Dunn, who leaves a widow and several small children, had been estate carpenter to the Earl

of Ranfurly for over three years. He had been a section leader in the Dungannon Battalion, U.V. F. and had volunteered with the Dungannon contingent on 26th August 1914, which joined the 6th Battalion Royal Inniskilling Fusiliers. He afterwards transferred to his present regiment. He had had four years service in the 1st (Volunteer) Battalion Royal Berkshire Regiment in England, of which county he was a native.[110]

Corporal Dunn was one of the founder members of the Dungannon Workers Union, No. 1 Branch. Following his death the branch, chaired by Mr Eugene McGurk, adopted a resolution of sympathy with the deceased soldier's widow and children. A memorial service for Corporal Dunn was held in Northland House, as reported in the *Belfast Newsletter* on 11 September 1915:

Through the kindness of the Countess of Ranfurly, a memorial service in connection with the death of Corporal Frederick J. Dunn, 5th Battalion Royal Irish Regiment, who was killed in action at the Gallipoli Peninsula on 16th ult., was held yesterday in Northland House, Dungannon. Corporal Dunn had been the estate carpenter for the Earl of Ranfurly, and had been an efficient section leader in the Dungannon Battalion U.V.F. prior to volunteering on the outbreak of the present war. The service, which was conducted by Rev Canon T. J. McEndoo M.A., was attended by the household staff and demesne employees and their families, and the deceased soldier's widow and children were also present. The hymn "O God, our help in ages past" And the special hymn "Loving Shepherd of Thy sheep" were sung, and prayers from the Burial Service and the 15th chapter of 1st Corinthians were read. An address was given by Rev F S Morrow, B. A. from the words of the Burial Service. "In the midst of life we are in death." The speaker making appropriate reference to Corporal Dunn having given his life for his country.

Corporal Frederick James Dunn has no known grave but his name appears on the Helles Memorial, Gallipoli. He is also remembered on St. Anne's Parish Church Roll of Honour.

Staff Sergeant Major Robert Sloan, Canterbury Regiment (New Zealand), had been born in Dungannon in 1884. He had served with the 16th Queen's Lancers during the Boer War and subsequently emigrated to New Zealand, where he served as Staff Sergeant Major of the 8th Canterbury Mounted Regiment. Reports of his death appeared in the *Belfast Newsletter:*

> *Mr Robert Sloan, Elm Lodge, Dungannon has received intimation that his son Robert has been killed in action in the Gallipoli Peninsula on 21st August, when serving with the New Zealand contingent. The deceased had served throughout the South African war with the Royal Irish Rifles and afterwards joined the 16th Lancers, in which corps he obtained the rank of sergeant-major. After his term of service had expired he went out to New Zealand and for three years acted as instructor in the local defence force there. On the call to arms sounding in New Zealand he volunteered. He leaves a widow and two children. A brother of the deceased Trooper Wm Sloan, 6th Inniskilling Dragoons has been missing since 6th November last, when he was doing duty in France with the 2nd Life Guards. Another brother, Private Thomas Sloan volunteered at the outbreak of hostilities, and joining the Army Veterinary Corps, is now on active service in France with the Mobile Veterinary Section.*[111]

Staff Sergeant Major Robert Sloan is buried in Hill 10 Cemetery, North Anzac, Gallipoli. He is also remembered on Dungannon War Memorial.

Private John Cullen (6560), 1st Battalion Royal Inniskilling Fusiliers, was killed in action on 21 August 1915. Aged 50, Private Cullen was one of the oldest men from Dungannon to be killed in action during the war. He lived at "Fair View," Ann Street. Private Cullen has no known grave but his name appears on the Helles Memorial, Gallipoli.

Private Bernard Fitzpatrick (4426), 1st Battalion Royal Inniskilling Fusiliers, was killed in action on the Gallipoli Peninsula on 21 August 1915. He was serving in the same battalion as his brother Private James Fiztpatrick. A further brother Private Frank Fitzpatrick, 2nd Battalion Royal Dublin Fusiliers was killed in action in France in June 1915. Private Bernard Fitzpatrick has no known grave but his name appears on the Helles Memorial, Gallipoli. He is also remembered on Dungannon War Memorial.

Private Robert Jeffs (46463), Royal Army Medical Corps, died of enteric fever on 29 August 1915 on the Gallipoli Peninsula. Private Jeffs prior to enlistment had been employed as a linen lapper at Drogheda with Messrs Dickson & Co., Milltown, Dungannon. He enlisted on 14 November 1914. Private Robert Jeffs has no known grave, but his name appears on the Helles Memorial, Gallipoli. He is also remembered on St. Anne's Parish Church Roll of Honour and Dungannon War Memorial.

Both Private Jeffs and Corporal McReynolds were remembered in the parish church during regular worship shortly after their death:

> *Rev F. S Morrow, B. A. preaching on Sunday in St Ann's Parish Church, Dungannon, said he had again to refer to the loss of two more members of the congregation who had gone forth and died in the service of their country. Corporal Robert McReynolds, Highland Light Infantry, had fallen in battle and Private Robert Jeffs, Royal Army Medical Corps, had succumbed to disease. Their bodies lay in soldier's graves far away from home beneath the grass of the Dardanelles. They had died fighting the battle of freedom, and no life blood was poured out in vain which was shed in defence of so noble a cause. The "Dead March" in Saul was rendered at the close of the service the congregation standing.*[112]

Private Patrick Birney (2883), 5th Battalion Connaught Rangers, died of illness after contracting dysentery in the Dardanelles. He had been born in Dungannon about 1877 and at the outbreak of war was living in Belfast where he enlisted. Private Birney had been hospitalised back to England and died on 9 September 1915. His grave is in Weston Mill Cemetery, Plymouth. His son Patrick was at the front from 1914 and was killed in action on 30 January 1917 serving with the Royal Inniskilling Fusiliers and is remembered on the Thiepval Memorial.

Private Thomas Joseph Sheridan (17684), 5th Battalion Royal Inniskilling Fusiliers, died of wounds he received in the Dardanelles on 12 October 1915. Born in Brackey, Sixmilecross, Private Sheridan is recorded as the son of James and Mary Sheridan, Mullyconnor, Dungannon. He is buried in the Alexandria Chatby War Memorial Cemetery, Chatby, Alexandria, Egypt. His brother Private James Sheridan died of wounds in October 1918. James had been serving with the 2nd Battalion Royal Dublin Fusiliers at the time of his death.

Private Edward Hughes (1307), 7th Battalion Royal Munster Fusiliers. died in hospital in Glasgow on 23 December 1915 from wounds he had received during the Dardanelles Campaign. Born around 1895 near Coalisland, Edward had enlisted for the term of the war. He had been married and was living in Bellshill, Glasgow. Edward is buried in Bothwell Park Cemetery, Bellshill, Glasgow, and is also remembered on Dungannon War Memorial.

Evacuation from Gallipoli

By the autumn of 1915 the Suvla offensive had become bogged down. The 10th (Irish) Division was moved from Gallipoli in September 1915. Having lost at least 3,000 men, it was only a shadow of the Division that had landed in Suvla Bay on 7 August 1915. A Dungannon man who served throughout the Suvla offensive was Private Atkinson Connelly from Tamnamore. Atkinson was only 16 when he enlisted. He left a note for his mother telling her that he had decided to forge his age and join the Army. He walked the twelve miles from Tamnamore to Armagh and joined the 5th Battalion Royal Irish Fusiliers in which he trained as a Lewis Gunner. Following the Gallipoli campaign, Atkinson went with the 10th (Irish) Division to Salonika in October 1915. Atkinson Connelly on his return from the war joined Tamnamore LOL 513 and Moygashel RBP 1052.

In November 1915 the decision was taken to evacuate all the allied troops from Gallipoli. In stark contrast to the landings, the evacuation was spectacular success. It was completed by early January 1916, with not a single life lost.

By the end of the campaign some 559,000 allied personnel had been deployed in Gallipoli, comprising 420,000 British and Empire troops, 80,000 French, 50,000 Australians and 9,000 New Zealanders. The allies suffered approximately 250,000 casualties, including 58,000 who were killed. The Turks and Germans, who had some 300,000 to 400,000 men engaged in the campaign, lost 87,000.

Other Theatres of War

The First World War was the first truly global conflict and the fighting extended far beyond the Western Front to Africa, Middle East and the Balkans. Men from Dungannon served King and Country in all of these battle zones.

African Campaigns

While the campaigns in South West Africa and East Africa commenced in 1914 they ran through into 1915. The allies suffered defeats during the early stages of the South West Africa campaign, but by June 1915 the power of numbers prevailed and the colony surrendered.

Two local men that took part in that offensive were Troopers Robert Daniel and Jack Burrowes. Robert who was in business in South Africa enlisted with Kaiffrarian Rifles at East London at the outbreak of the war and shortly afterwards was with the regiment in the operations against German South West Africa.

Trooper Jack Burrowes wrote home to friends in Dungannon and his account was published in the *Belfast Newsletter* on 10 June 1915:

Trooper Jack Burrowes, 1st Imperial Light Horse, writing from Rossing, German S. W. Africa to friends in Dungannon says – Just a line from the desert to say we are busy chasing square-heads (Germans) both night and day in this God-forsaken country, as they are always retreating and popping up again. When I returned to South Africa from Ireland I butted into this little lot (which as a Volunteer regiment is second to none anywhere), and arrived here via Walfish Bay. We are now guarding water holes and railway lines, and engaged at patrolling and scouting. This place is the limit as far as climate and vegetation are concerned. The whole country for about 150 miles inland from the sea is desert, and being undeveloped and not even prospected, water holes are scarce, and any that exist have been poisoned by the Germans as they retreated. The chief difficulty is transport, and new railway lines required to be made before the troops can move. These lines require thousands of infantry to keep them swept clear of sand, as the sand dunes are always moving and cover up the track, all guiding marks being obliterated in a few hours time. This desert country presents the appearance of having been at one time burned to the ashes. Hills, mountains and valleys are all coloured grey and drab, and the only signs of life are the flies and mosquitoes, which have here developed a faculty of torturing the white man to a degree unknown in any other part of the world I have been in. We have a visit twice a week from a German Taube, which up to the present has not done us any great damage; but its appearance, generally about daylight, throws the camp into great excitement, as no matter where you are it always seems to be just overhead. The German game is to abandon the roads and passes through which we are likely to come and lay contact mines. These have caused many casualties, but we now bring along goats and donkeys and send them over the ground first. This part of the country has been described as a land of sin, sorrow and sore eyes, and many men have gone totally blind, so now we use green veils over our helmets and wear smoked glass goggles.

Others with connections to Dungannon who took part in this campaign were the three Morrison boys, nephews of Mr W. J. Orr, J. P., Lisnacroy Dungannon. All three served with the South African Army. Edward Morrison served through the German South West Africa campaign under General Botha, while his other brothers Norman and Walter would see action on the Western Front. The Belfast Newsletter on 1 November 1915 reported that Private Walter Morrison, Cape Peninsular Rifles, who had been educated at Dungannon Royal School was visiting Dungannon.

The campaign in East Africa was a completely different affair as the Germans remain undefeated throughout the duration of the war. . Under the command of Lettow-Vorbeck the Germans only belatedly surrendered on the 25 November 1918. with Lettow-Vorbeck returning to Germany a national hero.

Lieutenant G. Norman Proctor who was with the Kashmir Rifles was present in German East Africa with the Indian Expeditionary Force. He had been promoted Captain and appointed special officer of the Kashmir Imperial Troops. Captain Proctor's two brothers also served with the colours. They were the sons of the late Mr James E. Proctor, Limavady and of Mrs Proctor, Tullydoey Moy County Tyrone.

Somaliland

Captain C. A. Howard, 32nd Lancers, Indian Army, who was in charge of the Camel Corps in Somaliland sent his father a detailed account of his service.:

A most interesting account of the fighting at Shimberberris has been received by Major R. Howard J.P. Annaginny House, Dungannon, from his eldest son who is in charge of the Camel Corps which forms part of the force operating against the Mad Mullah in Somaliland. The communication which is dated 27th February, contains the following:-
We had a much better show at Shimberberris last time than the first. We first of all went for the forts we had attacked and burnt before on top of the hills. There were only a few dervishes about, who disappeared into the caves down below on the hillside as we came along. We blew up all the forts with guncotton, and destroyed the foundations where they had actually started to build new forts. We were scarcely under fire, except for snipers from the caves below. We camped last night at the foot of the hill. A rather amusing, if somewhat grim, incident occurred here. We could hear the dervish scouts moving about during the night, and sent out a few illalos or tribal scouts to chase them off. These fellows caught a dervish, and came in and told us about it in the morning. We asked them for proof, whereupon they produced a great black leg hacked off below the knee. These illaloes are the bravest men in the world. They live in constant touch with death, and they constantly face the most horrible risks. If they are caught they die the most horrible death imaginable. There is no quarter asked or given between the dervishes and tribesmen. The next morning we marched round the bottom of the hills and arrived before Shimberberris about midday. We halted a couple of hours and picketed our animals. About 2 pm we advanced from here on foot. When we got near the hills we could see a fort about half way up the hillside on the right of the re entrant, and one similarly placed on the left. Right away in the background, at the angle of the re-entrant, was a third fort. Both sides of the re-entrant were riddled with caves. The third fort was over the water, which is always the deciding factor in this country. In other words, you can practically always defeat your enemy by holding the water. The colonel decided to send one company round to the fort on the right, and another to the left, whilst the remainder of the corps, with two guns advanced up the riverbed. The companies on the right and left had a very steep climb, but got up near their forts without incident,

178

when a heavy fire suddenly broke out from the caves. This cave fighting is the most dangerous and, at the same time, unsatisfactory form of warfare in the world. The enemy is under cover in the darkness of the cave, whilst the attacker is fully exposed to him, without being able to see anything. The forts on the right and left were found unoccupied whilst the one in the centre, which was occupied, was partly broken in by the guns, thus allowing a charge of guncotton to be laid in comparative safety. The guncotton was entirely successful, bringing down most of the fort and burying all the occupants in the debris. We next turned our attention to the caves, and although we had rifle fire, machine guns, and big guns on them for three hours, the dervishes fought on to the bitter end; and although we killed them nearly all there were still men firing at us from the caves when we went away. Such is fanaticism. These men have no fear of death, and they are probably the bravest and most stubborn fighters in the world. We captured a small dervish boy in one of the caves afterwards, and although he had a bullet clean through his thigh, he was quite unconcerned and walked 40 miles into Buras afterwards. There are no Red Cross nurses or hospitals for them. If they are hit they get better as best they can, or die; no one minds in the very least which they do. They breed a mighty hard race. The worst and biggest cave was on the right behind the fort, and it was here that Lowry Corry was badly wounded and several men killed and wounded, without being able to achieve anything. The colonel thereupon decided to try them with bombs. This was where I came in as I am in charge of the bomb department. The cave in question had a mouth about 25ft high and probably 30 ft wide with an enormous great boulder in front. To get into the cave it was necessary to climb up this boulder. From there it was evident that the cave was not very deep, but there were two long narrow passages to the right and left of the mouth. The dervishes retired into these passages as soon as anyone came near the cave and were thus able to cover the entrance without being seen themselves. It was comparatively easy to bomb the left passage, but I had to run the gauntlet on the right. I was fortunate enough to escape with a graze on the hand and a few small splinters in my arm. However, there was no more firing from that cave and when we visited it a week later we found splashes of blood all over it. We retired to our camp just before dark, but there were still shots coming from some of the caves as we drew off. We placed a party over the water and next morning the few remaining dervishes had evacuated the post. We marched back to Buras; but no sooner had we arrived than an alarmist message came in saying the dervishes were coming back in force. There was nothing for it but to return to Shimberberris, where we did. When we got there we found it was a false alarm. However, we didn't mind as it gave us an opportunity of examining the caves, & c; but as the fight had taken place a week before and a lot of the dead had not been removed, it was impossible to enter most of them. Thus ended the fourth and I hope, the last battle of Shimberberris.[113]

Captain C. A. Howard, was wounded at Shimberberris and returned home to Dungannon to recuperate from his injuries before returning to command the Camel Corps in Somaliland.

Serbia, Macedonia and Salonika

When the 10th (Irish) Division left Gallipoli it was heavily depleted and was sent to Salonika to recuperate. For instance, the 5th Battalion Royal Irish Fusiliers had only 140 fit men, one of whom was Atkinson Connelly from Tamnamore. He had managed to get through the Gallipoli campaign relatively unscathed, but his recuperation time was short lived as by the end of October his regiment were on the move to Serbia. Moving into Serbia was difficult as the roads were more like paths, if they existed at all. By December it became evident that the Serbians forces had been broken, and with the Bulgarians entering the war on the German side, the only option was withdrawal. The 10th (Irish) Division were for a time in the highlands of Macedonia, where the weather was extremely cold. This took its toll on the Division. The Belfast Newsletter carried the following reports about Dungannon men who suffered in the severe weather:.

Lance Corporal John Williamson, 5th Battalion Royal Irish Fusiliers, has written to his mother at Brooke Street, Dungannon, intimating that he has arrived at the Military Hospital, Devonport, suffering from frost bite and a dislocated knee caused by slipping in the snow in Macedonia.[114]

On 5 January 1916 the Belfast Newsletter reported that Lance Corporal John Williamson had returned home to Brooke Street, Dungannon, to recover from the injuries that he had suffered in Macedonia:

Private Arthur McGuckian, Royal Dublin Fusiliers, has intimated to his mother at Linfield Street, Dungannon that he is in hospital in Alexandria suffering from exposure occasioned by the recent campaign in

Macedonia. He states that the snow was four and five feet deep, and that the country was full of lakes and rivers, roads being an unknown quantity. Private McGuckian was "gassed" in France some six months ago.[115]

Private Robert Taylor, 1st Battalion Royal Inniskilling Fusiliers, has also arrived at Devonport military Hospital suffering frost bite sustained in Macedonia. He belongs to Moygashel, Dungannon, and sustained no fewer than seven wounds caused by shrapnel shell, fire at Festubert in May last with the 2nd Battalion.[116]

Another who returned home with the effects of illness from Macedonia was Major Robert J Howard, 9th Battalion The King's Own (Royal Lancaster Regiment). Major Howard had previous military experience with the Highland Light Infantry (Territorial Force), and on volunteering at the commencement of the war was posted to the Royal Lancaster Regiment. He saw considerable service both in France and in Serbia, where he was attached to the Serbian Headquarters Staff. He was invalided home to Annaginny House, Carland, Dungannon owing to an attack of dysentery, contracted while serving with the Balkan Expeditionary Force. At the outbreak of the war, Major Howard was chairman of Dungannon Rural District Council and a member of the Tyrone County Council. The Howard family had a strong military tradition.

Nurses

Some women from Tyrone, including Dungannon served as nurses during the war. Amongst them was Miss Isabella Dickson. The Belfast Newsletter on 17 February carried the following article just prior to her departure for the Western Front:

> *Miss Isabella Dickson, a North of Ireland lady, who was for some years on the nursing staff at the Tyrone County Infirmary, is about to relinquish her duties as cadet's nurse at the Royal Naval College, Osborne to take up an important post in France. Miss Dickson went to the Royal Naval College, Osborne in May1907, and has done splendid service there, winning the highest compliments for her attention and devotion. Hundreds of cadets have passed through her hands, including the Prince of Wales and Prince Albert. Both the late King Edward and King George have visited the sick quarters at the college, and highly complimented Miss Dickson on her highly efficient performances of the duties of cadet's nurse.*

Other like Miss Maud Burgess, the daughter of Dr. R Burgess J. P. Coagh, Miss Venables, daughter of Mr W. J. Venables, solicitor, Cookstown and Miss M. E. Proctor, of Tullydoey, Moy, offered their services as nurses and were accepted by the War Office. All three took up duty at the 3rd London General Hospital, Wandsworth. Miss Burgess and Miss Venables were trained for UVF Hospital work, obtaining first aid and nursing certificates. All of these women had brothers serving King and Country.

On 9 March 1915 the Belfast Newsletter reported that two members of the family of the Rev. William Clements, Benburb had the rare honour of being mentioned in the same despatches for services in the medical and nursing fields:

> *Among those whose names were mentioned in Field Marshall Sir John French's despatches is Miss May Clements, daughter of the Rev. Wm. Clements, minister of Benburb, who was gazetted matron at the outbreak of the war, and is now in charge of one of the principal base hospitals in France. Among those recommended by Sir John French for gallant and distinguished conduct in the field is Lieutenant-Colonel R. W. Clements, R.A.M.C. It is a rare, as it is a high honour to find two members of a family*

*mentioned in the same despatches, and the numerous friends of Rev. Mr.
Clements will join in congratulating him on the distinctions which have
been conferred simultaneously on Colonel and Miss Clements.*

One of the most fascinating stories concerning local nurses relates to
Miss Beatrice Kerr of Cookstown. The daughter of John Kerr, Beatrice
had been on the staff of Mrs St. Clair Stobart's Hospital with the Serbian
Army. Below are extracts of articles from the Belfast Newsletter and
Nursing Mirror telling of her experiences in 1915.

*Information has just been received in Cookstown that Miss Beatrice Kerr,
daughter of, Mr John Kerr, of Cookstown, who was on the staff of Mrs St.
Clair Stobart's, Hospital with the Servian Army has been captured by the
Austrians. Apparently all the rest of the staff got safely away in the retreat.
Miss Kerr has been on active service since the beginning of the war.*[117]

*The "Nursing Mirror" states that information has been received at
Cookstown by the father of Miss Beatrice Kerr, who was lately attached
to the staff of Mrs. St. Clair Hobart's Hospital, that she has been captured
by Austrians. No details are forthcoming as to how Nurse Kerr, who has
been in Servia since the beginning of the war, became separated from
the rest of her party, who appear to have got away safely.*[118]

*Information has just been received in Cookstown that Miss Beatrice Kerr,
who was with Mrs St Clair Stobart's Mission in Servia, and was reported
missing on 6th November, has reached London safely. She is the daughter
of Mr John Kerr of Moy Street, Cookstown and Nurse Kerr, who has a
large private practice in Cookstown. At very early age Miss Kerr qualified
in her mother's profession, and practised for some time in London, at the
same time studying for the diploma of sanitary science. In 1912 she was
appointed health visitor for East Ham under the Notification of Births Act
1912. When Mrs Stobart's organised a mission to work in Servia, where
the sanitary conditions were terrible. Miss Kerr volunteered and was given
three months leave by East Ham Council at half pay – the only
remuneration she received for her services, as her position was honorary.
The leave was then extended to six months but she was then unable to
return. The party left in April, travelling via Salonica and Kiagnzevate,
where the people were dying in thousands of disease. The hospital had
forty large tents, and did so good work that the King of Servia decorated*

the staff. After the Hospital work Miss Kerr organised twelve dispensaries in the country for the treatment of disease, and was preparing to follow the army in its expected advance when the reverse came and part of the staff was cut off by the Austrians. No news had since been received from her until the telegram announcing her arrival in London, but from reports of the Servian Relief Fund it appears that five or six British units were cut off in the territory captured by the enemy. They seem however to have made their way across Albania which Mr Foster Fraser describes in "Savage Europe" as dangerous even in times of peace for travellers without a strong escort and Montenegro to the sea, where they travelled overland in charge of Sir Ralph Paget. Miss Kerr is expected home shortly.[119]

Miss Beatrice Kerr, who was with the Stobart Hospital in Servia as honorary sanitary adviser, and whose capture by the Austrians was unofficially reported on 8th November, arrived home in Cookstown on the 29th ult. Dressed in the field uniform of the Stobart staff, and wearing the decoration bestowed on her by King Peter, she looked little the worse of the exposure and fatigue she endured when crossing the mountains of Montenegro, 8,000 feet high, with the fugitives from Servia.[120]

The story of Beatrice Kerr illustrates the tough conditions and dangers the nurses faced in the battle zone. It epitomises the sacrifices they made to serve King and Country.

Chapter 3

1916
The Road to the Somme

The Western Front, January to June 1916

Despite the disappointments of 1915, the allies entered the new year with renewed optimism. They had decided to launch a major offensive in the Somme region in the summer of 1916. The first half of the year was taken up with preparing for the Somme offensive, although a number of smaller scale raids and engagements were undertaken. Much emphasis was placed on ensuring that the men at the frontline could be supplied with ammunition, food and clothing. The development of a highly sophisticated supply chain was central to fighting the war.

Although January 1916 was a relatively quiet month for the British troops, some Dungannon men were injured. One interesting casualty was Lieutenant R. C. McMillan, RAMC, who kept the piece of shell which wounded him as a souvenir. The *Belfast Newsletter* reported on 13 January 1916:

> Lieutenant R. C. McMillan, R.A.M.C., who has been wounded in France, is a native of Dungannon. In a letter to a relative in Church Street, he says that he had gone up to an aid station with a wounded officer and after a time the Germans began shelling. He received a wound in the leg from a piece of shell, which cut his top boots, but he has retained the fragment as a souvenir. Lieutenant McMillan has been in the R.A.M.C. since October 1915, and is attached to a battalion of the Welsh Regiment.

Another local man injured during January was Noble Galbraith of Newmills. He previously served with the colours in India, and was now a shoeing-smith with the 120th Battery Royal Field Artillery. Having been home for a few days leave at Christmas 1915, he was wounded soon after he returned to the front. Writing to his wife at Newmills, Dungannon, he told her that he had been wounded on 15 January and was in the 8th General Hospital, Rouen. He was acting as stretcher-bearer, bringing in wounded, when a shell exploded near him and he was struck by fragments in the neck and legs. Prior to the war he had been employed at the Carland Quarries, Dungannon.

On a different note, the *Belfast Newsletter* on 7 January reported that the Rev. J. Dwyer Kelly, Chaplain to the Forces, had been mentioned in Sir John French's latest despatch. A native of Dungannon, he was a Wesleyan chaplain at the Curragh before going to France.

Honours bestowed on men connected with Dungannon were announced in the *Belfast Newsletter* on 14 January 1916:

> *The following have been appointed Companions of the Distinguished Service Order:*
>
> > *Major James Glendinning Browne, Army Service Corps, eldest son of Major James Browne, and a member of the well known Dungannon family.*
>
> *New Companions of the Order of the Bath are:*
>
> > *Colonel Edward George Browne, Army Medical Service, youngest son of the late Mr. William Browne, Dungannon, and a member of a family of soldiers which has distinguished itself in the present campaign."*

During January 1916 the Tyrones assisted with the building of railways behind the lines for the movement of supplies and men. They also cut wood, which was used to reinforce the trenches. The Tyrones had now been in France for over three months, and were entitled to home leave. The first of the men to go on leave left on the 29 January 1916

At the end of January the troops belonging to the 36th (Ulster) Division and the 16th (Irish) Division received a visit from the Lord Primate of the Church of Ireland, Most Rev. Dr. Crozier. While visiting the Ulster Division he was accompanied by Sir James H. Stronge, Bart. D. L. and they were the guests of Major-General Nugent. The Primate visited each battalion, and the brief addresses he delivered were of a very cheery and stimulating character. His Grace was very much impressed by what he saw, especially by the excellent spirit which seemed to animate all ranks.

The following is an account of Dr Crozier's visit to the 16th (Irish) Division:

> *His Grace the Lord Primate (Most Rev. Dr. Crozier), continuing his visit to the front, spent part of last week with the 16th (Irish) Division, as the guest of General Hickie. On Monday, 31st January, he went amongst the regiments at headquarters, speaking in his own happy genial manner to various units. The men everywhere gave him the heartiest welcome, and did not conceal their delight at having amongst them a distinguished*

fellow countryman. Differences of faith or politics were forgotten in the pleasure of meeting so thorough an Irishman as Dr. Crozier. On Tuesday, the 1st inst., the Primate's programme included a journey to some distant regiments of this division, and also a visit to the part of the trenches held by them. While at the 16th headquarters the Primate had an opportunity of addressing a large number of the members of his church at a meeting in a schoolhouse. The men were cheerful and happy in spite of much discomfort and strenuous labours. They deeply appreciated the rousing and inspiring words spoken to them by the head of their Church. His Grace also visited the field hospital there. An assembly to meet the Primate of the men of the Artillery Brigade, to which his gallant son, Major Barton Crozier, D.S.O., belongs, was arranged for Thursday, the 3rd inst., by Rev. J. Blackbourne. The tireless energy of his grace excited the wonder of even the men accustomed to the arduous life at the front. He travelled more than 1,000 miles by motor in France. Very highly prized was his affectionate, breezy energetic companionship. The Irish soldiers everywhere were intensely touched by his presence, recognising it as a proof of the thought taken for them by the Church and people at home. His Grace expressed his unconcealed delight at the great privilege he has enjoyed of meeting face to face his cheerful and heroic fellow countrymen who are in arms in a foreign land. He has been particularly grateful to find that the chaplains with the Irish regiments are highly valued and respected, and are accomplishing a noble work.[1]

In early February two Castlecaulfield men serving in the colours had something to celebrate. Firstly, Lieutenant David Williamson the son of Mr J. Moore Williamson, Foxhill, Castlecaulfield was promoted to the rank of Captain in the Army Veterinary Corps, backdated to the 1 August 1915. On the outbreak of war, Williamson had been called up and attached to the Royal Field Artillery and went out to the front with the original BEF. Secondly, Lieutenant W. H. D. Bennett who was serving with the 13th Canadian Infantry (Royal Highlanders of Canada) got married in Bangor. Lieutenant Bennett, the eldest son of Mr W. S. Bennett, Primrose Hill, Castlecaulfield, married Miss Ira Kathleen Millen the youngest daughter of the late Mr. Thomas Millen, Ballywildrick, Macosquin.

On 5 February 1916 the Tyrones received orders directing them into the reserve line at Beaussart. For over a week the battalion assisted in mining and tunnelling operations. Although the Tyrones were in relative safety,

Dungannon men in other battalions were casualties. One of those wounded was Private John Donaldson, 3rd Battalion Royal Inniskilling Fusiliers. The *Belfast Newsletter* reported this on 3 February 1916 that John wrote to his brother Mr. William Donaldson in Dungannon saying that he was in hospital in France suffering from wounds and had lost a finger on his right hand.

Another report in the *Belfast Newsletter* on 11 February 1916 recorded that Private Joseph Beggs of the 9th Battalion Royal Inniskilling Fusiliers (Tyrone Volunteers) had arrived home in Dungannon. Joseph had previously served fourteen years with the Royal Inniskilling Fusiliers prior to re-enlisting in October 1914. He had been invalided home due exposure in the trenches. Prior to the war he was in the employment of the Dungannon Urban District Council and also a member of the Dungannon Battalion UVF.

Reports from the front in February 1916 continued to bring news of Dungannon casualties, but thankfully relatively few deaths. These included the following notification of the wounding of Lance-Sergeant James Caddoo:

> *Mrs Caddoo, 28, Brooke Street, Dungannon, has received intimation that her husband, Lance-Sergeant James Caddoo, 10th Battalion Royal Irish Rifles (South Belfast Volunteers), has been wounded by shrapnel in France. The wound was severe, but the shrapnel has been removed. Previous to volunteering, Lance-Sergeant Caddoo was in the employment of Messrs, Dickson & Co., linen manufacturers, Dungannon.[2]*

On 29 February it was announced in the *Belfast Newsletter* that:

> *Surgeon-General James G. MacNeece, C. H., Army Medical Service, is retained on active list under the provisions of Articles 120 and 322, Royal Warrant for Pay and Promotion, and to be supernumerary. Surgeon-General MacNeece, who resided at Moville, is a son of the late Rev. James MacNeece, of Dungannon.*

During March 1916 reports were received of the wounding of Captain Robert Danson Cunningham, 10th Battalion The King's Liverpool Regiment (Liverpool Scottish). Cunningham had close family ties with Dungannon. He was the nephew of Colonel John S. Irwin C.B,

Dungannon and Mr Averell Lloyd, JP, Tamnamore, Moy. Indeed Captain Cunningham served in the Liverpool Scottish along with his cousin Lieutenant R. Averell Lloyd, of Irish rugby fame. The *Belfast Newsletter* reported on 10 March that Captain Cunningham had been wounded in the throat and face on 1 March. He had just returned to duty a fortnight earlier, having recovered from gunshot wounds to both thighs. Captain Robert Danson Cunningham was later awarded the Military Cross.

Another relation of the Lloyds of Tamnamore who served King and Country was Captain John Dunwoodie Martin McCallum, 8th Battalion Royal Irish Rifles (East Belfast Volunteers). His wife was the eldest daughter of Mr Lindsay Hill Lloyd and granddaughter of Mr Richard Lloyd, Tamnamore, County Tyrone. Major McCallum had been well known in athletic and cricket circles, being a useful wicketkeeper and capable batsman. McCallum obtained a commission in the 8th Battalion Royal Irish Rifles and was promoted to the rank of Captain on 3 November 1914. Having served as Adjutant, he was promoted to the temporary rank of Major by April 1916.

During March 1916 the Tyrones would see more action in the front line trenches, which placed them in considerable danger. A report in the *Belfast Newsletter* on 21 March 1916 detailed the very lucky escape three local men had while on duty in a forward listening post (sap):

> *Sergeant Edward Lucas, Parkanaur, and Privates Harry Hobson and Ted McNeill, Dungannon, all of whom belong to the 9th Battalion Royal Inniskilling Fusiliers (Tyrone Volunteers), have had a very narrow escape in the trenches in France. While on sap duty they were subjected to shell fire from the Germans. A large piece – weighing above 2lbs – of a shrapnel shell skimmed over the parapet and, knocking the steel helmet off Sergeant Lucas, buried itself about a foot and a half in the bottom of the trench between Privates Hobson and McNeill.*

During March it was also reported that Private Thomas Daly of the 6th Battalion Connaught Rangers had been wounded in France and was in hospital. Thomas was the son of the late Mr. John Daly who was the former proprietor of the Dungannon Saw Mills. Notification of Private Daly's wounding was sent to his aunt Miss Jane Daly, Union Place, Dungannon.

Reports of an unfortunate accident involving Dungannon man Trooper Harry Hamilton of the 6th (Inniskilling) Dragoons Service Squadron were received in the town at the end of March 1916. Trooper Hamilton met with a severe riding accident in France and had been hospitalised suffering from severe injuries to the head and legs.

News was also received of local men who had received promotions. Lieutenant Charles Newell of the Royal Engineers, who was the eldest son of Joseph Newell, Dungannon, was promoted to the rank of Captain with effect from 7 March 1916. Captain Newell had gone to France in September 1915. The *Belfast Newsletter* on 22 March 1916 reported that Lieutenant Harold Saunderson Sugars, RAMC, was also promoted to the rank of Captain. Captain Sugars had been born in Dungannon in 1882 and like his two older brothers was educated at the Royal School Dungannon. During his time at the Royal School he was a talented rugby forward. Harold went on to study medicine at Trinity and continued his rugby career playing for a number of clubs, including Trinity and Lansdowne. Having made his debut for Ireland against New Zealand in 1905; Sugars was capped three times. After graduating from Trinity, he joined the Colonial Medical Service, working in the Malay (Kra) Peninsula in Southeast Asia. During 1915 Sugars was released from his duties to join the RAMC. His two brothers also served the colours, Lieutenant John Charles Sugars with the Royal Field Artillery and Lieutenant Thomas Jones Sugars in the Canadian Irish Guards.

On 3 April the *Belfast Newsletter* announced that Lieutenant Joseph Marmion, RAMC, from Dungannon was promoted to the rank of Captain. Marmion had served in the Gallipoli campaign during 1915.

Throughout April 1916 a number of local men were wounded at the front:

> *Private William Victor Gallagher, Royal Inniskilling Fusiliers, formerly a rural postman at Moy, County Tyrone, has written his father, Mr W. A. Gallagher, Moy, stating that he is now in hospital in Chelsea, suffering from wounds in the legs and arms.*[3]

> *Mr. Joseph Atkinson, Atkinsallagh Glebe, Coalisland, has received official intimation that his son, Private Fred Atkinson, Royal Inniskilling Fusiliers, has been wounded in action.*[4]

To have been wounded and afterwards "gassed" and now again wounded has been the experience of Private Robert Cardwell, machine gun section, Royal Irish Fusiliers, a native of Coalisland. He is now in hospital suffering from a very severe wound in the head, caused by having been struck by a portion of shell fired from an enemy aircraft.[5]

Second Lieutenant Whiteside Macky, Royal Irish Rifles, officially reported wounded is a son of Rev. D. T. Macky, minister of Newmills Presbyterian Church, Dungannon, He was educated at Dungannon Royal School, and at McCreas, Magee College, Londonderry, where he held the Fullarton Scholarship for two years, subsequently proceeding to Trinity College, Dublin, where he joined the Officers' Training Corps. An enthusiastic member of the Ulster Volunteer Force, he obtained a commission on 28th January 1915, in the 17th (Reserve) Battalion Royal Irish Rifles, then under Colonel R. H, Wallace, C.B., and received his preliminary training at the Officers School of Instruction in Queen's University of Belfast. He was recently posted to one of the service battalions at the front.[6]

Captain R. N. A. Bailey, Highland Light Infantry, who is officially reported wounded, is a son of Rev. W.H. Bailey, M.A. of Clogher Presbyterian Church, and a nephew of Rev. W. J. Lowe, M.A., D.D., Belfast, and general secretary of the Presbyterian Church in Ireland. He was educated at Dungannon Royal School, and was formerly in the service of the Belfast Banking Company Ltd, having been stationed at the Ballymena and Portrush branches. He enlisted in a Public Schools Battalion, and at the beginning of 1915, obtained a commission in the Highland Light Infantry.[7]

Mrs James Watt, Dunsirk, Dungannon, has received intimation that her brother, Private Joseph Ferguson, Canadian Infantry, has been wounded in the right leg by shrapnel. He is a native of Dunsirk, and had emigrated to Vancouver, where he volunteered shortly after the commencement of the war.[8]

Lieutenant R. D. Greer of the Royal Irish Fusiliers was wounded on 27 April 1916. He was a grandson of the late Mr William J Greer, J.P., Rhone Hill, Moy and the youngest son of the Rev. Fergus Greer. Greer was wounded when a shell exploded in the trench he was occupying, burying him and several of his colleagues in debris. Lieutenant Greer was unconscious for some days, but the *Belfast Newsletter* on 25 May 1916 reported he was making good progress towards recovery in a London hospital.

Another Moy man, Private Peter McGuigan was also wounded on 27 April 1916:

> *Mr Thomas McGuigan, 1 Bread Street, Belfast, has been officially notified that his brother, Private Peter McGuigan, Royal Dublin Fusiliers was wounded and gassed on the 27th ult., and is now in hospital. Two other brothers, Privates Henry and John McGuigan, are serving with the Royal Irish Fusiliers, the former having been wounded three times within the past year. They are natives of Dungannon district, and belonged to Moy Company of the National Volunteers, Henry being an instructor.*[9]

The month of May began with the Tyrones in billets at Martinsart Wood, where they provided working parties for the Royal Engineers. On 5 May the Tyrones, despite being out of the line, came under attack from a German aeroplane which dropped two bombs killing one man and a number of transport mules. The next night the Tyrones were back in the line getting ready to embark on a raid on enemy trenches on the night of 7/8 May. The exploits of the Tyrones was reported in the *Belfast Newsletter* on 19 May:

> *The daring exploit of the Tyrones has been made the subject of a special order of the day issued by Major General O. S. W. Nugent, D.S.O., commanding the Division, and was as follows- "A raid on the German trenches was carried out at midnight on ----- by the 9th Battalion Royal Inniskilling Fusiliers. The raiding party consisted of Major W. J. Peacocke, Captain J Weir, Lieutenant W. S. Furness, Second Lieutenant L. W. H. Stevenson, Second Lieutenant R. W. McKinley, Second Lieutenant J Taylor and 84 other ranks. The raid was completely successful, and was carried out exactly as planned. Six German dugouts, in which it was certain there were a considerable number of men, were thoroughly bombed, and a machine gun was blown up, while a lively bombing fight took place between the blocking detachments of the raiding party and the Germans. Having accomplished the purpose of the raid, the party was withdrawn, with the loss of one man killed and two wounded. The raid was ably organised by Major Peacocke, and was carried out by the officers and men of the party exactly in accordance with the plan, and the discipline*

and determination of the party was all that could be desired. The Divisional Commander desires that his congratulations should be extended to all who took part in it. Brigadier General Hickman, in a special brigade order, says the arrangements and plans reflect the greatest credit on Colonel Ricardo, Major Peacocke, and other officers concerned. The whole scheme was executed with great dash and determination, cool judgement, and nerve.

The achievements of the Tyrones not only came to the attention of Sir Douglas Haig, but also to the people at home. Their achievements were of great interest and a source of pride to those attending the half yearly meeting of the County Tyrone Grand Orange Lodge in Dungannon in May 1916:

The recent achievements of the Tyrone Battalion of the Royal Inniskilling Fusiliers at the front were referred to at the half yearly meeting of the County Tyrone Grand Orange Lodge, held in Dungannon yesterday, under the chairmanship of Mr. Anketell Moutray D. L., County Grand Master, and the following resolution was unanimously adopted on the motion of Lieutenant Colonel R. T. G. Lowry, D. L. Pomeroy House seconded by Mr Barry Meglaughlin, Dungannon. "That this County Grand Lodge desire to send Colonel Ricardo and the officers and non commissioned officers and men of the Tyrone Volunteers their hearty congratulations on the high honour recently paid to them by the Commander in Chief, which has filled the brethren of their native county with pride.[10]

In a reply to the County Grand Lodge Lieutenant-Colonel A. Ricardo thanked them for their kind words, but also issued an appeal for men to join the 12th Battalion Royal Inniskilling Fusiliers:

Lieutenant-Colonel A. Ricardo, commanding the 9th Battalion Royal Inniskilling Fusiliers (Tyrone Volunteers), writing to the secretary of the County Grand Orange Lodge of Tyrone (Mr C. B. M. Chambre, J.P.), in acknowledgement of a resolution congratulating the battalion on its achievements in the field makes an earnest appeal for more recruits for the reserve battalion, the 12th Royal Inniskilling Fusiliers. "To us at the front" (he writes) "it is unthinkable that the men of Tyrone will allow strangers to fill the gaps caused in our ranks by this terrible war. It looks as if the time cannot be far distant when the Allies will advance to final victory. In this advance the Tyrones hope to bear an honourable part, and they confidently expect that Tyrone will do its duty by seeing that sufficient reinforcements are available to replace those who fall fighting for King and country.[11]

This raid on the enemy line had been a huge success for the Tyrones, but a number of them had been killed and wounded. It was the first raid to be carried out by the Ulster Division and a huge sense of pride had been felt that the Tyrones had been chosen to carry it out. The Tyrones were relieved from the front line on the night of 8/9 May and went to billets at Forceville, where they would remain for the rest of the month.

News was still filtering back to Dungannon about local men wounded at the front in France. The following are a few examples of reports that appeared in the press:

Trooper William Watt, Canadian Mounted Rifles, has been severely wounded in the side and thigh, and is now in hospital in England. The third son of Mr. Joseph Watt, Dungannon, he has two brothers in the service squadron of the 6th (Inniskilling) Dragoons and the reserve squadron of the North Irish Horse, while his elder sister, Nurse Sarah Watt, is in a VAD hospital in Wiltshire.[12]

Intimation has been received in Dungannon of casualties to several local soldiers of the Royal Inniskilling Fusiliers. Private David Glass, Milltown, Dungannon, has been slightly wounded, and Private William Smith, son of Mr Samuel Smith, Union Place, Dungannon, and 24 Sandy Row, Belfast, has been struck by shrapnel in the face and back.[13]

Private Joseph Watt, Royal Inniskilling Fusiliers, has been wounded. Previous to volunteering he resided at Redford, Moy, and was a member of Moy L.O.L. 90, and Moy Company, Dungannon Battalion U.V.F.[14]

Other men reported wounded during the month of May were Private Jack Williamson of the Royal Inniskilling Fusiliers and Private Henry Hull of the Cycling Corps, attached to the Royal Inniskilling Fusiliers. The reports of them being wounded appeared in the *Belfast Newsletter* on 18 and 22 May 1916 respectively:

Mr Andrew Williamson, Benburb, Moy, has been notified that his son, Private Jack Williamson, Royal Inniskilling Fusiliers, was wounded on the

7th inst. He was a member of the Benburb Company, Dungannon Battalion, U.V.F., and Benburb L.O.L., No 4. Prior to volunteering he was employed in Messrs. McKean's Weaving Factory.

Intimation has been received by Mrs Hull, Gortnaskea, Coalisland, that her husband, Private Henry Hull, Cycling Corps attached to the Royal Inniskilling Fusiliers, has been wounded. Prior to volunteering he was in the employment of Messrs. John Stevenson & Co. Ltd., Coalisland.

With the Somme offensive looming, the preparation of the men for the attack was underway. While the Tyrones obviously did not know their exact targets or the date of attack, they must have realised that an important engagement was about to take place given that they spent much of their time between 11 and 31 May practising attacks over dummy trenches at the Clairefaye training ground.

The spirits of the Tyrones during May 1916 were described in a letter sent from the front by the Rev. W. J. Robinson to Mr James Nixon, Park Road, Dungannon:

Mr. James Nixon, Park Road, Dungannon, having been instrumental in raising a substantial sum to purchase cigarettes for the 9th Royal Inniskilling Fusiliers (Tyrone Volunteers), has received a letter of acknowledgement from Rev. W. J. Robinson, chaplain to the Forces (formerly Methodist minister in Dungannon). The rev. gentleman says "The battalion you are interested in raided the enemy trenches lately in first-class style, and have been singled out for special praise. The weather is wet and cold at present, but will soon be warm enough every way – temperature and fighting both. The men are fearless and by no means downhearted Full of hope and fight, they are.[15]

As May came to a close reports of more local casualties were received in Dungannon. Private Robert Wigton of the 9th Royal Inniskilling Fusiliers was reported wounded in the *Belfast Newsletter* dated 29 May. He was the youngest son of the late Mr. William Wigton, Cavan, Killyman, Dungannon and was a member of Killyman LOL 206. Also listed in the report as wounded were Sergeant James Anderson, Altmore, Pomeroy, Private J Williamson, Benburb, Moy and Private Absalom Keightly, Langford Street, Belfast, but formerly of Coalisland.

It was also reported in the *Belfast Newsletter* on 23 May 1916 that Dr. George A. Campbell had obtained a commission in the RAMC and would take up duty in a couple of weeks time. He was the son of Mr. John Campbell, Eglish, Dungannon, and had been practising medicine in London for some time.

In early June further casualties from the Dungannon area were reported:

> *Mr Thomas Simons, Canary, Moy, has received official intimation that his son, Private John Simons, Royal Irish Fusiliers (County Armagh Volunteers) has been shot in the head and is at present in hospital.*[16]

> *Private Joseph McSorley, Royal Dublin Fusiliers, who has been wounded, belongs to Gortin district, County Tyrone, and volunteered in Dungannon on 13th November 1914.*[17]

> *Mr. Samuel McMenemy, Scotch Street, Dungannon, has received official notice that his second son, Private J. McMenemy, Canadians, has had his thigh fractured. Prior to joining the army he was employed at Eaton's in Toronto.*[18]

On 10 June the *Belfast Newsletter* reported that Private Robert Neville of the 49th Canadian Infantry was wounded in the thigh and foot by shrapnel in action at Mount Sorrel. Robert was the fourth son of James and Helena Neville, Moygashel House, Dungannon. Having been educated at the Royal School Dungannon, he decided to emigrate to Canada in 1913. Robert would enlist for King and Country on 5 May 1915 and the next day his older brother James also joined the same battalion. The brothers set off for Europe in June 1915 Following his wounding, Robert Neville spent some time recuperating in hospital in England before returning to the front, where he took part in the battle for Vimy Ridge in 1917. Private Robert Neville was killed on 1 October 1918.

Details of two other local men who had been wounded in France were received in mid June:

> *Mr James Moore, Crieve, Carland, Dungannon, received information some time ago that his younger son, Private N. S. Moore, Machine Gun Corps, attached to the Royal Inniskilling Fusiliers (Tyrone Volunteers), was*

missing, but he has now been informed that the soldier is in the First Canadian Hospital, "somewhere in France," suffering from pneumonia. Prior to volunteering for the war Private Moore was in the employment of Messrs D Brown & Sons, Donaghmore.[19]

Corporal William Whittle, Royal Inniskilling Fusiliers (Tyrone Volunteers), is in hospital suffering from injury to his eye, caused by a "lear shell." He is the son of the late Mr. Robert Whittle, Derryfubble, Moy.[20]

Private J Crawford, Donaghmore, and Private F Donaghy, Dungannon, appeared in the casualty lists of the Royal Inniskilling Fusiliers during June 1916, while Private J Morgan of Coalisland appeared in the Royal Irish Fusiliers casualty lists.

In addition, it was reported that Private George McCanley and Corporal Fred Johnston, had been wounded:

Mrs Samuel McCanley, Clare Terrace, Dungannon, received official intimation on Saturday that her son Private George McCanley, Royal Inniskilling Fusiliers (Ulster Division) has been wounded.[21]

Mr David Johnston, Broom Hill, Dungannon, has received intimation that his elder son, Corporal Fred Johnston, Royal Inniskilling Fusiliers (Ulster Division), has been wounded in action. He is a former Dungannon Royal School boy.[22]

Corporal Fred Johnston's brother, Private Edwin Charles Johnston, died of wounds on Saint Patrick's Day 1916. Fred after recuperating had returned to action with the Tyrones and was awarded a Military Medal in February 1918 and promoted to the rank of Sergeant.

The 30 June brought news of two men from Milltown, Dungannon having been wounded prior to the major Somme offensive. Private William Milligan and Private Samuel Gates, who were both in the Royal Inniskilling Fusiliers, were hospitalised in France and London respectively. Private Milligan was the son of Mr Thomas Milligan, and Private Gates was the son of Mr John Gates, who had also just received news that another son Private Matthew Gates, Royal Inniskilling Fusiliers, was in hospital in Salonika.

As June 1916 drew to a close two well known Dungannon men Captain Robert Stevenson and Lieutenant Brogden returned to duty on the Western Front, having been at home to recuperate from wounds they received in the Gallipoli campaign. This was reported in the *Belfast Newsletter*, as follows:

> *Two Dungannon officers, Captain Robert Stevenson, 6th Battalion Royal Inniskilling Fusiliers (the well-known linen manufacturer and ex-Rugby international and second in command of the Dungannon Battalion U.V.F.), who was wounded at the Dardanelles on 7th August last, and Lieutenant T. W. E. Brogden, 6th Battalion Royal Irish Rifles (nephew of Dr. Price, a former city organist of Belfast), who was also wounded at Gallipoli in August, have left for the front.*[23]

The Dungannon Fallen, January to June 1916

Captain William Thomas Lyons of the 10th Battalion Royal Welsh Fusiliers was killed in action on 3 March 1916. Born in Belfast he was educated at Methodist College and the Royal School Dungannon. William joined the Queen's University Officer Training Corps in May 1913 and in December 1914 he received a commission to the 10th Battalion Royal Welsh Fusiliers. By September 1915 he had achieved a promotion to the rank of Adjutant, having been promoted to Lieutenant and Captain earlier in the year. William was an excellent linguist, being able to speak four languages. The *Belfast Newsletter* on 8 March 1916 reported his death, as follows:

> *Captain William Thomas Lyons, adjutant of the 10th (Service) Battalion Royal Welsh Fusiliers, who was killed in action in France on 4th inst., was the eldest son of Mr. and Mrs. William Lyons, 21 Kerrsland Drive, Strandtown, Belfast. He was educated at the Methodist College, Belfast and Royal School, Dungannon, and commenced his business career in the counting-house of Messrs. James Lindsay & Co., Limited, Donegall Place, where he held the position of foreign correspondent for 11½ years. About four years ago he became accountant and office manager of the Jaffe Spinning Company, Limited, Newtownards Road, and was assistant secretary when he obtained his commission in December 1914. He joined the battalion, then commanded by a distinguished County Derry officer, Colonel W. R. H. Beresford-Ash, at Bournemouth, and was*

promoted to the rank of lieutenant on 5th June, 1915. He qualified with first class honours at the Hythe School of Musketry in July, and was subsequently given command of a company, being appointed adjutant to the battalion in September. Captain Lyons spoke four languages, and was particularly fluent in French, while he held several diplomas for accountancy and commercial work. He formerly taught bookkeeping in the Municipal Technical Institute, Belfast and the Bangor and Ballyclare Technical Schools. He was also a well known as an elocutionist, being one of Mr William Pyper's gold and silver medallists, and was a member of Masonic Lodge No. 372. Captain Lyons joined the Belfast University Officers' Training Corps in May 1913, and became a first-class signaller in November 1914. He was 35 years of age.

Captain William Thomas Lyons is buried in Spoilbank Cemetery, Ypres, Belgium.

Private Hamilton Patterson McReynolds (23188) of the 9th Battalion Royal Inniskilling Fusiliers died of wounds on the 12 March 1916. Hamilton was born around 1896 at Donaghey, Sherrygroom, Dungannon. He joined the 12th Battalion Royal Inniskilling Fusiliers on 15 May 1915 and was later posted to the 9th Battalion. Hamilton was a member of LOL 126 and had been an active member of the Sherrygroom section of the UVF. Private McReynolds had been very seriously wounded on 9 March 1916 by shrapnel and failed to recover from these injuries. The *Belfast Newsletter* reported his death, as follows:

Mr Hugh McReynolds, Donaghey, Sherrygroom, Dungannon, has been notified that his son, private Hamilton McReynolds, has died from wounds received in action in France on 12th March. Private McReynolds was 19 years of age.[24]

Lieutenant-Colonel Ricardo wrote to Private McReynolds' father conveying the sympathy of all ranks to him and advising him that every effort had been made to save his son. Hamilton is buried in Doullens Communal Cemetery Ext 1, Doullens, Somme, and is also remembered on the Cenotaph in Stewartstown and on Donaghendry Parish Church Roll of Honour.

Private Edwin Charles Johnston (26383) of the 7th Battalion Royal Inniskilling Fusiliers, 16th (Irish) Division, died of wounds on 17 March

1916. Private Johnston's father initially received notification that his son had been hospitalised in France due to an accidental fall:

> Mr David Johnston, Altnavannog, Dungannon, has received official intimation that his second son, Private Edmund Johnston, 7th Battalion Royal Inniskilling Fusiliers, is in hospital in France, suffering from serious fracture of the skull, caused by an accidental fall in the trenches. He was a member of Derrycreevy section, Dungannon Battalion U. V. F., and his elder brother, Fred Johnston, an old Dungannon Royal School boy, is in France with the Ulster Division.[25]

Private Edwin Johnston actually died of shrapnel wounds a week after receiving them, as was confirmed by an officer in the Royal Inniskilling Fusiliers:

> Mr David Johnston, Broomhill, Altnavanog, Dungannon, has received a letter from an officer in the Royal Inniskilling Fusiliers, stating that his son, Private Edwin Johnston, was wounded by shrapnel in the first line trenches and died a week later in hospital. It had previously been reported that deceased had met, his injuries through accidentally falling into a trench.[26]

Private Edwin Charles Johnston is buried in Lillers Communal Cemetery, Lillers, Pas-de-Calais. He is also remembered on Dungannon War Memorial.

Captain Frederick John Duggan of the Royal Field Artillery was killed in action on 21 March 1916. A native of Clones in County Monaghan, Frederick Duggan's connection with Dungannon was that he was educated at the Royal School. On leaving school he enlisted as an army cadet in the Royal Field Artillery, Woolwich, London. Captain Duggan was mentioned in despatches during his service for King and Country. While on enemy observations duties he was fatally wounded by a German sniper. The *Belfast Newsletter* on 28 March 1916 reported his death, as follows:

> News was received in Clones yesterday morning of the death in action in France of Captain Fred J Duggan, Royal Field Artillery, son of Mr Creighton Duggan, Clones. The sad message had been forwarded to the late Captain Duggan's widow, who resides in London, by his Colonel,

who, in expressing deep regret at his death, said he was one of the very best, and loved by all the officers and men. Captain Duggan, who was in his 34th year, was educated at Dungannon Royal School and afterwards at Woolwich. He married in 1905, Edith Emily, only daughter of the late Thomas Albert Bampfield Cogan, of Bristol, and leaves two sons. He has a younger brother in the Royal Engineers.

Captain Frederick Duggan is buried at Erquinghem-Lys Churchyard Extension, Armentieres.

Lance Corporal John (Jack) Fitzsimmons (14610) of the 10th Battalion Royal Irish Rifles was born in Dungannon around 1871. Prior to the war the family had moved to Belfast where he worked as a commercial traveller. Before enlisting in Belfast, Jack had gained some military experience with the Belfast UVF. Following his wounding at the front he was sent to hospital in Huddersfield, but died on 22 March 1916. Lance Corporal John (Jack) Fitzsimmons' body was returned to Belfast and he was subsequently buried in the City Cemetery.

Corporal Henry Mitchell Kelly was serving with the Black Watch when he was killed in action on 3 April 1916. Born in Castlecaulfield about 1892, he worked in the drapery business prior to the war. His work had taken him to J. S. Anderson & Son, Coleraine, and it was in that town he enlisted. A letter to Corporal Kelly's mother indicates that he had only recently gone to the front. The *Mid Ulster Mail* on 22 April 1916 carried the following detailed letter from his captain:

Dear Mrs Kelly, last Monday evening, 3rd April, the enemy sprang a mine and the vibration brought down part of our trench, killing and hurting some of my men. Your son was at his post waiting and watching, and I am very sorry to inform you that he was in the place most affected. His comrades went to his assistance at once, but I deeply regret to inform you we found he had laid down his life for his country. He had only recently joined us, and in addition to favourable reports from the Home Battalion, we were impressed by his fine physique and ability. As his company commander, I feel his loss greatly, and as a fellow countryman I offer you my deepest sympathy, in which my brother officers join me. He was buried last evening, and the service was conducted by one of our chaplains in a small village well back, where there is a graveyard for our troops. I shall take steps to have you informed of the name of the village later. Believe me, yours truly, W P Campbell, Captain.

Corporal Henry Mitchell Kelly is buried in the Maroeuil British Cemetery, Maroeuil, Pas-de-Calais. He is also remembered on Dungannon War Memorial and in Lower Clonaneese Presbyterian Church.

Major Robertson Stewart Smyth of the Royal Army Medical Corps died of wounds in a London hospital on 5 April 1916 as a result of suffering gas poisoning in December 1915 and January 1916. Born in Warrenpoint, Major Robertson had been educated at the Royal School Dungannon, where he had developed a keen interest in rugby. He played for the school and Dungannon Rugby Club. He continued his rugby career at Trinity College Dublin. Smyth was capped three times for Ireland and also represented the Barbarians and British Lions. His death was reported in the *Belfast Newsletter* on 6 April 1916:

> *The death occurred suddenly, yesterday, in a nursing home in London, of Major Roberston Stewart Smyth, M.D., Royal Army Medical Corps, who was invalided home from the Front in December last. The late Major Smyth was the fourth son of the late Mr. Wm. Smyth, Brookfield, Banbridge, and was educated in Dungannon Royal School and Trinity College, Dublin. He was a former captain of Dublin University Rugby Club and represented Ireland in several international matches. He entered the Royal Army Medical Corps in July 1905, and was promoted to the rank of captain in January, 1909, obtaining his majority in October last. He went to France in September 1914, and served on the western front continuously until December 1915, when he was invalided home, subsequently relinquishing his commission on the ground of ill health. Major Smyth was mentioned in despatches by Field Marshall Viscount French for gallant and distinguished service in the field. He was a brother of Captain E. F. Smyth, 11th Battalion Royal Irish Rifles (South Antrim Volunteers), who is at present home on leave, and a cousin of Captain C. B. F. Smyth D.S.O., Royal Engineers.*

Major Robertson Stewart Smyth had been mentioned in the despatches of Sir John French for distinguished service. Following his death Smyth's body was returned home and he was buried in the family plot in Banbridge Town Cemetery.

Private Thomas Houston (20305) of the 9th Battalion Royal Irish Fusiliers died of wounds on 10 April 1916. Born in Eglish, he was the brother of

Mrs D Ellison, Feeney's Lane, Dungannon. The *Belfast Newsletter* on 13 June 1916 reported:

> *Mrs D Ellison, Feeney's Lane, Dungannon, has received intimation that her brother, Private Thomas Houston, died on 10th ult. of wounds received. He was a native of Culcairn, Elm Park, Killylea.*

Private Thomas Houston is buried in Doullens Communal Cemetery Ext 1, Doullens, Somme.

Private Samuel Birney (21012) of the 9th Battalion Royal Inniskilling Fusiliers was killed in action on 22 April 1916. Born in Campsie, Omagh, County Tyrone he was the brother of Miss A Birney, The Rectory, Dungannon. Private Samuel Birney is buried in Authuile Military Cemetery, Authuile, Somme.

Private John Weir (9596) of the 8th Battalion Royal Dublin Fusiliers was killed in action on 29 April 1916. The son of John and Margaret Weir he was born in Mullyrudden, Carland, Dungannon around 1896. He enlisted for King and Country in January 1915, aged 19. Private John Weir has no known grave, but is remembered on the Loos Memorial, Loos, Pas-de-Calais and also on Dungannon War Memorial.

Private Hugh McAlindon (24559) of the 8th Battalion Royal Dublin Fusiliers died of wounds received on the Western Front on the 29 April 1916. Hugh had been born in Coalisland around 1889 and was the son of Alexander and Catherine McAlindon. The family at some point moved to Port Glasgow. Enlisting for service he suffered the effects of gas poisoning and succumbed to his injuries, aged 27. Hugh is buried in Vermelles British Cemetery, Lens, Pas-de-Calais and is also remembered on Port Glasgow War Memorial.

Private Francis Jones (26543) of the 8th Battalion Royal Inniskilling Fusiliers, 16th (Irish) Division, died of wounds on 30 April 1916. Originally from Aughnacloy he had been living in Dungannon prior to enlisting at Omagh in September 1915. His sister Miss Lizzie Jones who was living in Scotch Street, Dungannon, received intimation of her brother's death. Private Francis Jones is buried in Chocques Military Cemetery, Bethune, Pas-de-Calais and is also remembered on Dungannon War Memorial.

Corporal Alexander Loughran (15403), 14th Battalion Durham Light Infantry, was born in Castlecaulfield around 1890. Prior to the war Alexander was working in Hamsterley Colliery, County Durham and enlisted in September 1915 in Newcastle on Tyne. The *Belfast Newsletter* carried this notification of his death on 2 June 1916:

> *Mr Joseph Loughran, farmer, Kilyberry, Castlecaulfield, County Tyrone, has received official intimation that his son Corporal A. Loughran Durham Light infantry, has died of wounds. He was a member of Kilnaslee Temperance L.O.L. No. 364 (Castlecaulfield District).*

Corporal Alexander Loughran died of wounds on 10 May 1916 and is buried in Lijssenthoek Cemetery, Poperinghe, West-Vlaanderen, Belgium. He is also remembered on Dungannon War Memorial and on the Roll of Honour of Castlecaulfield Presbyterian Church.

Private James Woods (22851), 7th Battalion Royal Inniskilling Fusiliers, 16th (Irish) Division, was killed in action on 22 May 1916. James was said to have been born in Eglish in 1900. Enlisting in Dungannon in June 1915 he would only have been 15 if this birth year is correct. James had received wounds to his hand and returned to duty just a short time prior to his death. The *Belfast Newsletter* reported Private James Woods' death on 9 June 1916:

> *Private James Woods, Royal Inniskilling Fusiliers, who belongs to Mullboy, Dungannon, was killed in action on 22nd ult. He was 18 years of age.*

Private James Wood is buried in Philosophe British Military Cemetery, Mazingarbe, Pas-de-Calais and he is also remembered on Dungannon War Memorial.

Private James Watson Hetherington (16431) died on 3 June 1916 while serving with the 7th Battalion Canadian Infantry. James had been born around 1884 to James and Jane Hetherington, Killyman Street, Moy. James had seen military experience with the Royal Inniskilling Fusiliers prior to his emigration to Canada. He enlisted in Vancouver on the outbreak of hostilities, with the first Canadian contingent. James had seen action on the Western Front from February 1915 and had been quite seriously wounded at the Battle of Ypres in April 1915. Having been hospitalised in England he returned home to the Moy to recuperate and despite being marked for home duty he returned to his regiment on the Western Front. The *Belfast Newsletter* printed notification of Private Hetherington's death on 17 June 1916:

> *Mrs Hetherington, Killyman Street, Moy, has received official intimation that her eldest son, Private James Heatherington, Canadian, Infantry, has been killed in action. He was one of three brothers serving with the colours, and had been in Canada for the past nine years.*

The Hetherington boys played their part in serving King and Country, as all five brothers enlisted in the colours. James the eldest made the ultimate sacrifice with the Canadian Infantry. His brother Robert served with the Royal Navy, Richard and Samuel both enlisted to the Ulster Division and served with the Tyrones, while Frederick joined another battalion of the Royal Inniskilling Fusiliers.

In a letter to the *Tyrone Courier*, Robert Hetherington wrote:

> *I often think of the slackers back home; how shamed they should be of their cowardice, and how small they will surely appear in the eyes of the heroes on their victorious return from this most bloody war. I am both pleased and proud to say there are no cowards in our family, as I would rather be doing my duty just here than bear the disgrace of the slackers at home. Of course I do not refer to married men with young families, nor an only son with a widowed mother to look after. I hear from my brothers very regularly, and am glad to say not one of them would change place with the cowards they have known so well in days gone by, and who were then so apparently very loyal. I sincerely hope conscription will soon be passed in Ireland; then we will get a good laugh at these cowards who will then be obliged to don the khaki, much to their sorrow. In any case, if God spares us to come home again, we'll be able to hold up our heads and look everyone straight in the face, and say we at least have done our duty like men.[27]*

The Hetherington boys were also active member of the loyal institutions in the Moy area. Prior to emigrating to Canada, James was a member of Moy LOL. 90, R.B.P. 77 and Moy Conservative Flute Band. His brothers Robert, Richard and Samuel were also members of Moy L.O.L. 90, Moy Conservative Flute Band and Moy UVF Company.

Private James Watson Hetherington is buried at Railway Dugouts Burial Ground, Ypres, Belgium and he is also remembered on Moy War Memorial.

Corporal Ernest Oliver (472017) of the 16th Battalion Canadian Infantry died on 13 June 1916. Born in Beragh in 1889 he was the son of Samuel and Elizabeth Oliver. Prior to emigrating to Canada, Ernest served with the North of Ireland Imperial Yeomanry. In Canada he worked as a clerk. Answering the call of King and Country, he enlisted in Saskatoon on 12 July 1915. Ernest died at Tyillebeke near Ypres and having no known grave he is remembered on the Menin Gate Memorial. Ernest parents moved to Coalisland and he is also remembered on the family headstone in Brackaville Parish Church

Private Michael Irwin (25518), 9th Battalion Royal Inniskilling Fusiliers, was born in Benburb around 1888 and was killed in action on 23 June 1916. Michael had been living in Hexham-on-Tyne at the commencement of hostilities, but travelled to Finner Camp to enlist. He may have enlisted during a recruiting drive for the Tyrones on Tyneside, which resulted in a number of men from the area joining the battalion. Michael, with his comrades, had taken up a position in Thiepval Wood in preparation for the Battle of the Somme when he was killed. At this time the British were laying down a continuous artillery barrage in preparation for the great offensive. The Germans replied with merciless accuracy on the British front line. Private Irwin is buried in Authuile Military Cemetery, Authuile, Somme and is also remembered on Hexham War Memorial.

2nd Lieutenant Arthur Henry Tottenham of the 2nd Battalion Royal Inniskilling Fusiliers was killed in action on 27 June 1916. The son of Lowry Cliffe Loftus Tottenham, he was born in Roscommon around 1896. Arthur's father had been a District Inspector in the Royal Irish Constabulary prior to retiring to the Grange, Moy. He was educated in Mostyn House Preparatory School, Chester and St Bees School in Cumbria. Having just left school, he volunteered on the outbreak of the war. Arthur entered Sandhurst and received his commission on 20 October 1915. During the Easter Rising in April 1916, Arthur saw service in Dublin with the Inniskillings. Subsequently he went to France to serve with the 2nd Battalion Royal Inniskilling Fusiliers. Arthur had four other brothers who were also serving in the colours. Two brothers were in the Loyal North West Mounted Police (The Mounties) in Canada and Edwin Lowry served with the 8th Loyal North Lancashires.

The Tottenham family suffered a double blow in June 1916. Confirmation that Edwin had been killed in Mesopotamia in April 1916 arrived during the same week that they received notification of Arthur's death.

2nd Lieutenant Arthur Henry Tottenham is buried in Bouzincourt Communal Cemetery Extension, Bouzincourt, Somme. He is also remembered on Moy War Memorial and Dungannon War Memorial. His brother, Edwin has no known grave but is remembered on Basra War Memorial, Dungannon War Memorial and Moy War Memorial.

The Battle of the Somme, 1 July 1916

The Somme offensive was one of the largest battles that took place during the Great War. It lasted from 1 July 1916 until the 18 November 1916, and saw some million men wounded or killed. It was one of the bloodiest battles ever fought. The allies began to plan for the Somme offensive in December 1915. The original plan was for the French to lead the offensive, with the British acting in a supporting role. However the German onslaught at Verdun, launched in February 1916, forced the allies to change their plans. French troops were redeployed to defend Verdun, thus the Somme became largely a British offensive.

In preparation for the attack tunnellers planted mines under the German positions which were set to explode at the beginning of the offensive. An artillery barrage the like of which had never been seen before commenced on 24 June, continuing 24 hours a day for a seven days. The German artillery, however, responded with as much ferocity as the allies.

The Battle of the Somme commenced on the morning of 1 July 1916. Five French divisions attacked the German lines on the right wing of the British formations, astride the River Somme. The British launched a diversionary attack using two divisions from the 3rd Army at Gommecourt, but the main thrust of the attack was undertaken by the British 4th Army between the villages of Serre and Maricourt. Some 12 British divisions, amounting to 100,000 men, took part in the first day of the battle. Among them were the men of the 36th (Ulster) Division, but it should be remembered that Ulstermen also served in other divisions.

The Germans had also been busy making plans. Their plan was one of unyielding defence. General Erich von Falkenhayn had drawn up a construction plan in early 1915 to strengthen trench defences and protect his men. His plan saw barbed wire defences in front of the German lines double in width, with double and triple thickness barbed wire being used. He developed a frontline trench system that consisted of three trenches: the first being for sentries; the second for the main garrison force; and the third for reserves. Probably the most effective defence systems that Falkenhayn developed was a series of mined bunkers and tunnel complexes dug some 20 to 30 feet deep and fit to hold upwards of 25 men along the trench system. These defences were reinforced and strengthened by carefully sited machine guns bunkers that allowed the gunner a clear view over "No Man's Land."

Unfortunately for the allies the artillery bombardment of the German lines had not achieved its objectives. The bombardment certainly disrupted the German supply lines and caused enough casualties to concern its commanders, but when the British began their advance the Germans carried out a well rehearsed drill of climbing up from their deep protective bunkers to man the smashed in trenches.

The effectiveness of the German bunker system and devastating effect of their machine gun posts were vividly described in a first hand report from an unnamed wounded young Irishman published in the *Belfast Newsletter* on 6 July 1916:

> *His regiment left the trenches to attack as steadily as if on parade. In rushing the German second line devilish machine guns were encountered, but despite the terrific fire the trench was carried, and many Germans were captured in dugouts. The dug-outs were a revelation, being deep caves, concrete lined, and practically shell proof. The man was wounded when crawling through some wire. He encountered some of his comrades just where they emerged from the first German trench. He thought they were stopping before rising to come on, but getting nearer he was horrified to find they been cut down by machine gun fire.*

Prior to the commencement of the battle, Lieutenant-General Sir George Richardson KCB received the following letter dated 30 June 1916 from Major General Oliver S. W. Nugent DSO, General Officer Commanding the Ulster Division:

> *Dear Sir George – Before you get this we shall have put the value of the Ulster Division to the supreme test. I have no fears of the result. I am certain no General in the armies out here has a finer Division, fitter or keener.*
>
> *I am certain they will be magnificent in attack, and we could hardly have a date better calculated to inspire every national tradition amongst our men of the North.*
>
> *It makes me very sad to think what the price may be, but I am sure the officers and men think nothing of that. They only want to be let go. – Believe me, yours sincerely,*
>
> *(Signed) O. S. Nugent* [28]

The Ulster Division was about to face its first major test, but Nugent was confident that his men would be up to the challenge. He issued the following Special Order to the officers and men on 30 June 1916:

On the eve of the offensive for which the Ulster Division has trained and waited for so many months. I wish that every officer and man of the Division should know how absolutely confident I feel that the honour of the British Army and the honour of Ulster are in safe keeping in their hands.

It has been my privilege to command the Division in France during the past nine months, during which time I have had various opportunities of seeing that it has been steadfast in defence and gallant in minor offensives.

The time has now come to show to the world the qualities which fit it for the great offensive about to open.

Much is expected of the Ulster Division, and I am certain that the expectation will be fulfilled. Resolution, self-reliance, and the spirit which knows no surrender and no defeat are present in full measure, and will bear fruit on the battlefield that will redound to the credit of our country.

Nine months ago the King, after his inspection of the Division, desired me to write and tell him how it bore itself in its first great encounter with the enemy.

I hope that I shall be able to write and tell him how the men of the Ulster Division bore themselves like men in the day of battle, and did all that was expected of them.

To every officer and man of the Division I wish success and honour.

O. S. W. Nugent
Major General Commanding Division [29]

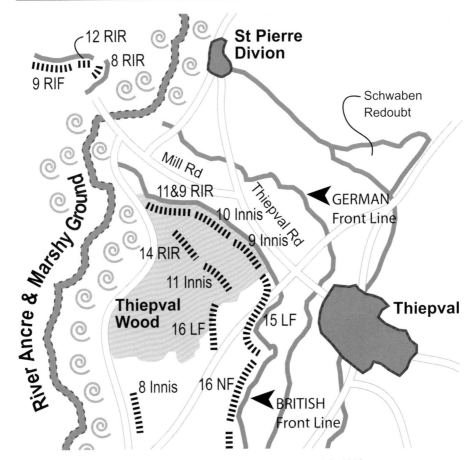

36th (Ulster) Division Battle Formation on 1 July 1916

The Somme offensive began at 7.30am on the morning of 1 July. The 36th (Ulster) Division attacked the Germans along the Ancre River between Beaumont Hamel and Thiepval. The 9th Battalion Royal Inniskilling Fusiliers (Tyrones), as part of the 109th Brigade, was given the honour of leading the charge on the right flank of the Division from Thiepval Wood. The 109th Brigade broke through the German lines and managed to capture an important enemy strongpoint, the Schwaben Redoubt. These Ulstermen, which included many from Dungannon, advanced further than any other contingent on 1 July. However, because the 32nd Division's attack on the village of Thiepval had failed, the 109th Brigade were left exposed to fire on both flanks. By early afternoon it became obvious that the Ulster Division could not sustain this advance. They were running out of ammunition and supplies and were forced to give up virtually all the ground they had gained. Fresh troops came forward to relieve the Ulstermen. The Ulster Division had suffered heavily, with 2,000 men killed and 3,500 wounded. Nugent's faith in his men had been justified. He was proud of the courage and discipline they had shown, but was saddened by the heavy losses endured. Nugent expressed his feelings in the Special Order of the Day which he issued on 3 July:

The General Officer Commanding the Ulster Division desires that the Division should know that, in his opinion, nothing finer has been done in the war than the attack by the Ulster Division on the 1st July.

The leading of the company officers, the discipline and courage shown by all the ranks of the Division will stand out in the future history of the war as an example of what good troops, well led, are capable of accomplishing.

None but troops of the best quality could have faced the fire which was brought to bear on them and the losses suffered during the advance.

Nothing could have been finer than the steadiness and discipline shown by every battalion, not only in forming up outside its own trenches, but in advancing under severe enfilading fire.

The advance across the open to the German line was carried out with the steadiness of a parade movement, under a fire both from front and flanks which could only have been faced by troops of the highest quality.

The fact that the objects of the attack on one side were not obtained is no reflection on the battalions which were entrusted with the task.

They did all that man could do and, in common with every battalion in the Division, showed the most conspicuous courage and devotion.

On the other side, the Division carried out every portion of its allotted task in spite of the heaviest losses.

It captured nearly 600 prisoners, and carried its advance triumphantly to the limits of the objective laid down.

There is nothing in the operations carried out by the Ulster Division on the 1st July that will not be a source of pride to all Ulstermen.

The Division has been highly tried, and has emerged from the ordeal with sustained honour, having fulfilled, in every particular, the great expectations formed of it.

Tales of individual and collective heroism on the part of officers and men come in from every side, too numerous to mention, but all showing that the standard of gallantry and devotion attained is one that may be equalled, but is never likely to be surpassed.

The General Officer Commanding deeply regrets the heavy losses of officers and men. He is proud beyond description, as every officer and man in the Division may well be, of the magnificent example of sublime courage and discipline which the Ulster Division has given to the Army. Ulster has every reason to be proud of the men she has given to the service of our country.

Though many of our best men have gone, the spirit which animated them remains in the Division, and will never die

L. J. COMYN, Lt-Col., A.A. and Q.M.G., 36th Division. 3rd July, 1916 [30]

The Ulster Division's Heroism

The achievements of the Ulster Division were widely recognised. The first indications of their heroism came in a report from *The Times*, carried in the *Belfast Newsletter* on 4 July 1916:

The heroism and self sacrifice of the Ulstermen in particular continues to be the theme of mournful praise and henceforth in Ulster the 1st of July will have a new and more glorious, if more sorrowful, meaning, into which no shade of contention can enter.

Many accolades were paid to the Ulster Division concerning their actions on 1 July 1916. A letter written on 3 July by a distinguished English Staff Officer to Lieutenant Colonel Fred Crawford was reported in the *Belfast Newsletter* on 7 July 1916 under the title "The Most Gallant Men in the World." it stated:

The Division has been through an ordeal by fire, gas and poison. It has behaved marvellously, and has got through all the German lines.
Our gallant fellows marched into a narrow alley of death, shouting "No Surrender" and "Remember the Boyne."
I wish I had been born an Ulsterman, but I am proud to have been associated with these wonderful men – the most gallant in the world. I fully realise how you feel where you are.
Many a family in Ulster will have lost a son or a father out here. I do not believe men ever passed to another world in so glorious a light.
After the day before yesterday I hope I may be allowed the rest of my life to maintain my association with the Ulster Province.

The following famous eyewitness account of the battle by Captain Wilfrid Spender, who was on the Ulster Division's Headquarters staff, was published in the *Belfast Newsletter* on 7 July 1916:

I am not an Ulsterman, but yesterday, the 1st July, as I followed their amazing attack I felt that I would rather be an Ulsterman than anything else in the world.

My position enabled me to watch the commencement of their attack from the wood in which they had formed up, but which long prior to the hour of the assault was being overwhelmed with shell fire, so that the trees were stripped, and the top half of the wood ceased to be anything but a slope of bare stumps with innumerable shell holes peppered in the chalk. It looked as if nothing could live in the wood, and indeed the losses were heavy before they started, two companies of one battalion being sadly reduced in the assembly trenches.

When I saw the men emerge through the smoke and form up as if on parade, I could hardly believe my eyes. Then I saw them attack, beginning at a slow walk over "No Man's Land," and then suddenly let loose as they charged over the two front lines of enemy trenches, shouting "No surrender, boys."

The enemy's gunfire raked them from the left, and machine guns in a village enfiladed them on the right, but battalion after battalion came out of the awful wood as steadily as I have seen them at Ballykinlar, Clandeboye, or Shane's Castle. The enemy's third line was soon taken, and still the waves went on, getting thinner and thinner, but without hesitation.

The enemy's fourth line fell before these men, who would not be stopped. There remained the fifth line representatives, and the neighbouring corps and division, who could not withhold their praise at what they had seen, said no human beings could get to it until the flanks of the Ulster Division were cleared. This was recognised, and the attack on the last German line was countermanded. The order arrived too late, or perhaps the Ulstermen, mindful that it was the anniversary of the Boyne, would not be denied, but pressed on. I could see only a small portion of this advance, but could watch our men work forward, seeming to escape the shell fire by miracle, and now, much reduced indeed, enter the fifth line of the enemy's trenches, our final objective. It could not be held, however, as the Division had advanced into a narrow salient.

The corps on our right and left had been unable to advance, so that the

215

Ulstermen were the target of the concentrated hostile guns and machine guns behind and on both flanks. Although the enemy in front were vanquished and retreating, the order to retire was given, but some preferred to die on the ground they had won so hardly. As I write they still hold the Germans two first lines, and occasionally batches of German prisoners are passed back over the deadly zone. Over 500 have arrived, but the Ulstermen took many more who did not survive the fire of their own German guns.

My pen cannot describe adequately the hundreds of heroic acts that I witnessed, nor how quickly a relieving force was organised of men who had already been fighting for thirty-six hours to carry ammunition and water to the gallant garrison still holding on.

The Ulster Division has lost very heavily, and in doing so has sacrificed itself for the Empire. The Ulster Volunteer Force, from which the Division was made, has won a name which equals any in history. Their devotion, which no doubt has helped the advance elsewhere, deserves the gratitude of the British Empire.

The Gallantry of the Tyrones

The gallantry of the 109th Brigade, which included the Tyrones, was commended by their commanding officer Brigadier General R.G. Shuter, DSO in the Order of the Day issued on 3 July 1916:

The Brigadier-General Commanding wishes to express his warm congratulations and high appreciation to all ranks of the Brigade on their gallant hearing and conduct during the great attack on the 1st July.

The advance of the Brigade was so dashing, so resolute, and determined that it was entirely irresistible and carried all before it, chasing the enemy in all directions, and taking approximately 400 prisoners.

Each Battalion of the Brigade, as we anticipated by all those who knew the grit and sterling qualities of the men of the Ulster Division, vied with each other in deeds of personal gallantry and bravery, and the Brigade carried out to the letter the task which was entrusted to it of taking "U" line. In so doing the Brigade covered itself with undying fame and glory, and its dashing, determined advance and behaviour will undoubtedly go down in history as its share of the work of the great Ulster Division of Irishmen.

Unfortunately, we have sustained grievous casualties, but the Brigadier-General hopes that when the ranks are presently filled with drafts that, wherever these may come from, the survivors of the original Brigade will do their utmost to instil their own magnificent fighting spirit into the new arrivals, as by so doing this they will be offering the most fitting tribute to their gallant dead comrades and friends who have fallen in honour on the field of battle, and who have left behind them such a splendid fighting record for those who come after them to live up to and emulate.

A. C. Richardson, Captain
Brigade Major, 109th Brigade [31]

The outstanding conduct and gallantry of the Tyrones during the attack on 1 July is graphically described in the following account written by the commander of the 9th Battalion Royal Inniskilling Fusiliers, Lieutenant-Colonel A. St. Ricardo, DSO:

Just now it is a hard struggle between pride and sorrow, and every moment the latter surges up, and it takes a mighty effort to keep our chins up, but we shall see it through and begin again, however hard. Out of 19 officers who went over 12 have gone, the very best, and all dear pals; four came back untouched and three wounded got back. One of these lay out for twenty-four hours; and on for forty-eight; whilst the casualties in the rank and file were numerous.

Early on the 1st July the boys were convinced the date had been chosen for their special benefit – the battle began. Every gun on both sides fired as fast as it could, and during the din our dear boys just walked out of the wood and out through lanes in our wire. I shall never forget for one minute the extraordinary sight, The Derrys, on our left, were so eager they started a few minutes before the ordered time, and the Tyrones were not going to be left behind, and they got going without delay. No fuss, no shouting, no running, everything orderly, solid and thorough, just like the men themselves. Here and there a boy would wave his hand to me as I shouted good luck to them through my megaphone, and all had a happy face. Most were carrying loads. Fancy advancing against heavy fire carrying a heavy roll of barbed wire on your shoulders.

The leading battalions suffered comparatively little getting out, but when they came close to the German front line they came under appalling machine gun fire, which obliterated whole platoons. And, alas for us, the division on our right could not get on, and the same happened the division on our left. So we came in for the concentrated fire of what would have been spread over three divisions, had our neighbours been all Ulstermen. But every man who remained standing pressed on, and without officers or non-commissioned officers they "carried on", faithful to their job. Not a man turned to come back, not one. Eventually small knots belonging to all the battalions of the division (except two) gathered into the part of the German third line allotted to the division and began to consolidate it. Major John Peacocke, a cousin of Lady Carson, a most gallant and dashing officer, was sent forward after the advance to see how matters stood. He took charge, and gave to the representatives of each unit a certain task in the defence.

The situation after the first few hours was indeed a cruel one for the Ulster Division. There they were, a wedge driven into the German lines, only a few hundred yards wide, and for fourteen hours they bore the brunt of the German machine gun fire and shell fire from three sides, and even from behind they were not safe. The parties told off to deal with the German first and second lines had in many cases been wiped out, and the Germans sent parties from the Ranks in behind our boys. The division took 300 prisoners, and could have taken hundreds more, but could not handle them. Major Peacocke sent back many messages by runners. I sent off every man I had, my own servant, my shorthand clerk, and so on to get water at the river; the pipes had long before been smashed. On their way many, including both above named, were killed by shell fire. In the end, at 10.30 p.m. they had got to the third line at 8.30 a.m. – the glorious band in front had to come back. They fought to the last and threw their last bomb, and were so exhausted that most of them could not speak. Shortly after they came back help came, and the line they had taken and held was reoccupied without opposition, the Germans, I suppose, being as exhausted as we were. Our side eventually lost the wedge like bit after some days. It was valueless, and could only be held at very heavy cost.

We were withdrawn late on Sunday evening very tired and weary.

There are many instances of outstanding gallantry but it is almost impossible to collect evidence. We may here more of it when some of our wounded come back to us. These are a few instances taken haphazard:-

Corporal Thos. McClay, Laghey, County Donegal, assisted Second Lieutenant Lawrence to take twenty prisoners. He conveyed them single handed over "No Man's Land" and then returned to the German third line, all under very heavy fire. When he returned he had been fighting, hard for ten hours.

Company Sergeant-Major Ed. Chapman, Dublin, was wounded early in the day, but carried on throughout and refused to go back.

Private Thos. Gibson, of Coalisland, saw three Germans working a machine gun. He attacked them single-handed and killed them all with his clubbed rifle, thereby saving many lives.

Corporal John Conn, Caledon, came across two of our machine guns out of action. He repaired them under fire and wiped out a German flanking party. He carried both guns himself part of the way back, but had to abandon one, being utterly exhausted.

Sergeant James McPike, Dungannon did splendid work throughout, and set a fine example.

Lance Corporal Daniel Lyttle, Leckpatrick, Strabane, when trying to save two machine guns from the enemy, found himself cut off. He fired one gun until the ammunition was exhausted then destroyed both guns, and bombed his way back to the rest of the party. He had always been to the fore in many a tight place.

Sergeant Samuel Kelly, Belfast, volunteered to take a patrol to ascertain how things were going on our right. Corporal Daniel Griffiths, Dublin; Lance Corporal Lewis Pratt, Cavan; and Private Wm. Abraham, Ballinamallard, went with him. The latter was killed, but the remainder got back with valuable information. Sergeant Kelly did great work; to the last in organising and encouraging his men.

Corporal Daniel Griffths, Lance Corporal Lewis Pratt, with Private Fred Carter, Kingstown, bombed and shot nine Germans who were trying to mount a machine gun.

Private Samuel Turner, Dundrum, and Private Clarence Rooney, Clogher, forced a barricaded dug-out, captured 10 Germans, and destroyed an elaborate signalling apparatus, thereby preventing information getting back.

Lance Corporal Wm. Neely, Clogher; Private Samuel Spence, Randalstown; Private James Sproule, Castlederg; and Private Wm. R. Reid, Aughnacloy were part of a blocking party. Their officer and more than half their party was killed, but they held on and covered the retirement of the main party, eventually retiring in good order, fighting every inch of the way.

Private Fred Gibson, Caledon, pushed forward alone with his machine gun, and fought until his ammunition was done. It is feared he was killed subsequently.

Private James Mahaffy, Caledon, was badly wounded in the leg early in the day, and was ordered back. He refused to go and continued to carry ammunition for his machine gun.

Lance Corporal John Hunter, Coleraine, succeeded in picking off several German gunners. His cool and accurate shooting at such a time was remarkable.

Private Robert Monteith, Lislap, Omagh, had his leg taken off above the knee. He used his rifle and bayonet as a crutch and continued to advance. It is feared he succumbed later.

Private Wallie Scott, Belfast, whilst alone met five Germans. He captured them single handed and marched them back to the German second line to where a sergeant had a larger party gathered.

Sergeant George McKinstry, Dunagnnon, was wounded and able to walk back, but he preferred to remain with Captain Muriel, who was wounded, all night.

Corporal Thomas Dickson, Lisnahull, Dungannon, did very fine work throughout the fight.

Private Joe O'Brien, Eglniton, Derry; Private David Mulligan, Belfast; Private John Scott; Everton; Private Richard Yates, Liverpool, Private James Mendin, Belfast; Private John Armour Glasgow; and Lance Corporal John R Graham, Ardstraw, all carried messages continuously during the five day bombardment and during the 1st and 2nd July, always under heavy shell fire. Their gallant work greatly assisted the keeping up of communications. These are just a sample. Those in hospital could tell of many splendid deeds. [32]

Another report of the exceptional deeds of the Tyrones came from the officer commanding the Royal Artillery Brigade, which had supported their advance on 1 July. In a letter to Lieutenant-Colonel Ricardo, he wrote:

My fellows will be more than pleased to hear their work was so well done. Their whole hearts were in it, for the feeling everyone in the right group had was that to work with the – Brigade – and I may say, especially with the Royal Inniskilling Fusiliers (Tyrones) – was always to be on the road to victory. We all knew how splendidly all your battalions would do, and the fact that our relations have always been so cordial lent fresh skill to every single detachment. I had the privilege of seeing the advance, and I cannot tell how indescribably proud and thrilled I was at the way the whole attack was carried through. It was simply magnificent. The enforced later withdrawal of your brigade was like a blow in the face to us, the feeling of sympathy was so personal and so close. We all want you to know that when we ever do get a chance to get our own back we want to prepare the way and support the attack behind your gallant battalions. We all live with you in mourning for those who have gone. We all feel we have lost some very dear friends. I couldn't help thinking of what Rupert Brooke wrote as an epitaph

> *"If I should die, think only this of me,*
> *That there's some corner of a foreign field*
> *That is for ever England:"*

None of your sportsmen died without knowing that that was so. [33]

A further report of the important role played by the Tyrones in the Somme offensive, written by an officer who witnessed their advance, was published in the *Belfast Newsletter* on 28 August 1916:

He says – Holding the "pride of place", the leading battalion on the right of the Division was the Tyrone Battalion of the Royal Inniskilling Fusiliers. They gave good cause for the Tyrone that bred them to have a special pride in them and they added to the glories of the illustrious regiment to which they are so proud to belong. The objective was the German third line. Certain points in the German lines had been named after places we know so well at home. Someway or somehow we were to reach a point christened Lisnaskea. The sun rose and ushered in a glorious day. One forgot the strain of imminent battle, and felt that it was good to be alive. Word quickly flew round. The attack was to be launched at 7.30. At 6.25 a hurricane bombardment commenced. Innumerable guns rained their missiles on the German lines. The huge 15 m. and the small gun spoke together, and for 65 minutes this relentless tornado swept the German lines. At 7.15 our men debouched from their trenches under cover of this fire, and took up their position in front of our wire, through which lanes had been cut. At 7.30 the bugle sounded the assault. The two leading companies advanced in perfect line, followed by the supporting companies in artillery formation. Running across "No Man's Land" there was a sunken road. No man can picture the magnificent sight of our men advancing in unwavering lanes as if on parade. So perfect was their discipline that, not-withstanding the withering fire brought to bear on them from Thiepval, they would have carried out any drill movements. At the sunken road both shell and machine gun fire grew intense. Men fell by the score. Still the line advanced. There was none of the heat and fury of the charge, but a calm, restrained, and deliberate advance in face of a pitiless fire. Until they reached the German wire the leading companies did not stutter so much as those in rear. On approaching the Germans "A" line those still standing swept on with irresistible determination. They charged the machine guns which the enemy had mounted on their parapets. On they pushed over the support line towards "B" line, known as the Crucifix line. Sweeping over the "B" line with numbers dwindling at every step they still went on. Enfiladed with machine-gun fire from the right, and facing with a magnificent courage the fire poured into them by the German gunners holding the "C" line, the remnant reached their objective "Lisnaskea". A mere handful of men under Second-Lieutenant McKinlay held on for about an hour in face of superior numbers . . . . . Our men were forced to withdraw to the Crucifix line, where the supporting battalions were endeavouring to establish themselves. Here throughout the day the men toiled hard, reversing the German trench and consolidating the position to meet the inevitable counter-attack. At ten in the morning Major Peacocke, second in command faced the merciless fire which swept "No Man's Land" an succeeded in reaching the Crucifix line and took charge. At about 3 pm in the afternoon the enemy fiercely bombarded the piece of trench we were holding with high explosive and shrapnel, and simultaneously attacked with bombs on our right: but we held on till ten p.m., when our bombs became exhausted. Many attempts had been made to continue the supply, but carriers could not live through the fire sweeping the path they had to follow. We were compelled to fall back.

The Dungannon Casualties, 1 July 1916

As already mentioned, the Ulster Division suffered many casualties at the Somme. On the eve of battle the Tyrones had 22 officers and 680 men. On being relieved on the night of 2 July 1916 the roll call showed that 16 officers and 461 men were killed, wounded, or missing.

Details of the Ulster Division's casualties started to appear in articles in the *Belfast Newsletter* on 7 July 1916 and continued to do so for several weeks. There were also references to soldiers who served in other divisions. The following is a list of the many men from the Dungannon district reported wounded or missing who appeared in these articles. Additional information found about any of these individuals during the research for this book has been included.

1) Private Thomas Slater, Royal Inniskilling Fusiliers, Milltown Dungannon, wounded.

2) Sergeant George McKinstry, Royal Inniskilling Fusiliers, Milltown Dungannon, wounded. He was a member of Moygashel LOL 708.

3) Lance Corporal Thomas McIntyre, 9th Inniskilling Fusiliers (Tyrone Volunteers), Linfield Street Dungannon, wounded.

4) Private Thomas Daly, 6th Battalion Connaught Rangers, Union Place Dungannon, Wounded.

5) Second Lieutenant Arthur A. Andrews, Royal Irish Fusiliers, wounded in the thigh. He was the second son of Mr Alexander Andrews, Stuart Place, Dungannon, and received his commission on 23 August 1915. Prior to the war he was in the employment of the Belfast Banking Company in Coleraine and Belfast. He was educated at Dungannon Royal School.

6) Second Lieutenant Gilbert Evelyn Barcroft, Royal Inniskilling Fusiliers (County Tyrone Volunteers), wounded in the head. He was sent to hospital in Bristol before returning home to recuperate. He was the only son of the late Mr. Frederick Barcroft, Stangmore Lodge, Dungannon. Second Lieutenant Barcroft had close links with Bernagh LOL 429.

7) Second Lieutenant Ernest Daniel, Royal Irish Rifles, wounded (shell shock). He was sent to No. 20 General Hospital Camiers, France. Ernest was the youngest son of Mr. Robert Daniel J.P., Derryvale, Newmills and one of five brothers who served the colours

8) Private William J. V. Archer, Royal Irish Rifles, Bush Road, Dungannon, wounded. He was a member Bush LOL 163.

9) Private William Blair, Tyrone Volunteers, Bovean, Moy wounded.

10) Private Enoch Bowen, Tyrone Volunteers, Tamnamore Moy wounded.

11) Private Samuel Clarke, Tyrone Volunteers, Carrickaness, Benburb, wounded.

12) Private Hugh Harris, Y.C.V., Gortnagglush, wounded.

13) Private Richard Jenkinson, Tyrone Volunteers, Lisnaclin, shell shock.

14) Private Samuel Lambe, Tyrone Volunteers, Lisnahull Dungannon, wounded. He was a member of Dungannon Holdfast LOL 1620.

15) Private Robert Montgomery, Tyrone Volunteers, Coalisland, wounded. He was a member of Coalisand LOL 93 and after the war became Worshipful Master, before emigrating to Australia.

16) Sergeant J. F. McAllister, R Engineers, wounded.

17) Private Wm. McConaghy, Tyrone Volunteers, wounded.

18) Corporal David McDaniel, Royal Irish Fusiliers, wounded (second time). He was the son of Mr Thomas McDaniel, farmer, Tullyvannon, and one of four brothers who served in the colours.

19) Private James McGerr, Tyrone Volunteers, Milltown, Benburb, wounded.

20) Private Samuel McGuor, Tyrone Volunteers, Gortavoy Pomeroy, wounded (second time).

21) Lance-Corporal William McMenemy, Tyrone Volunteers, Henry Street, Dungannon, wounded. He was a member of Dungannon Holdfast LOL 1620.

22) Corporal James McPeake, Tyrone Volunteers, Linfield Street, Dungannon, wounded.

23) Private John Joseph O'Neill, Royal Inniskilling Fusiliers, Lisnastraine, Coalisland, wounded.

24) Corporal Frederick S. Patterson, Tyrone Volunteers, Drumreagh, Newmills, wounded. One of his brothers was a prisoner of war in Germany, and another brother died while undergoing training.

25) Corporal Harry Robinson, County Down Volunteers, Benburb, Moy, wounded.

26) Private Nathaniel Stothers, Tyrone Volunteers, Lisnamonaghan, Castlecaulfield, wounded.

27) Private Gervais Williamson, Tyrone Volunteers, Forthill Farm, Castlecaulfield, wounded.

28) Private Joseph Young, Tyrone Volunteers, Milltown, wounded.

29) Sergeant George Belshaw, Royal Inniskilling Fusiliers, Tyrone Volunteers, Coolhill, Dungannon, wounded. He was a member of Moygashel LOL 708.

30) Private Robert Carroll, Tyrone Volunteers, Castlecaulfield, wounded.

31) Corporal Harry Cullen, Tyrone Volunteers, Moygashel, wounded. He was a member of Moygashel LOL 708.

32) Sergeant Richard Gallery and Corporal R. Gallery, Tyrone Volunteers Castlecaulfield, wounded.

33) Private George Bell, Tyrone Volunteers, Drumkirk, Castlecaulfield, wounded.

34) Private James Kelly, Tyrone Volunteers, Castlecaulfield, wounded.

35) Corporal Thomas Lawson, Royal Inniskilling Fusiliers, wounded. He was the youngest of the five soldier sons of Mr. Wm. J. Lawson, Milltown.

36) Lance Corporal Robert J. Leckey, Tyrone Volunteers, Perry Street, Dungannon, wounded. He was a member of Dungannon Holdfast LOL 1620.

37) Sergeant Edward Lucas, Tyrone volunteers, Parkanaur, Castlecaulfield, wounded.

38) Private Wm. Millar, Tyrone Volunteers, Milltown, wounded.

39) Private Thomas Orr, Tyrone Volunteers Moygashel, wounded. He was a member of Moygashel LOL 708.

40) Private George Reilly, Tyrone Volunteers Moygashel, wounded.

41) Private Jas Fitzpatrick, Royal Inniskilling Fusiliers, Donaghmore Road, Dungannon, wounded.

42) Private David Lambe, Tyrone Volunteers, Lisnahull, wounded.

43) Private Robert Cobain, Royal Irish Rifles, Cavankeeran Pomeroy, wounded.

44) Private Robert Irwin, Tyrone Volunteers, Altmore, Pomeroy, wounded.

45) Private William Forsythe, Royal Irish Rifles, Pomeroy Demense, wounded.

46) Private Samuel Gates, Tyrone Volunteers, Milltown, shell-shock.

47) Private John Rainey, County Armagh Volunteers, Charlemont, Moy, wounded.

48) Private David Cullen, Tyrone Volunteers, Moy, wounded.

49) Private Thomas McGinnis, Tyrone Volunteers, Moygashel wounded.

50) Private Robert Fulton, Tyrone Volunteers, Tullyaghbeg Newmills, wounded.

51) Private Samuel Heatherington, Tyrone Volunteers, Killyman Street, Moy, wounded. He was a member of Moy LOL 90.

52) Private Harry Hobson, Tyrone Volunteers, Killylack Dungannon, wounded.

53) Private William Hobson, Killylack Dungannon, missing.

54) Private George Marshall, Tyrone Volunteers Legane Dungannon, wounded and missing.

55) Corporal James McPeake, Linfield Street Dungannon, wounded. He was a member of Dungannon Holdfast LOL 1620.

56) Private James Gray, Doneydade, Dungannon, shell-shock.

57) Private John Latimer, Glencon, Newmills Dungannon, wounded.

58) Private William Lockhart, Annahoe, Dungannon, severely wounded. He was a member of Dungannon Holdfast LOL 1620.

59) Private Robert Braiden, Tyrone Volunteers, Barrack Street Dungannon, shell-shock.

60) Private Dawson Colgan, Tyrone Volunteers, Moy, wounded.

61) Private John Cumberland, Tyrone Volunteers Kilnacart, Dungannon, missing. He was a member of Kilnacart LOL 296.

62) Private James Cumberland, Tyrone Volunteers Kilnacart Dungannon, wounded. He was a member of Kilnacart LOL 296.

63) Private George Farr, Tyrone Volunteers, Mulnagore, Dungannon, missing.

64) Private David Johnston, Inniskilling Fusiliers, Killymeal, Dungannon, wounded.

65) Private Samuel Simpson, Tyrone Volunteers, Greenhail, Moy, wounded.

66) Private Albert Stevenson, Tyrone Volunteers, Aughnacloy Road, Dungannon, wounded.

67) Private Joseph Stephenson, Tyrone Volunteers, Dungannon, wounded. He was a member of Dungannon Total Abstinence LOL 1229.

68) Private Guy Williamson, Tyrone Volunteers, Forthill Farm, Castlecaulfield, wounded.

69) Second Lieutenant John Kelly, Black Watch, wounded. The son of the late Mr. James Kelly, Derrybean, Dungannon. Kelly had served in the 11th Hussars as a non-commissioned officer but subsequently received a commission in October 1915 to the Black Watch. His commission was awarded for service in the field.

70) Sapper William Lewis, Royal Engineers, Ulster Division Park Road, Dungannon, wounded.

71) Private John Arthurs (Junior), Royal Inniskilling Fusiliers, Anne Street, Dungannon severely wounded.

72) Private Samuel Heggarty, Tyrone Volunteers, Glencon, Newmills, Dungannon, wounded.

73) Private John McGrath, Tyrone Volunteers, wounded. The *Belfast Newsletter* reported on 10 August 1916 that he was a prisoner of war at Minden, Westphalia, that his wounds were healing and the Germans were kind to him. Private John McGrath was the son of William McGrath, Barrack Street, Dungannon.

The *Mid Ulster Mail* on 16 September 1916 reported the return of a number of men to Dungannon to recuperate from the wounds they have received during the Somme offensive:

Sergeant George McKinstry, Royal Inniskilling Fusiliers, who was severely wounded in the back on 1st July, and has obtained a very favourable

*record from Lieutenant-Colonel Ricardo, D.S.O. for his devotion to duty
on that occasion has returned home to Milltown, Dungannon to recover
from his wounds. Corporal Thomas Lawson (one of the five soldier sons
of Mr William Lawson, Milltown, Dungannon) wounded in the hand and
previously wounded at Gallipoli; Private Harry Hobson, Killylack,
Dungannon wounded in the abdomen; Signaller William McConaghy,
Market Square, Dungannon shot through the left shoulder; Private David
Lambe, Lisnahull, Dungannon, suffering from bullet wounds in the leg,
have also returned home. All these soldiers belong to the Royal
Inniskilling Fusiliers. Signaller McConaghy was one of the few
Dungannon men who succeeded in reaching the German third line on
the 1st July and held on there until the retirement was ordered. He was
wounded at the second line about eleven o'clock and Rifleman W. J. V.
Archer (son of Mr Samuel Archer, Bush Road, Dungannon), was wounded
beside him at the same time. Both of them had to lie out until the
following morning when they were picked up and brought to the Field
Station.*

The Dungannon Fallen, 1 July 1916

The following is a list of the men from Dungannon and District who
died as a result of the assault on the Somme on 1 July 1916 arranged
alphabetically.

Rifleman Robert Anderson (16153), 9th Battalion Royal Irish Rifles was
killed in action serving King and Country on the first day of the Somme.
Robert prior to the war worked in Dickson and Company, Weaving
Factory, Milltown, Dungannon and had been the bandmaster of the
Dungannon Conservative Flute Band for many years. He had also been
Deputy Master of Dungannon Holdfast LOL. 1620. Private Robert
Anderson has no known grave, but is remembered on the Thiepval
Memorial, Thiepval, Somme and on Dungannon Holdfast LOL 1620
Roll of Honour.

Private Robert Anderson (14744), 11th Battalion Royal Inniskilling
Fusiliers (Donegal and Fermanagh Volunteers) was born in Dungannon
around 1891. The family had moved to Londonderry by 1901 and it was
here that Robert enlisted to serve the colours. Robert was killed in action
on the first day of the great offensive. He has no known grave, but is

remembered on the Thiepval Memorial, Thiepval, Somme and the War Memorial in the Diamond, Londonderry.

Private Robert Henry Anderson (16873), 9ᵗʰ Battalion Royal Inniskilling Fusiliers (Tyrone Volunteers) was killed in action on the 1 July 1916. He was born in Dungannon around 1887 and lived with his family at Derrygortreavy. Prior to the war he worked in a mill as a flax dresser. Robert's brother Private William Anderson, Beechvalley, Dungannon, also served in the same battalion during the Somme offensive. William was reported missing, but had in fact been taken prisoner during the battle. Private Robert Henry Anderson is buried in Mill Road Cemetery, Thiepval, Somme and is also remembered on Dungannon War Memorial.

Private Robert Baxter (16168), 1ˢᵗ Battalion King's Own Scottish Borders, died of wounds on 2 July 1916. Born in 1893 in Dungannon the family had moved to Belfast by 1901. Prior to the war Robert worked as a farm servant at Killantrae, Port William, Wigtownshire, Scotland. Here he enlisted to serve the colours. Robert is buried in Acheux British Cemetery, Albert, Somme.

Private William Best (11182), 9ᵗʰ Battalion Royal Inniskilling Fusiliers gave his life for King and Country on 2 July 1916. He was born in Partick, Lanarkshire, Scotland around 1879. By 1901 Robert and his widowed mother were living in Drumcoo, Derrygortreavy, Dungannon. Prior to war William worked as a chauffeur for Robert Hamilton Scott, Elm Lodge, Bush and he was an active member of the Bush Company UVF, which his employer commanded. William was also an officer bearer in Dungannon Volunteer LOL 178 and was also a Sir Knight in Golden Knights of Dungannon RBP 52. He joined the Tyrones in Dungannon.

Corporal R Hamilton wrote a letter to William's sister, Miss Best, Drumcoo, Dungannon, following his death:

I exceedingly regret to have to convey to you the distressing news that your brother, Private Wm. Best, was killed in action on Sunday (2 July) night. But I feel it was my duty to do so as he was one of my best friends. Our battalion went into the trenches on Friday night to lead the great attack for the Ulster Division in the big advance. They fought like lions and the immortal charge shall never be forgotten. Your brother was struck by fragments of a shell while in the act of carrying water to the wounded heroes. I was speaking to him before he went into the trenches on Friday night, and little did I think that we would not meet again. You can always cherish the thought that he died a hero's death fighting for his King and country, and that he laid down his life for his friends. He was a staunch comrade and a true friend, and my heartiest sympathy is with you in your great loss and sad bereavement.[34]

Private William Best has no known grave. He is remembered on the Thiepval Memorial, Thiepval, Somme, as well as Dungannon War Memorial and St. Anne's Parish Church Roll of Honour.

Private Enoch Bowen (12766), 11th Battalion Royal Inniskilling Fusiliers (Donegal and Fermanagh Volunteers) was born around 1898. The son of John and Elizabeth Bowen, Tamnamore, Moy he grew up in a large family of farming stock. Enoch prior to the war had been an active member of the Killyman Company UVF. Private Enoch Bowen died of wounds received during the 1 July offensive, but it was not until August 1916 that his sister Mrs McMinn, Derrylee, Moy received official intimation of his death. Enoch is buried in Connaught Cemetery, Thiepval, Somme and is also remembered on Dungannon War Memorial.

Lance Corporal George Burrows (17838), 9th Battalion Royal Inniskilling Fusiliers (Tyrone Volunteers), was born in Donaghmore around 1894. Prior to the war George Burrows was in the employment of Lord Ranfurly and had been the personal attendant to Viscount Northland at the UVF camp of instruction held at Baronscourt in 1913. George was a member of A Company Dungannon Battalion UVF, Cullenfad LOL 39 Castlecaulfield and Dungannon Star of the East Temperance RBP 523. He died serving King and Country on 1 July 1916 and has no known grave, but is remembered on the Thiepval Memorial, Thiepval, Somme. George is also remembered on the Castlecaulfield Parish Church Roll of Honour and Dungannon War Memorial.

Private Robert Carson (17524), 9th Battalion Royal Inniskilling Fusiliers (Tyrone Volunteers), was born in Derryscallop, Moy around 1896. Robert enlisted at Moy along with his older brother William. Unfortunately for the family both would be killed in action on 1 July 1916. Private Robert Carson has no known grave but is remembered on the Thiepval Memorial, Thiepval, Somme and Moy War Memorial.

Private William Carson (17523), 9th Battalion Royal Inniskilling Fusiliers (Tyrone Volunteers), was born in Derryscallop, Moy around 1896. William enlisted at Moy in November 1914 along with his younger brother Robert. Prior to the outbreak of hostilities William was a member of the local UVF Company and both brothers made the supreme sacrifice for King and Country being killed in action on 1 July 1916. Private William Carson has no known grave but is remembered on the Thiepval Memorial, Thiepval, Somme and Moy War Memorial.

Second Lieutenant William John White Carson, 14th Battalion Royal Irish Rifles was born around 1887 in Belfast, County Down and was killed in action on 1 July 1916. William's connection with Dungannon is that he was educated for a period of time at the Royal School Dungannon. The *Belfast Newsletter* carried the following article regarding Second Lieutenant William John White Carson on 8 July 1916:

> *Second Lieutenant W. J. W. Carson, Royal Irish Rifles (Young Citizen Volunteers), missing is a son of Mr W. M. Carson, Estate Agent. Rosemary Street, and Tareen House, Old Cavehill Road, Belfast. He was educated at Dungannon Royal School and after taking his degree in surveying at a London college went into business with his father. He received his commission in the Young Citizen Volunteers from the old public School Boys Battalion and was reported missing after Saturday's (1 July) action.*

Second Lieutenant William John White Carson has no known grave, but is remembered on the Thiepval Memorial, Thiepval, Somme.

Lieutenant Alfred Middleton Blackwood Rose-Cleland, 1st Battalion Royal Dublin Fusiliers, was killed in action on 1 July 1916. Born around 1895 he was the son of Henry Sommerville Rose-Cleland, a linen merchant, and Elizabeth Rose-Cleland. Alfred grew up at Altnavannog, Bernagh and was educated at Dungannon Royal School. The *Belfast Newsletter* on 10 July 1916 carried the following article regarding Lieutenant A. M. B. Rose-Cleland:

> *Mr Henry S Rose-Cleland, Redford House, Moy was notified by the War Office on Saturday evening that his only child, Second Lieutenant Alfred M. Rose-Cleland, Royal Dublin Fusiliers was killed in action on the 1st inst. (July). The deceased officer was educated at Dungannon Royal School and at St Columba's College, Rathfarnham, County Dublin. At the*

commencement of the present war he was in employment of the well known firm of McLaughlin & Harvey, Ltd., contractor and builder, Belfast, and was working at Rocking, near Braintree, Essex, but he came home and enlisted in the 9th Battalion Royal Inniskilling Fusiliers (County Tyrone Volunteers). He served some months at Finner Camp, and was a lance corporal when gazetted as second lieutenant in February 1915. He was the lineal descendant of a Scottish noble family of great antiquity, one of his ancestors being cousin of the famous Sir William Wallace, the hero of Scotland, while another fought at Flodden Field in defence of James IV of Scotland. A more immediate ancestor while filling the office of High Sheriff of County Down in 1805, presided at the historic election for that county between Lord Castlereagh who brought about the Legislative Union and Colonel John Meade, which lasted twenty one days.

Lieutenant Alfred Middleton Blackwood Rose-Cleland is buried in Auchonvillers Military Cemetery, Auchonvillers, Somme and is also remembered on Moy War Memorial.

Private James Cumberland (11554), 9th Battalion Royal Inniskilling Fusiliers (Tyrone Volunteers), was one of three brothers serving with the Tyrones. James and his brother John are likely to have enlisted together given their consecutive regimental numbers. Along with his brother, James was killed in action during the first day of the Battle of the Somme. The Cumberlands were a patriotic family. In addition to their three sons, William John and Mary Cumberland had also six nephews serving in the colours. James grew up at Kilnacart, Derrygortreavy, Dungannon and with his brother was a member of the Derrygortreavy

Brothers Pte's John and James Cumberland
killed in action 1 July 1916

Company of the Dungannon Battalion UVF and also Kilnacart

LOL 296. The *Belfast Newsletter* on 14 August 1916 carried a letter to James and John's mother from Colonel Ricardo:

> *I fear I have only bad news to send you. Your boys John and James took part in the great attack on July 1st, and were last seen gallantly advancing with their company against the German trenches. The Ulster Division got to the place they were told to win, but owing to those on the right and left of us being unable to get forward we had to come back, after holding on for fourteen hours, and all our bombs being expended. When the roll was called both your boys were missing, and I greatly fear they must have fallen in the very severe fighting that took place. I doubt if they were taken prisoners, for "No Surrender" was the feeling that day in the Ulster Division, and I should be wrong if I encouraged you to hope that they have survived. They were very gallant lads, and they helped to bring honour on the Ulster Division. They fell doing their duty to the last, and will be an example to their friends and neighbours for all time.*

Private James Cumberland has no known grave, but is remembered on the Thiepval Memorial, Thiepval, Somme and Dungannon War Memorial.

Private John Cumberland (11553), 9th Battalion Royal Inniskilling Fusiliers (Tyrone Volunteers), was one of three brothers serving with the Tyrones. John was killed in action during the first day of battle, along with his brother James. The son of William John and Mary Cumberland, John was reared at Kilnacart, Derrygortreavy, Dungannon. Prior to the war John was a member of the Derrygortreavy Company of the Dungannon Battalion UVF and also belonged to Kilnacart LOL 296. The *Mid Ulster Mail* on 12 August 1916 carried the following article:

> *Mr W. J. Cumberland, Kilnacart, Dungannon, whose three sons joined the Tyrone Battalion Royal Inniskilling Fusiliers, has received on Tuesday official intimation that his two sons John and James Cumberland are missing. Mrs Cumberland has also received the following letter from Captain T. Robinson of that battalion - I am very sorry indeed to hear that your sons are wounded and missing. Your three boys were in my company from the time they joined the 9th Battalion up to a couple of months ago when I was sent home from France. Your boys were a great help to me and I always found them smart, clean and obedient lads and everything that soldiers ought to be. I trust that you may soon have good*

news from the one who is missing and that the one who has been wounded is not seriously injured, and that you may soon have him home with you for a rest. I had all the Dungannon boys in my company and during my 24 years army experiences I never found braver or better lads. Dungannon may well be proud of them.

Private John Cumberland has no known grave but is remembered on the Thiepval Memorial, Thiepval, Somme and Dungannon War Memorial.

Captain William Tillie Dickson, 1st Battalion Royal Inniskilling Fusiliers, died on 9 July 1916 of wounds that he sustained at the Battle of the Somme. Born around 1887 he was the son of James and Annabelle Dickson. His father was a local linen manufacturer and Member of Parliament. Educated at Uppingham School, Rutland, near Leicester, he returned to work with his father in the family business, Dickson & Co. Prior to the war William was an active member of East Tyrone Unionist Association, Masonic Lodge No. 9 Dungannon, Bush LOL 163 and commanded C Company of the Dungannon UVF Battalion.

Captain William Tillie Dickson was reported wounded in the *Belfast Newsletter* on 8 July:

Lieutenant W. T. Dickson, Royal Inniskilling Fusiliers, severely wounded, is now in hospital. He is the eldest son of Mr James Dickson, J. P. Milltown House, Dungannon, and before the war was engaged with his father in the linen business. He was a prominent member of the U.V.F., and commanded C Company of the Dungannon Battalion. He was one of the first to volunteer at the outbreak of war, enlisting as a private in the 6th Inniskillings, and accompanied his battalion in the Dardanelles. He was invalided home from the Gallipoli Peninsula, and on recovery was posted to one of the line battalions.

However on 13 July 1916 the *Belfast Newsletter* reported his death:

Deep sorrow has been caused in Dungannon by the death from wounds received in action of Captain William Tillie Dickson, the eldest son of Mr and Mrs James Dickson, of Milltown House. Captain Dickson was wounded during the attack on the German trenches on the 1st July, and succumbed to his injuries on Sunday last. The deceased officer, who was educated at Uppingham was prominently identified with the Ulster Volunteer movement previous to the war. He had command of C

Company of the Dungannon battalion, and by his keenness and ability he brought the men under his care up to a very high state of efficiency in regard to drill and discipline. He volunteered for the Army at the commencement of the war, and took part in the landing at Suvla Bay. Subsequently he was invalided home, but returned to the fighting again in February last. Before joining the Army Captain Dickson was associated with his father in the linen business. He married a daughter of Mr. Edward Coey D. L., of Merville, Whitehouse, who will have the sympathy of the entire community in the sad bereavement, which has befallen her. The deceased's younger brother, Second Lieutenant Harold Dickson, Royal Dublin Fusiliers is at present serving in France.

A special memorial service was held for Captain William Tillie Dickson in First Dungannon Presbyterian Church, this was well attended. Special music was rendered including the hymns " Now the Labourer's Task is Over" and "For All Thy Saints Who From Their Labours Rest". The Reverend Stanley W. Thompson paid tribute to Captain Dickson and also referred to two other members of the congregation who had laid down their lives in service of the colours. Second Lieutenant William Porter and Private Richard Averall. Another memorial service for Captain Dixon was held in Whitehouse Presbyterian Church.

Captain Dickson's brother and sister also served in the war. His brother Lieutenant T. C. H. Dickson of the Royal Dublin Fusiliers was wounded in mid August 1916. William's sister, Miss Jessie Dickson, was on the staff of the UVF hospital at Pau, France and then later transferred to the hospital at Arc-en-Barrios.

Captain William Tillie Dickson is buried in Beauval Communal Cemetery, Beauval, Somme. He is remembered on Dungannon War Memorial.

Private George Dilworth (17526), 9th Battalion Royal Inniskilling Fusiliers (Tyrone Volunteers) was killed in action on 1 July 1916. Born in Killyman, George enlisted at Moy for service with the Tyrones. Private George Dilworth has no known grave but is remembered on the Thiepval Memorial, Thiepval, Somme and Dungannon War Memorial.

Private William Duke (11482), 9th Battalion Royal Inniskilling Fusiliers (Tyrone Volunteers), was born in Milltown, County Armagh around 1889. By 1901 the family was living at Charlemont, Moy. By 1914

William was a member of the Moy Company UVF, and resided at the Grange, Moy. He was killed on battle during 1 July 1916, but has no known grave. Private William Duke is remembered on the Thiepval Memorial, Thiepval, Somme and Moy War Memorial.

Private George Farr (11193), 9th Battalion Royal Inniskilling Fusiliers (Tyrone Volunteers), was born in Drumglass, Dungannon. The family at some point moved to Crossdernot, Dungannon. George enlisted to serve the colours in Dungannon. His brother had been killed some years earlier in the South African War. George was killed on the first day of the Somme offensive. On receipt of intimation that George Farr had been killed in action, his brother Robert who resided at Tullynisken Rectory would enlist with the Royal Inniskillings Fusiliers. He would also lose his life in the war. Another brother James who lived in New Zealand served in the Wellington Regiment. Private George Farr has no known grave, but is remembered on the Thiepval Memorial, Thiepval, Somme and Dungannon War Memorial.

Lance Corporal John M. Fulton (17664), 14th Battalion Royal Irish Rifles, was born in Dungannon. Enlisting in Belfast he was killed in action on 1 July 1916. Lance Corporal John M Fulton is buried in Mill Road Cemetery, Thiepval, Somme.

Private William Gallagher (13345), 9th Battalion Royal Inniskilling Fusiliers (Tyrone Volunteers) was born in Killyman. William worked to Mr T. W. Douglas, Culnagor as a labourer prior to the war. He was a member of Killyman LOL 33 and was living in the Moy area when he enlisted at Dungannon. Private William Gallagher was killed in action on 1 July 1916 and is buried in Mill Road Cemetery, Thiepval, Somme. He is remembered on Dungannon War Memorial.

Private William Harbinson (11200), 9th Battalion Royal Inniskilling Fusiliers, (Tyrone Volunteers) was killed in action on 1 July 1916. Born in Dungannon around 1890 he was educated at Drumglass School. William's brothers also served the colours during the war. Indeed, it was his brother Thomas who served in the same battalion who wrote home to tell his mother that William had been killed in action while serving in the Transport Section of the battalion. Private William Harbinson has no known grave, but is remembered on the Thiepval Memorial, Thiepval, Somme, as well as St Anne's Parish Church Roll of Honour and Dungannon War Memorial.

Private Robert Irwin (16877), 9th Battalion Royal Inniskilling Fusiliers (Tyrone Volunteers), was born in Benburb. The son of William Irwin, Robert travelled to Finner Camp in County Donegal to enlist. Prior to the war he had been a member of the Benburb Company, Dungannon Battalion UVF and was one of many local men who lost their lives on 1 July 1916. Private Robert Irwin has no known grave but is remembered on the Thiepval Memorial, Thiepval, Somme.

Private Absalom Keightley (22841), 9th Battalion Royal Inniskilling Fusiliers (Tyrone Volunteers), was born in Coalisland around 1886. The family moved to Belfast and it was here he enlisted to serve his country. Private Absalom Keightley lost his life on 1 July 1916 and has no known grave but is remembered on the Thiepval Memorial, Thiepval, Somme,

Private Samuel Lambe (11911), 9th Battalion Royal Inniskilling Fusiliers (Tyrone Volunteers), was born in Dungannon around 1896. The son of Thomas Henry and Jane Lambe, Samuel at the age of 13 was working as a mill worker and living with the family at Lisnahull, Dungannon. Samuel Lambe enlisted at Dungannon and he would serve in the Tyrones along with his brother David. Despite being reported as wounded and in hospital, Samuel Lambe was actually killed in action during the great charge made by the Tyrones on 1 July 1916. His brother David was wounded in the same attack and subsequently sent to hospital in England. The *Tyrone Courier* on 31 August 1916 published an extract of a letter sent by Lieutenant-Colonel Ricardo DSO, Officer Commanding the Tyrone Volunteers to Samuel's parents:

> *He helped to uphold the honour of his regiment and to make the Ulster Division famous. He was a good soldier and will be missed by us all. Please accept the sincere sympathy of all ranks in the battalion in your sorrow.*

Private Samuel Lambe has no known grave, but is remembered on the Thiepval Memorial, Thiepval, Somme. He is also commemorated on the Dungannon Holdfast LOL 1620 Roll of Honour and Dungannon War Memorial.

Sapper William J. Lewis (64673), 122nd Field Company, Royal Engineers, Ulster Division, was born in Drumlea, Omagh. The family moved to Dungannon at some point and prior to the war William worked in Hale, Martin & Co. Ltd, Spinning Mill, Dungannon. He was an active member of C Company Dungannon Battalion UVF. William was attached to the 12th Battalion Royal Irish Rifles on 1 July when he lost his life in battle. The *Mid Ulster Mail* on 30 September 1916 reported:

> *The mystery surrounding the fate of Sapper William Lewis, Royal Engineers, who had been officially reported as wounded and missing since the 1st July has been solved. His father, Mr. James Lewis, Park Road, Dungannon, has received a letter from the young man's officer, Lieutenant Young, stating that the body of his son had been found in No Man's Land by the Black Watch on the 16th inst. (September) and had been suitably interred. His identification disc, pocket book, and ring, had also been found.*

Sapper William J. Lewis has no known grave, but is remembered on the Thiepval Memorial, Thiepval, Somme.

Private George Marshall (13551), 9th Battalion Royal Inniskilling Fusiliers (Tyrone Volunteers), was born in Belfast around 1895. The family had moved to Legane, Ballymagran, Dungannon by 1901. George enlisted in Caledon to serve King and Country and lost his life on 1 July 1916. George's father, Mr T. C. W. Marshall was the vice-chairman of Dungannon Board of Guardians. Private George Marshall has no known grave, but is remembered on the Thiepval Memorial, Thiepval, Somme, and Dungannon War Memorial.

Private Richard McIntyre (G/21639), 9th Battalion Royal Irish Fusiliers (Armagh Volunteers), was born in Dungannon around 1892. Prior to the war Richard was a seamen working on the Anchor Line and on returning home volunteered to serve King and Country, enlisting at Portadown. Richard's three brothers also served the colours, following in the footsteps of their father who had been a sergeant in the Army. Richard's eldest brother was a career soldier, having served with the Royal Garrison Artillery and subsequently had left for the front with the 2nd Inniskillings. Another brother Joseph had been a reservist and left for the front at the beginning of the war, also with the 2nd Inniskillings. Both of these brothers were wounded in May 1915 at the Battle of Festubert. A third brother Thomas served with the Tyrones and was wounded on 3 July as the battle still raged on the Somme. The McIntyre's would lose two sons to the war Richard at the Somme and Joseph in 1917. Private Richard

McIntyre is buried in Ancre British Cemetery, Beaumont-Hamel Somme and is remembered on St. Anne's Parish Church Roll of Honour.

Lance Corporal William McMenemy (19349), 9th Battalion Royal Inniskilling Fusiliers (Tyrone Volunteers), was born in Dungannon around 1885. Prior to the war William lived with his wife in Henry Street, Dungannon, and worked for Stevenson and Co Ltd. He was a drill instructor in B Company Dungannon UVF. He had previous military experience with the Royal Inniskilling Fusiliers, being a time expired soldier and enlisted to serve King and Country again at Bundoran, County Donegal. Initially William had been reported wounded along with J. McVey, Caledon, and J. J. O'Neill, Coalisland, but Colonel Ricardo in a letter to his wife published in the *Tyrone Courier* on 31 August 1916 explained that:

> *Lance Corporal Wm. McMenemy, Tyrone Volunteers, who had been previously reported wounded and missing, cannot be traced after every possible inquiry and that it is feared he fell on 1st July, and offering the sympathy of all ranks of the battalion in her sorrow.*

Lance Corporal William McMenemy has no known grave but is remembered on the Thiepval Memorial, Thiepval, Somme. He is also remembered on Dungannon Holdfast LOL 1620 Roll of Honour and Dungannon War Memorial.

Private Lewis Meenagh (6977), 1st Battalion Royal Inniskilling Fusiliers was born in Drumglass, Dungannon around 1882. By 1901 Lewis is recorded as working as a linen lapper for Stevenson & Co, linen manufacturers, Dungannon. By 1911 he was living in Beragh, married with a new born baby girl, Margaret, and working as a postman. On the outbreak of hostilities Lewis was called up on the Army Reserve and enlisted to serve the colours at Omagh. Lewis to France with the 2nd Battalion Royal Inniskilling Fusiliers and was wounded in July 1915 at Festubert. The following article was printed in the *Tyrone Courier* on 9 September 1915 under the title "A Gallant Inniskilling":

> *Mr John Meenagh, house painter, Georges Street, Dungannon, has received the following letter from his brother, Private Lewis Meenagh, 2nd Battalion Royal Inniskilling Fusiliers, a former employee of Messrs. Stevenson and Son, linen manufacturers Dungannon, who is at present in hospital in London suffering from wounds received in Festubert on*

22nd July:- "I received the Courier all right and was glad to see it. I was wounded at Festubert on 22nd July. I have seen some hard fighting since the beginning of the war and have come through some stiff engagements, including the retreat from Mons, and as for the good old Inniskillings, out of 1400 of us, there only remains about 500. We made a terrible charge against the Germans on 15th May at Festubert and lost very heavily, 850 being killed or wounded. We carried three lines of German trenches at the point of the bayonet along with the Worcesters; we were the first to attack and they were our supports. The attack was carried out with great success and we got great praise from General French and others who said we were second to none in the British army. I have been strongly recommended for the D.C.M. for building an observation post at St Marguerite on La Basse side under heavy shell fire, thereby saving a brigade from being cut up. I have learned nothing about it since as I have been wounded. We have had some hardships but were always cheerful, anxious to give the Huns a good "licking" and if spared to return I hope to help to do that. We would like to get at the Kaiser in Berlin; we would make him sorry for all his doings. If the Germans fought fair as they ought to do, the war would have been finished by now. I am getting the best of treatment in hospital here and get motor-rides around London, and hope to be all right again very soon.

Lewis Meenagh would return to the Western Front and by the time the Battle of the Somme came round he was serving with the 1st Battalion Royal Inniskilling Fusiliers (29th Division) who attacked the village of Beaumont Hamel on 1 July along with the Royal Newfoundland Regiment. Lewis was killed in this attack, leaving a wife, daughter and son. His son was killed serving the colours during the Second World War.

Private Lewis Meenagh is buried in the Y-Ravine Cemetery, Beaumont Hamel, Somme. He is remembered on St. Anne's Parish Church Roll of Honour and Dungannon War Memorial.

Rifleman Frederick William Moore (412), 13th Battalion Royal Irish Rifles, was born in Seapatrick, County Down about 1898. By 1911 Frederick was living in Market Square, Dungannon and working as a drapers apprentice for Menary Brothers in the town. Frederick Moore would enlist into the 36th (Ulster) Division at Banbridge and would serve with D Company, 13th Royal Irish Rifles. Rifleman Frederick Moore has no known grave, but is remembered on the Thiepval Memorial, Thiepval, Somme.

Private Edward Murphy (11269), 9th Battalion Royal Inniskilling Fusiliers (Tyrone Volunteers), was born around 1886 in Clonfeacle. Edward was living in Benburb prior to the war and was an active member of Benburb Company UVF. He enlisted to serve the colours in Dungannon. Edward was killed in action on 1 July 1916 and like so many of his comrades has no known grave, but is remembered on the Thiepval Memorial, Thiepval, Somme.

Private Charles O'Neill (4427), 1st Battalion Royal Inniskilling Fusiliers, was born in Dungannon around 1894. Charles grew up in Anne Street, Dungannon and worked as a tinsmith in his early days. At some point prior to the war he enlisted with the Royal Inniskilling Fusiliers and was serving with them in India on the outbreak of the war. Charles arrived on the Western Front in October 1914 and would serve there continuously until he returned home to Dungannon in the summer of 1915 having been wounded in Flanders in May. Charles brother Francis is believed to have also served in the colours during the war. Private Charles O'Neill was killed in action on the first day of the Somme and has no known grave. He is remembered on the Thiepval Memorial, Thiepval, Somme and Dungannon War Memorial.

Private William James Orr (11906), 9th Battalion Royal Inniskilling Fusiliers (Tyrone Volunteers), was born around 1896 in Killyman. Brought up for a period of time in Belfast, he returned with his family to reside in the Ballynakelly area. William worked for John Stevenson & Co., Coalisland, and was also an active member of the Ballynakelly UVF before he enlisted for King and Country at Omagh. Killed in action on 1 July 1916, Private William James Orr has no known grave, but is remembered on the Thiepval Memorial, Thiepval, Somme and Dungannon War Memorial.

Captain James Claude Beauchamp Proctor, 10th Battalion Royal Inniskilling Fusiliers (Derry Volunteers), was killed in action during the first day of the Battle of the Somme. Born in June 1885 in County Londonderry, he was educated at Reading School Berkshire and Trinity College, Dublin. He volunteered on the outbreak of war and was gazetted Captain of the 10th Battalion Royal Inniskilling Fusiliers (Derry Volunteers) on 21 September 1914. The *Belfast Newsletter* on 7 July 1916 carried the following report:

Captain James Claude Beauchamp Proctor, Royal Inniskilling Fusiliers (Derry Battalion), who was killed on the 1 July, was the eldest son of the late Mr. James E. Proctor, solicitor, Limavady, and of Mrs Proctor, Tullydoey House, Moy. He was educated at Reading School, Berks, concluding his collegiate career at Trinity, Dublin, where he obtained his M. A., and subsequently his I.L.D. He was an Auditor of the Solicitors Debating Society in Dublin, and practised as a solicitor in association with his father in Limavady for a time. He afterwards went to the Bar, and became a member of the North West Circuit. He was an ardent Unionist in politics, a member of the Ulster Unionist Council, organiser and secretary of the local Unionist club, and the co-organiser and secretary of the U.V.F. He was second in command of the North Londonderry Regiment, U.V.F., and on the outbreak of war he obtained a commission in the 10th Inniskillings, Ulster Division serving at Finner, Randalstown, and Seaford before proceeding to the Front. The deceased has two brothers serving with the colours – Major G. Norman Proctor (East Africa) and Edwin V. Proctor (Australian Force, Egypt), and his younger sister is a military nurse.

Captain James Claude Beauchamp Proctor is buried in Mill Road Cemetery, Thiepval, Somme. He is remembered in Drumachose Parish Church, Limavady and Benburb Parish Church. He is also commemorated on the Barrister's Roll of Honour, Four Courts, Dublin, and Moy War Memorial.

Second Lieutenant William Porter, 6th Battalion Royal Inniskilling Fusiliers, was attached to the 1st Battalion of this regiment when he was killed in action during the first day of July at the Battle of the Somme. Born in Belfast around 1884, William attended the Royal School Dungannon before emigrating to Canada. The *Belfast Newsletter* on 7 July 1916 carried the following article:

Second Lieutenant William Porter, Royal Inniskilling Fusiliers, killed in action, was the youngest son of Mr William Porter, Beechview, Balmoral Avenue, Belfast, and a brother-in-law of Mr R. W. Bingham, B.A., and Headmaster of Dungannon Royal School. The late Second Lieutenant Porter was severely wounded in the chest during the landing at Suvla Bay in August last and after his recovery was engaged on the Irish west coast defences and ultimately was attached to a battalion serving in France. He evinced the greatest possible interest in the U.V.F. movement, having returned specially from Canada to take part in it, and was a half company commander in the "A" company, Dungannon Battalion. He was a keen and popular sportsman and an enthusiastic Rugby footballer.

Second Lieutenant William Porter had enlisted as a Private with over a 100 men from Dungannon UVF on the outbreak of hostilities. He quickly received a Commission and saw his first action in the Dardanelles where he was wounded and returned to Dungannon to recuperate. On recovery he was posted to the west of Ireland before returning to the Western Front. William is buried in the Ancre British Cemetery, Beaumont-Hamel, Somme. He is remembered on the St Anne's Parish Church Roll of Honour and Dungannon War Memorial.

Private Peter Rafferty (27405), 1st Battalion Royal Inniskilling Fusiliers, was born in Coalisland around 1895. Prior to the war Peter worked in the brick yard as a labourer and on the outbreak of hostilities enlisted in Dungannon. He was killed in action serving at Beaumont Hamel on 1 July 1916. Private Peter Rafferty is buried in the Y-Ravine Cemetery, Beaumont Hamel, Somme and is remembered on Dungannon War Memorial.

Private Alexander Skiffington (3790), 1st Battalion Royal Inniskilling Fusiliers, was born in Dungannon around 1890. By the age of 18 Alexander was residing at the Army Barracks, Gortmore, Omagh, probably having enlisted into the Regular Army. On the outbreak of the war he was called up with the special reserve and served the colours with the Inniskillings. He lost his life on 1 July 1916. Private Alexander Skiffington has no known grave, but is remembered on the Thiepval Memorial, Thiepval, Somme and Dungannon War Memorial.

Lance Corporal Samuel Smith (11222), 9th Battalion Royal Inniskilling Fusiliers (Tyrone Volunteers), was born in Scotland around 1895. His family subsequently moved to Derrycreevy, Benburb and it was here that Samuel would grow up. A member of the Benburb Company UVF. Samuel would enlist to serve the colours when the call to the volunteers came. He enlisted in Dungannon and lost his life on 1 July 1916. Lance Corporal Samuel Smith has no known grave, but is remembered on the Thiepval Memorial, Thiepval, Somme.

Private Robert Somerville (16033), 10th Battalion Royal Inniskilling Fusiliers (The Derrys) was killed in battle on 1 July 1916. Born in Ayr,

Scotland around 1898, the family initially moved to Belfast before settling in Dungannon. Prior to the outbreak of war he was in the employment of Miss Lyle, Laurel Hill, Coleraine and was an active member of the Coleraine UVF. On the formation of the 36th (Ulster) Division he enlisted at Donegal. At the end of 1915 Robert suffered shrapnel wounds and was hospitalised at Le Havre. Private Robert Somerville is buried in Connaught Cemetery, Thiepval, Somme.

Private James Stewart (22930), 9th Battalion Royal Inniskilling Fusiliers (Tyrone Volunteers), was born at Tullynisken around 1876. Prior to the war he worked in Derryvale Linen and Finishing Works, and was living at Farlough with his wife and two sons. James had held the offices of Secretary of Newmills LOL 183 and Worshipful Master of Bush RBP No. 4. He was also an Inspector for the East Tyrone Unionist Association and an active member of Newmills UVF Company. On the outbreak of war he joined the Tyrones in Dungannon. Private James Stewart lost his life on the first day of the Somme offensive. He has no known grave, but is remembered on the Thiepval Memorial, Thiepval, Somme. He is also remembered on the Newmills Parish Church Roll of Honour, Newmills LOL 183 Roll of Honour and Dungannon War Memorial.

Private Henry Strain (20787), 9th Battalion Royal Inniskilling Fusiliers (Tyrone Volunteers), was killed in action on 1 July 1916. Born in Dungannon Henry enlisted with the Tyrones in Omagh. Private Henry Strain has no known grave, but is remembered on the Thiepval Memorial, Thiepval, Somme and Castlecaulfield Parish Church Roll of Honour.

Private William Stratton (14930), 11th Battalion Royal Inniskilling Fusiliers (Donegal and Fermanagh Volunteers), was killed in action on 1 July 1916. Born in Killyman, William enlisted in Belfast. He is buried in Connaught Cemetery, Thiepval, Somme.

Private William James Stratton (16132), 9th Battalion Royal Irish Fusiliers (Armagh Volunteers), was killed in action on 1 July 1916. Born around 1893 in Derrycurry, County Armagh he had formerly served with the Mid Ulster Royal Artillery. William enlisted at Monaghan town. On his death William's wife was living at Derrygalley, Moy. Private William James Stratton has no known grave, but is remembered on the Thiepval Memorial, Thiepval, Somme.

Private Robert Thomas Taylor (3718), 1st Battalion Royal Inniskilling Fusiliers, died on 3 July of wounds he received during the Somme offensive. Before the war, Robert was an active member of the UVF in Moygashel and belonged to Moygashel LOL 708. Robert fought in several battles during the war. He was wounded at Festubert on the Western Front in May 1915. On returning to duty, he went to Macedonia with the 10th (Irish) Division. He suffered frostbite in Macedonia and was sent to Devonport Military Hospital in England. He would return to action in time to take part in the Somme offensive, where he lost his life. Following Robert's death, Moygashel LOL 708 passed a motion of sympathy to his widow, which was reported in the Mid Ulster Mail on 15 July 1916:

> The W.M., Br William Ardrey, referred to the heavy loss the lodge had sustained in the death in action of Lance-Corporal Robert Taylor. He proposed a resolution expressing the deepest sympathy be adopted and forwarded to Mrs Taylor, the bereaved widow. The resolution was seconded by Br. George Gallagher, secretary and adopted in silence, the members standing. The lodge then adjourned as a token of respect.

Private Robert Thomas Taylor is buried in Gezaincourt Communal Cemetery, Gezaincourt, Somme. He is remembered on the Dungannon War Memorial.

Trooper Alexander Watt (101), 6th Inniskilling Dragoons, was attached to 2nd Regiment, North Irish Horse when he was killed in action on 3 July 1916. Born around 1897 at Drumglass, Dungannon, the family lived in George Street in the town. On the outbreak of war Alexander enlisted in Dungannon. His two other brothers also served the colours, William with the Canadian Mounted Rifles and George with the North Irish Horse. His sister Sarah also volunteered, serving as a nurse with the Red Cross in England. Alexander was killed while bringing in wounded comrades from the battlefield at the Somme. Trooper Alexander Watt has no known grave, but is remembered on the Thiepval Memorial, Thiepval, Somme and St. Anne's Parish Church Roll of Honour.

Private Joseph Watt (17866), 9th Battalion Royal Inniskilling Fusiliers (Tyrone Volunteers), gave his life for King and Country at the Battle of the Somme on 1 July 1916. Born in Moy around 1881 Joseph was married and living at Altnavannog, Bernagh by 1901. Joseph enlisted in

Omagh to serve with the Tyrones. He was wounded in May 1916. Having recovered from his wounds he took part in the great offensive at the Somme, losing his life. Prior to the war Joseph worked for Mr Samuel Cummings. He had been an active member of the Moy Company UVF, Moy LOL 90, Derryoghill RBP 77 and Dungannon Temperance Flute Band.

The following letter from Lieutenant E. W. Crawford, acting adjutant, to Mrs Watt was published in the *Mid Ulster Mail* on 12 August 1916:

> *I regret to inform you that your husband, Private Joseph Watt, of my battalion, is missing since the 1st inst (July). He took part in the gallant attack made by the Ulster Division on that date. He was a good soldier and a loyal comrade, and his loss is keenly felt by all ranks in the battalion. Please accept my sincere sympathy in your great loss.*

Private Joseph Watt has no known grave, but is remembered on the Thiepval Memorial, Thiepval, Somme. He is also remembered on Dungannon War Memorial and Moy War Memorial.

Private Thomas Williamson (13703), 11th Battalion Royal Inniskilling Fusiliers (Donegal and Fermanagh Volunteers), was killed in action on 1 July 1916. Born in Canary, County Armagh he enlisted in Belfast to serve the colours. Private Thomas Williamson has no known grave, but is remembered on the Thiepval Memorial, Thiepval, Somme and Moy War Memorial.

Private Robert John Wilson (20268), 9th Battalion Royal Inniskilling Fusiliers (Tyrone Volunteers), died serving the colours on 1 July 1916. Born in Glasgow, Scotland around 1891 the family were residing at Mullaghadun, Bernagh by 1901. Robert was educated at Drumglass Boys National School and was living at Clare Terrace, Dungannon by 1911. He enlisted in Omagh shortly after the outbreak of the war. Private Wilson's mother thought that her son was wounded and in hospital following the attack at the Somme on 1 July. She was preparing for his homecoming when she received a letter from Colonel Ricardo confirming his death. These sad circumstances were reported in the *Mid Ulster Mail* on 26 August 1916, as follows:

> *A pathetic incident has just taken place in connection with the permission just given to National Schools to use the Union Jack to teach patriotism.*

Mrs Wilson, of Beech Valley, Dungannon, whose son, Private Wilson, aged 19, was a member of the Tyrone Volunteers, had purchased two large Union Jacks to decorate her dwelling house in honour of the home-coming of her son from the Front. He took part in the great advance on 1st July, but was one of those who sacrificed their lives for King and country. Mrs Wilson has now presented the flags to Mr. Thornberry, Principal of Drumglass Boys School, where the boy was educated, to hang on the walls as an incentive to the pupils and in memory of her brave son.

Private Robert John Wilson has no known grave, but is remembered on the Thiepval Memorial, Thiepval, Somme, St. Anne's Parish Church Roll of Honour, Dungannon Holdfast LOL 1620 Roll of Honour and Dungannon War Memorial.

Second Lieutenant Matthew John Wright, 14th Battalion Royal Irish Rifles (Young Citizen Volunteers), made the ultimate sacrifice for King and Country at the Somme on 1 July 1916. The son of a Presbyterian clergyman he was born in Newtownards around 1888. Prior to the war Matthew had worked for a period of time for John Stevenson Ltd, Coalisland before moving to the employment of James P. Corry, Belfast. He enlisted as a private in the 14th Battalion Royal Irish Rifles in early October 1914 and applied for a commission some weeks later. He received his commission as a Second Lieutenant in January 1915 and went to France with the Ulster Division in October 1915. Matthew was on leave at home in Newtownards in May 1916, but returned to the Western Front by 27 May 1916. At the end of the war the Masonic Lodge in Newtownards was renamed in his memory. Second Lieutenant Matthew John Wright has no known grave, but is remembered on the Thiepval Memorial, Thiepval, Somme. He is also remembered on Newtownards First Presbyterian Church WW1 War Memorial.

Withdrawal of the 36th (Ulster) Division

On 2 July 1916 the Ulster Division, including the Tyrones, was withdrawn from the front line. It was soon transferred from France to Messines, Belgium, where it spent the remainder of 1916. Having suffered such heavy losses, the Division was a shadow of its former self. Work began immediately on reorganising the Division and replacing the men lost on the first day of the Somme with new recruits. The task of leading the new recruitment campaign for the Tyrones was lead by Thomas McGregor Greer of Tullylagan, Cookstown. Sir Edward Carson, the unionist leader, sent the following letter to Mr Greer emphasising the importance of this work:

ROYAL INNISKILLING FUSILIERS,

9th Battalion Recruiting Campaign.

5, EATON PLACE,
LONDON,
12th JULY, 1916.

Dear Mr. Greer,

      I am very pleased to hear that at the request of the officer commanding the 9th Inniskillings, you are taking up the question of recruiting for this Battalion in the County of Tyrone.

      Our old friends and comrades of the 36th (Ulster) Division have brought undying fame to Ulster and the Empire and it is the plain duty of those of their fellow-countrymen who can do so, to help to carry on the war, and to follow the example that they so nobly inaugurated.

      We must take care that that work has not been in vain, by sending men out to fill the place of our fallen heroes, and it would indeed be a lamentable chapter in the history of this great Division if, by reason of the sacrifices so willingly made, we were unable to take part in the final triumph and victory which assuredly awaits us if every man will do his duty.

      I know that many of our friends are naturally anxious for the safety and welfare of their families by reason of the late deplorable rebellion in Ireland, and the inadequate protection that was afforded through the laxity of the Government, but I think they may be assured that the Government is now fully alive to the elementary duty of protecting all those who are loyal in Ireland, and I have been assured that every step will be taken that is necessary to prevent such outrages in the future.

      The promise of the exclusion of the six counties, including County Tyrone, from the operation of the Home Rule Act, is an additional reason why we should wholeheartedly throw in our lot with all those who place country before party, and have firmly set themselves to see this war through to a successful conclusion.

I remain,
Yours sincerely,
(Signed) EDWARD CARSON.

Conclusion

This chapter has focused solely on the involvement of men from Dungannon and district in land operations on the Western Front up to 1 July 1916. Their activities in the other theatres of war, including at sea, during 1916 will be covered in the second volume of this series.

The Charge of the Ulster Division
at Thiepval July 1st 1916

Was ever a Charge in the world like this?
Shall ever a son of Ulster miss
A fame that is wholly and solely his-
A fame of sublimest splendour?
The lads who laughed in the face of Death!
Above the roar of he cannon's breath
Singing their sacred shibboleth
Of "The boyne!" and "No Surrender!"

Giant strong with the strength of Right-
Fired, by the souls of their sires to fight-
What cared they for the forman's might,
Or how many cannon's thundered?
Face to face with a hundred Huns,
Half-a0-score of Ulster sons
Silenced the thunder of he guns-
Ten-a match for a hundred!

Nought could stay them: nought could stop
Athirst for blood to the last red drop,
Charging along on the topmost top
Of the waves of Fire that bore them!
On, with a thirst that nought could quell,
Thro a hurricane-shower of shot and shell,
To fight- or fall, as their Fathers fell,
In the doughty days before them!

Marrily – every mother's son-
Laughing, as tho they fought for fun
With a song and a cheer they charged the Hun,
Marring his Maker's image!
Chaffing, as tho each shell might be
The whistle call of a Referee!
And the bloodiest tussle in History
Only-a Football scrimmage!

Into the Hell of "No Man's Land"
Thro poisoned air, at their soul's command,
And a shrapnel-storm that none could stand,
Charging. In wild derision.
Past Sentry Death, who, wondering, kept
His vigil there-on, on they swept,
Where never a man could live-except
Ulster's divine Division!

Flinging his fun in the face of Death-
Above the roar of the cannon's breath
Singing his cared shibboleth
Of "The Boyne!" and "No Surrender!"
Wherever a son of Ulster is,
Honour and Glory shall aye be his!
Was ever a fight in the world like this,
Or a charge of sublimer splendour?

SAMUEL K. COWAN, M. A.

Chapter Notes

CHAPTER 1

1	*Daily News & Leader, 5 August 1914*
2	*The Belfast Newsletter, 5 August 1914*
3	*The Belfast Newsletter, 11 August 1914*
4	*The Belfast Newsletter, 10 August 1914*
5	*Arthur Marwick, The Deluge (Penguin Books Ltd., Middlesex, 1967) p.34*
6	*The Belfast Newsletter, 28 August 1914*
7	*The Belfast Newsletter, 1 September 1914*
8	*The Belfast Newsletter, 23 September 1914*
9	*The Belfast Newsletter, 4 September 1914*
10	*The Belfast Newsletter, 4 September 1914*
11	*The Belfast Newsletter, 22 October 1914*
12	*The Belfast Newsletter, 13 November 1914*
13	*The Belfast Newsletter, 14 December 1914*
14	*W. J. Canning, A Wheen of Medals (W. J. Canning, Dunally Lodge, 2006) p.32*
15	*W. J. Canning, A Wheen of Medals (W. J. Canning, Dunally Lodge, 2006) p.33*
16	*The Belfast Newsletter, 3 Noveber 1914*
17	*The Belfast Newsletter, 3 November 1914*
18	*The Belfast Newsletter, 8 October 1914*
19	*The Belfast Newsletter, 4 December 1914*
20	*H. W. Wilson & J. A. Hammerlon, The Great War Volume 1 (The Amalgamated Press Ltd., London 1914) p.185*
21	*H. W. Wilson & J. A. Hammerlon, The Great War Volume 1 (The Amalgamated Press Ltd., London 1914) p.185*
22	*The Belfast Newsletter, 12 October 1914*
23	*The Belfast Newsletter, 11 February 1915*
24	*The Belfast Newsletter, 20 November 1914*
25	*The Belfast Newsletter, 15 June 1915*
26	*The Belfast Newsletter, 8 October 1914*
27	*Friends of the Somme, Mid Ulster Branch, Dungannon War Dead, Website*
28	*The Belfast Newsletter, 14 November 1914*
29	*The Belfast Newsletter, 27 November 1914*
30	*The Belfast Newsletter, 27 November 1914*
31	*The Tyrone Courier, 13 April 1916*
32	*The Belfast Newsletter, 5 January 1915*

CHAPTER 2

1	*The Belfast Newsletter, 4 February 1915*
2	*The Belfast Newsletter, 8 February 1915*
3	*The Belfast Newsletter, 23 April 1915*
4	*The Belfast Newsletter, 28 April 1915*
5	*The Belfast Newsletter, 30 April 1915*
6	*W. J. Canning, A Wheen of Medals (W. J. Canning, Dunally Lodge, 2006) p.55*
7	*The Belfast Newsletter, 8 May 1915*
8	*The Belfast Newsletter, 14 May 1915*
9	*The Belfast Newsletter, 20 May 1915*
10	*The Belfast Newsletter, 21 May 1915*
11	*The Belfast Newsletter, 18 August 1915*
12	*The Belfast Newsletter, 18 September 1915*
13	*The Belfast Newsletter, 25 October 1915*
14	*The Belfast Newsletter, 23 October 1915*
15	*The Belfast Newsletter, 4 December 1915*
16	*The Belfast Newsletter, 27 December 1915*
17	*The Belfast Newsletter, 20 November 1915*
18	*The Belfast Newsletter, 20 January 1915*
19	*The Belfast Newsletter, 28 January 1915*
20	*The Belfast Newsletter, 18 February 1915*
21	*The Belfast Newsletter, 25 August 1915*
22	*The Belfast Newsletter, 29 March 1915*
23	*The Belfast Newsletter, 30 April 1915*
24	*The Belfast Newsletter, 4 May 1915*
25	*The Belfast Newsletter, 4 May 1915*
26	*The Belfast Newsletter, 7 May 1915*
27	*The Belfast Newsletter, 7 June 1915*
28	*The Belfast Newsletter 25 June 1915*
29	*The Belfast Newsletter, 24 July 1915*
30	*The Belfast Newsletter, 29 July 1915*
31	*The Belfast Newsletter, 7 September 1915*
32	*The Belfast Newsletter, 5 October 1915*
33	*The Belfast Newsletter, 3 November 1915*
34	*The Belfast Newsletter, 10 November 1915*
35	*The Belfast Newsletter, 2 December 1915*
36	*The Belfast Newsletter, 25 February 1915*
37	*The Belfast Newsletter, 24 March 1915*
38	*The Belfast Newsletter, 16 April 1915*
39	*The Belfast Newsletter, 29 March 1915*
40	*The Belfast Newsletter, 25 January 1915*
41	*The Belfast Newsletter, 5 February 1915*

42   *The Belfast Newsletter, 11 February 1915*

43   *The Belfast Newsletter, 6 February 1915*

44   *The Belfast Newsletter, 17 February 1915*

45   *The Belfast Newsletter, 17 February 1915*

46   *The Belfast Newsletter, 17 February 1915*

47   *The Belfast Newsletter, 8 February 1915*

48   *Dungannon Volunteer LOL 178, Private Minute Book*

49   *The Belfast Newsletter, 24 May 1915*

50   *The Belfast Newsletter, 11 February 1915*

51   *The Belfast Newsletter, 5 August 1915*

52   *The Belfast Newsletter, 11 May 1915*

53   *The Belfast Newsletter, 8 July 1915*

54   *The Belfast Newsletter, 2 June 1915*

55   *The Belfast Newsletter, 20 May 1915*

56   *The 1st Battalion - The Faugh a Ballaughs in the Great War*

        (Brigadier General A. R. Burrowes, CMG, DSO, Gale & Polden Ltd., Aldershot) p.30

57   *The Belfast Newsletter, 28 May 1915*

58   *The Belfast Newsletter, 9 June 1915*

59   *The Belfast Newsletter, 1 June 1915*

60   *The Belfast Newsletter, 18 October 1915*

61   *The Belfast Newsletter, 12 August 1915*

62   *The Belfast Newsletter, 15 September 1915*

63   *The Belfast Newsletter, 9 June 1915*

64   *The Belfast Newsletter, 25 June 1915*

65   *The Belfast Newsletter, 26 June 1915*

66   *The Tyrone Courier, 29 July 1915*

67   *The Belfast Newsletter, 12 May 1915*

68   *The Belfast Newsletter, 27 May 1915*

69   *The Belfast Newsletter, 3 June 1915*

70   *The Belfast Newsletter, 23 August 1915*

71   *The Belfast Newsletter, 30 August 1915*

72   *The Belfast Newsletter, 8 April 1916*

73   *The Belfast Newsletter, 1 June 1915*

74   *The Belfast Newsletter, 10 July 1915*

75   *The Belfast Newsletter, 29 March 1915*

76   *The Belfast Newsletter, 3 June 1915*

77   *The Belfast Newsletter, 4 October 1915*

78   *The Belfast Newsletter, 5 October 1915*

79   *The Belfast Newsletter, 8 November 1915*

80   *The Belfast Newsletter, 15 November 1915*

81   *The Belfast Newsletter, 30 December 1915*

82   *The Belfast Newsletter, 3 January 1916*

83   *The Belfast Newsletter, 12 November 1915*

84   *The Belfast Newsletter, 27 February 1915*

85   *The Belfast Newsletter, 15 November 1915*

86   *The Belfast Newsletter, 16 November 1915*

87   *The Belfast Newsletter, 24 November 1915*

88   *The Belfast Newsletter, 24 November 1915*

89   *The Belfast Newsletter, 13 October 1915*

90   *The Belfast Newsletter, 8 November 1915*

91   *The Belfast Newsletter, 16 November 1915*

92   *The Belfast Newsletter, 22 November 1915*

93   *The Belfast Newsletter, 26 November 1915*

94   *The Belfast Newsletter, 27 November 1915*

95   *The Belfast Newsletter, 4 January 1916*

96   *The Belfast Newsletter, 4 December 1915*

97   *The Belfast Newsletter, 4 June 1915*

98   *The Belfast Newsletter, 23 July 1915*

99   *The Belfast Newsletter, 21 July 1915*

100   *The Belfast Newsletter 13 September 1915*

101   *The Belfast Newsletter, 13 August 1915*

102   *The Belfast Newsletter, 13 September 1915*

103   *The Belfast Newsletter, 10 September 1915*

104   *The Belfast Newsletter, 25 August 1915*

105   *The Belfast Newsletter, 13 September 1915*

106   *The Belfast Newsletter, 29 September 1915*

107   *The Belfast Newsletter, 17 August 1915*

108   *The Belfast Newsletter, 28 August 1915*

109   *The Belfast Newsletter, 1 September 1915*

110   *The Belfast Newsletter, 2 September 1915*

111   *The Belfast Newsletter, 14 September 1915*

112   *The Belfast Newsletter, 21 September 1915*

113   *The Belfast Newsletter, 17 April 1915*

114   *The Belfast Newsletter, 30 December 1915*

115   *The Belfast Newsletter, 30 December 1915*

116   *The Belfast Newsletter, 30 December 1915*

117   *The Belfast Newsletter, 8 November 1915*

118   *The Belfast Newsletter, 22 November 1915*

119   *The Belfast Newsletter, 24 December 1915*

120   *The Belfast Newsletter, 3 January 1916*

CHAPTER 3

1   *The Belfast Newsletter, 7 February 1915*

2   *The Belfast Newsletter, 15 February 1915*

3   *The Belfast Newsletter, 11 April 1915*

4   *The Belfast Newsletter, 14 April 1915*

5   *The Belfast Newsletter, 11 April 1915*

6   *The Belfast Newsletter, 25 April 1915*

7   *The Belfast Newsletter, 26 April 1915*

8   *The Belfast Newsletter, 29 April 1915*

9   *The Belfast Newsletter, 18 May 1915*

10   *The Belfast Newsletter, 20 May 1915*

11   *The Belfast Newsletter, 12 June 1915*

12   *The Belfast Newsletter, 5 May 1915*

13   *The Belfast Newsletter, 17 May 1915*

14   *The Belfast Newsletter, 17 May 1915*

15   *The Belfast Newsletter, 23 May 1915*

16   *The Belfast Newsletter, 3 June 1916*

17   *The Belfast Newsletter, 7 June 1916*

18   *The Belfast Newsletter, 7 June 1916*

19   *The Belfast Newsletter, 15 June 1916*

20   *The Belfast Newsletter, 15 June 1916*

21   *The Belfast Newsletter, 3 July 1916*

22   *The Belfast Newsletter, 1 July 1916*

23   *The Belfast Newsletter, 27 June 1916*

24   *The Belfast Newsletter, 27 March 1916*

25   *The Belfast Newsletter, 21 March 1916*

26   *The Belfast Newsletter, 27 April 1916*

27   *The Tyrone Courier, 25 May 1916*

28   *The Belfast Newsletter, 4 July 1916*

29   *The Belfast Newsletter, 6 July 1916*

30   *The Belfast Newsletter, 8 July 1916*

31   *The Belfast Newsletter, 13 July 1916*

32   *The Belfast Newsletter 19 August 1916*

33   *The Belfast Newsletter 23 August 1916*

34   *The Tyrone Courier, 13 July 1916*

Orangemen in Service 1914 - 1918

First Name	Surname	Awards	Lodge No.	Lodge Name	Townland
Robert	Anderson		1620	Holdfast Dungannon	–
James	Anderson		1620	Holdfast Dungannon	–
William. J	Anderson		708/1620	Moygashel/Holdfast Dungannon	Beechvalley
William	Archer		163	Bush	Bush Road
Alexander	Ardrey		708	Moygashel	Moygashel
James	Arthurs		183	Newmills	–
Robert J	Averall		1620	Holdfast Dungannon	Milltown
George	Belshaw	DCM	708	Moygashel	Coolhill
J	Benson		1620	Holdfast Dungannon	–
William	Best		178	Dungannon Volunteers	Drumcoo
Andrew	Boyd		1229	Dungannon Total Abstinence	Union Place
H	Boyd		1620	Holdfast Dungannon	–
George	Burrows		39	Cullenfad	Donaghmore
George	Caddoo	MM	296	Killnacart	–
Hugh John	Cairns (Kearns)		93	Coalisland	Coalisland
Robert	Cardwell		93	Coalisland	–
Nathaniel	Clarke		856	Derrycreevy	–
Atkinson	Connelly		513	Tamnamore	Tamnamore
Thomas John	Cross		1229/178	Dungannon Volunteers	Market Square
Samuel	Cross		1229	Dungannon Total Abstinence	Market Square
Harry/Henry	Cullen		708	Moygashel	Moygashel
James	Cumberland		296	Killnacart	Kilnacart
John	Cumberland		296	Killnacart	Kilnacart
James	Davis		1620	Holdfast Dungannon	–
Joy	Davis		1620	Holdfast Dungannon	–
S	Davis		1620	Holdfast Dungannon	–
William Tillie	Dickson		163	Bush	Milltown
William R	Dickson		1620	Holdfast Dungannon	Ballysaggart
R J	Dixon		1620	Holdfast Dungannon	–
Joseph	Doonan	MM	Unkown	–	John Street
Fred	Doonan	MM	Unkown	–	John Street
John Alexander	Doonan		Unkown	–	John Street
J	Dougan		1620	Holdfast Dungannon	–
Wingfield	Espey		163	Bush	Lowertown
T	Ferguson		1620	Holdfast Dungannon	–
Thomas	Fox		708	Moygashel	Moygashel
William	Gallagher		33	Bogbawn - Killyman	Drumeenagh, Killyman
Thomas	Gallagher		856	Derrycreevy	Henry Street
T	Gracey		1620	Holdfast Dungannon	–
Adam	Harbinson		1620	Holdfast Dungannon	Beechvalley
William	Harbinson		1620	Holdfast Dungannon	Drumcoo
Thomas	Harbinson		1620	Holdfast Dungannon	–
Thomas	Henry		1620	Holdfast Dungannon	
James Watson	Hetherington		90	–	Killyman Street Moy
Samuel	Hetherington		90	–	Killyman Street Moy
R	Hodgett		1620	Holdfast Dungannon	
Garnet W	Irwin		1620	Holdfast Dungannon	Castle Hill Dungannon
John George	Jones		183	Newmills	–
Thomas Ucher Caulfield	Knox (Northland)		178	Dungannon Volunteers	–
Samuel Victor	Lambe		1620	Holdfast Dungannon	Lisnahull
J	Lecky		1620	Holdfast Dungannon	–
Robert J	Lecky		1620	Holdfast Dungannon	Perry Street

Rank	Battalion	Regiment	Killed / Wounded	Battle	Date of Death	Recorded / Cross Referenced
Private 16153	9th Batt	R Irish / R Inniskilling Fus	Killed	Somme	07/01/1916	1st Presbyterian Church
	9th Batt	R Inniskilling Fus	Wounded	–	–	1st Presbyterian Church
Private	9th Batt	R Inniskilling Fus	Pow	–	–	Drumglass Roll of Honour
Private	–	R Inniskilling Fus	Wounded	–	–	Drumglass Roll of Honour
–	–	Unknown	–	–	–	–
–	10th Batt	Royal Canadian Rgt	Killed	–	04/26/1915	Newmills Church of Ireland
Private	2nd Batt	R Inniskilling Fus	Killed	–	11/07/1914	1st Presbyterian Church
Sergeant Major	9th Batt	R Inniskilling Fus	Wounded	–	–	2nd Presbyterian Church
–	–	–	–	–	–	–
Lieutenant	9th Batt	R Inniskilling Fus	Killed	Somme	07/02/1916	St Annes Parish Church
Private	10th Batt	R Inniskilling Fus	Killed	Bourlan Wood	12/07/1917	St Annes Parish Church
–	–	–	–	–	–	Drumglass Roll of Honour
L/Corp 17838	9th Batt	R Inniskilling Fus	Killed	Somme	07/01/1916	Castlecaufield Parish Church
–	9th Batt	R Inniskilling Fus	Killed	–	07/28/1918	–
–	2nd Batt	R Inniskilling Fus	Killed	Festubert	05/16/1915	–
–	–	–	Wounded	–	–	–
–	–	Royal Field Artillery	–	–	–	–
Private	–	R Irish Fus	–	–	–	–
Private	9th Batt	R Inniskilling Fus	Killed	–	10/15/1918	St Annes Parish Church
–	9th Batt	R Inniskilling Fus	Wounded	–	–	Drumglass Roll of Honour
	9th Batt	R Inniskilling Fus	Wounded	–	–	Drumglass Roll of Honour
Private 11553	9th Batt	R Inniskilling Fus	Killed	Somme	07/01/1916	Eglish Church of Ireland
Private 11554	9th Batt	R Inniskilling Fus	Killed	Somme	07/01/1916	Eglish Church of Ireland
Corporal		North Irish Horse	–	–	–	Drumglass Roll of Honour
–	–	–	–	–	–	Drumglass Roll of Honour
–	–	–	–	–	–	Drumglass Roll of Honour
Captain	6th Batt	R Inniskilling Fus	Killed	Somme	07/09/1916	1st Presbyterian Church
Private	2nd Batt	R Inniskilling Fus	Killed	Festubert	05/15/1915	St Annes Parish Church
–	–	–	–	–	–	Drumglass Roll of Honour
Private	2nd Batt	Lon Irish / R Inniskilling Fus	–	–	–	Drumglass Roll of Honour
L/Corp	9th Batt	R Inniskilling Fus	–	–	–	Drumglass Roll of Honour
Private	2nd Batt	Lon Irish / R Inniskilling Fus	Killed	Palestine	12/23/1917	St Annes Parish Church
–	–	–	–	–	–	Drumglass Roll of Honour
Corporal	–	North Irish Horse	–	–	–	–
–	–	–	–	–	–	Drumglass Roll of Honour
–	–	–	–	–	–	Drumglass Roll of Honour
Private 13345	9th Batt	R Inniskilling Fus	Killed	Somme	07/01/1916	–
Private	2nd Batt	R Inniskilling Fus	Killed	–	10/14/1918	St Annes Parish Church
–	–	–	–	–	–	–
L/Corp	1st Batt	R Irish Fusiliers	–	–	–	Drumglass Roll of Honour
Private 11200	9th Batt	R Inniskilling Fus	Killed	Somme	07/01/1916	St Annes Parish Church
–	1st Batt	R Irish Fusiliers	–	–	–	–
Private	9th Batt	R Inniskilling Fus	–	–	–	1st Presbyterian Church
Private	7th Batt	Canadian Infantry	Killed	–	06/03/1916	Moy War Memorial
Private	–	R Inniskilling Fus	Wounded	–	–	–
–	–	–	–	–	–	Drumglass Roll of Honour
–	9th Batt	Royal Irish Fusiliers	Killed	–	08/26/2018	St Annes Parish Church
–	–	Army Service Corp	–	–	06/21/1918	Newmills Church of Ireland
–	2nd Batt	Coldstream Guards	Killed	La Basse	02/01/1915	St Annes Parish Church
Private	9th Batt	R Inniskilling Fus	Killed	Somme	07/01/1916	2nd Presbyterian Church
–	–	–	–	–	–	Drumglass Roll of Honour
L/Corp	–	R Inniskilling Fus	Wounded	–	–	Drumglass Roll of Honour

Orangemen in Service 1914 - 1918

First Name	Surname	Awards	Lodge No.	Lodge Name	Townland
W	Lecky		1620	Holdfast Dungannon	–
C	Lewis		1620	Holdfast Dungannon	–
R A	Lloyd		513	Tamnamore	Tamnamore
William	Lockhart		1620	Holdfast Dungannon	Annahoe
Robert	Lynn		93	Coalisland	Mousetown
William	Lynn		93	Coalisland	Mousetown
Joseph	Marsh		93/183	Coalisland/Newmills	–
George	Mc Kinstry		708	Moygashel	Moygashel
William	Mc Menemy		1620	Holdfast Dungannon	Henry Street
William	Mc Minn		93	Coalisland	–
James	Mc Peake		1620	Holdfast Dungannon	Linfield Street
Robert	Mc Reynolds		1620	Holdfast Dungannon	–
Robert	Mc Williams		1620	Holdfast Dungannon	–
John	Meenagh		1620	Holdfast Dungannon	–
Robert	Montgomery		93	Coalisland	Coalisland
Walter Augustus	Montgomery		183	Newmills	–
David	Montgomery		708	Moygashel	Moygashel
H	Moore		1620	Holdfast Dungannon	–
Thomas Henry	Morgan		183	Newmills	–
Charles	Newell		1620	Holdfast Dungannon	Perry Street
Harry/henry	Newell		1620	Holdfast Dungannon	Perry Street
Robert	Orr		708	Moygashel	Moygashel
Thomas	Orr		708	Moygashel	Moygashel
Alexander	Orr		708	Moygashel	Moygashel
Thomas	Patterson		183	Newmills	Drumreagh
William	Patton		183	Newmills	–
Joseph	Rainey		1620	Holdfast Dungannon	Killylack
George	Reilly		708	Moygashel	Moygashel
R H	Scott		163	Bush	–
Alexander	Shannon		708	Moygashel	Moygashel
Alexander	Smith		1620	Holdfast Dungannon	Royal School
William C	Steenson		1620	Holdfast Dungannon	Beechvalley
Joseph	Stevenson		1229	Dungannon Total Abstinence	Carricklongfield
James	Stewart		183	Newmills	Newmills
John	Stinson		1620	Holdfast Dungannon	Clonaneese
Robert Thomas	Taylor		708	Moygashel	Moygashel
William James	Telford		1620	Holdfast Dungannon	Mark Street
Robert	Thompson		708	Moygashel	Moygashel
Joseph	Watt		90	–	Redford, Moy
Patrick J	Weir		708/1620	Moygashel/Holdfast Dungannon	Boyds Square
W	Weir		1620	Holdfast Dungannon	–
Fredrick	Wigton		206	Killyman	–
Robert	Wigton		206	Killyman	–
Jack	Williamson		1620	Holdfast Dungannon	–
Robert J	Wilson		1620	Holdfast Dungannon	Clare Terrace
W E	Wolsey		1620	Holdfast Dungannon	–
J	Wolsey		1620	Holdfast Dungannon	–
Robert	Wylie		708	Moygashel	Moygashel

Rank	Battalion	Regiment	Killed / Wounded	Battle	Date of Death	Recorded / Cross Referenced
–	–	–	–	–	–	Drumglass Roll of Honour
–	–	–	–	–	–	–
–	10th	Kings Liverpool Rgt	–	–	–	–
Private	–	R Inniskilling Fus	Wounded	–	–	Drumglass Roll of Honour
Driver	87th Battery	Royal Field Artillery	Killed	Ypres	08/06/1915	–
Sergeant	2nd Batt	R Irish Fusiliers	Wounded	–	–	–
–	15th Batt	R Irish / R Inniskilling Fus	Killed	Cambrai	11/23/1917	Newmills Church of Ireland
	9th Batt	R Inniskilling Fus	Wounded	–	–	Drumglass Roll of Honour
Private	9th Batt	R Inniskilling Fus	Killed	Somme	07/01/1916	1st Presbyterian Church
Private	1st Batt	R Inniskilling Fus	Killed	–	11/22/1917	Newmills Church of Ireland
L/Corp	9th Batt	R Inniskilling Fus	–	–	–	Drumglass Roll of Honour
Corporal	–	Black Watch	Killed	Dardanelles	08/14/2015	St Annes Parish Church
–	1st Batt	Highland Light Infantry	Killed	–	08/14/2015	–
–	–	–	–	–	–	Drumglass Roll of Honour
Private	–	R Inniskilling Fus	Wounded	–	–	–
–	2nd Air Park	Royal Air Force	Killed	–	11/23/1918	Newmills Church of Ireland
–	–	–	–	–	–	–
–	–	–	–	–	–	–
–	49th Batt	Austrailian Infantry	Killed	–	04/08/1918	–
Lieutenant	–	Royal Engineers	Killed	–	03/24/1918	St Annes Parish Church
Trooper	–	North Irish Horse	–	–	–	Drumglass Roll of Honour
–	9th Batt	R Inniskilling Fus	Killed	–	04/25/1918	2nd Presbyterian Church
–	9th Batt	R Inniskilling Fus	Wounded	–	–	2nd Presbyterian Church
–	9th Batt	R Inniskilling Fus	–	–	–	2nd Presbyterian Church
11360	5th Batt	Royal Irish Rgt	Killed	–	02/08/1915	Newmills Church of Ireland
–	–	–	Killed	–	–	Newmills Church of Ireland
Private	6th Batt	R Inniskilling Fus	Wounded	Dardanelles	–	2nd Presbyterian Church
Private	–	R Inniskilling Fus	–	–	–	Drumglass Roll of Honour
Captain	9th Batt	R Inniskilling Fus	–	–	–	–
–	–	–	–	–	–	–
Private	9th Batt	R Inniskilling Fus	–	–	–	2nd Presbyterian Church
Private	9th Batt	R Inniskilling Fus	–	–	–	2nd Presbyterian Church
Private	9th Batt	R Inniskilling Fus	Killed	Messines	06/07/1917	St Annes Parish Church
Private 22930	9th Batt	R Inniskilling Fus	Killed	Somme	07/01/1916	Newmills Church of Ireland
–	17th Batt	Worcestershire Rgt	Killed	–	12/04/1918	–
L/Corp	1st Batt	R Inniskilling Fus	Killed	Somme	07/03/1916	2nd Presbyterian Church
Private	1st Batt	York & Lancaster Rgt	–	–	05/08/1915	St Annes Parish Church
–	–	–	–	–	–	–
Private	9th Batt	R Inniskilling Fus	Killed	Somme	07/01/1916	Moy War Memorial
–	9th Batt	R Inniskilling Fus	Killed	–	03/02/1917	St Annes Parish Church
–	–	–	–	–	–	–
27312	9th Batt	R Inniskilling Fus	Killed	–	03/29/1918	–
11227	9th Batt	R Inniskilling Fus	Killed	–	10/20/1919	–
–	–	–	–	–	–	Drumglass Roll of Honour
Private 20268	9th Batt	R Inniskilling Fus	Killed	Somme	07/01/1916	St Annes Parish Church
–	–	–	–	–	–	Drumglass Roll of Honour
–	–	–	–	–	–	Drumglass Roll of Honour
–	–	–	–	–	–	–

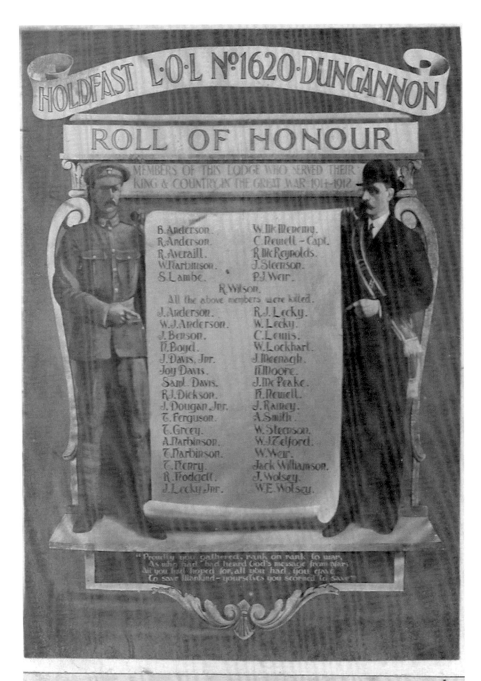

Drumglass Boys National School, Dungannon
Roll of Honour, 1914

Published in the Mid-Ulster Mail on Saturday 21 November 1914

Averill	Robert J	3rd	Batt. Inniskilling Fusiliers
Bell	William	1st	Batt. Royal Irish Fusiliers
Benson	Tom		HMS Jupiter
Cross	Samuel	9th	Batt. Inniskilling Fusiliers
Cullen	Henry		Inniskilling Fusiliers
Davis	James		North Irish Horse
Davis	Joy	67th	Company Army Service Corps
Dickson	Robert J	9th	Batt. Inniskilling Fusiliers
Dickson	William R	2nd	Batt. Inniskilling Fusiliers
Harbinson	Adam	3rd	Batt. Inniskilling Fusiliers
Harbinson	Tom	9th	Batt. Inniskilling Fusiliers
Harbinson	William	9th	Batt. Inniskilling Fusiliers
Hart	Tom	8th	Batt. Royal Irish Rifles
Hayes	Tom	2nd	Batt. Inniskilling Fusiliers
Hodgett	Gilbert	9th	Batt. Inniskilling Fusiliers
Jeffs	Robert		Army Medical Corps
Jenkinson	Richard	9th	Batt. Inniskilling Fusiliers
Johnston	John	3rd	Batt. Inniskilling Fusiliers
Leckey	John	9th	Batt. Inniskilling Fusiliers
Milligan	William	9th	Batt. Inniskilling Fusiliers
McCauley	George	9th	Batt. Inniskilling Fusiliers
McCrea	Robert		Royal Garrison Artillery
McKeown	William		Inniskilling Dragoons
McNeill	Edward	9th	Batt. Inniskilling Fusiliers
McPeak	James	9th	Batt. Inniskilling Fusiliers
Patton	Joe	6th	Batt. Inniskilling Fusiliers
Reid	Edward		BC Contingent, Canadian Regiment
Steenson	Robert	2nd	Batt. Royal Irish Fusiliers
Taylor	Robert	3rd	Batt. Inniskilling Fusiliers
Webb	James	9th	Batt. Inniskilling Fusiliers
Williamson	Alex R		Inniskilling Dragoons
Williamson	Jack		Royal Irish Fusiliers
Williamson	James	6th	Batt. Inniskilling Fusiliers
Wilson	Robert	9th	Batt. Inniskilling Fusiliers
Woolsey	Ed. W	6th	Batt. Inniskilling Fusiliers

Glossary and Abbreviations

Adjutant	An officer who assists the commanding officer in the details of his command.
AO	Army Order.
Bde	Brigade.
BEF	British Expeditionary Force.
BEF	Belfast Evening Telegraph.
Blighty	A wound serious enough to have one shipped to hospital in England. Battalion.
Bomb	Hand grenade.
Cadre	A small number of officers and men comprising the nucleus of a regiment.
CB	Confined to barracks.
Commission	Appointment as an officer.
Coy	Company.
CQS	Company Quartermaster Sergeant.
CSM	Company Sergeant Major.
CWGC	Commonwealth War Graves Commission.
DoW	Died of wounds.
Draft	A group of men sent as reinforcements.
Enfilade	A volley of gunfire directed along a line from end to end.
Fatigue	A party detailed to work on trench digging or other labour.
Flammenwerfer	Flame-thrower.
GHQ	General Headquarters.
GOC	General Officer Commanding (of a division).
Jack Johnson	A type of German artillery shell.
KIA	Killed in action.
KR/KRR	King's Rules and Regulations.
LOL	Loyal Orange Lodge.
LG	Lewis gun.
LG	London Gazette.
MGC	Machine Gun Corps.
MIC	Medal Index Card.
MMP	Military Mounted Police.
NCO	Non-commissioned officer - the rank between private and officer (usually sergeant, lance sergeant, corporal, lance corporal).
NIH	North Irish Horse.
OTC	Officer Training Corps.
Pillbox	A reinforced concrete defensive post.
Pineapple	A German ball grenade.
PoW	Prisoner of war.
Quartermaster	An officer responsible for the provision of food, clothing and equipment Royal Artillery.
RBP	Royal Black Preceptory.

RAF	Royal Air Force.
RAMC	Royal Army Medical Corps.
RE	Royal Engineers.
Redoubt	A fortified defensive post.
RFA	Royal Field Artillery.
RFC	Royal Flying Corps.
RGA	Royal Garrison Artillery.
RIF	Royal Irish Fusiliers.
RInnF	Royal Inniskilling Fusiliers.
RIC	Royal Irish Constabulary.
RIF	Royal Irish Rifles.
RIR	Royal Irish Regiment.
RSM	Regimental Sergeant Major.
SAA	Small arms ammunition.
Salient	Ground projecting into the area held by the enemy, and therefore subject to fire from the flanks.
Salve	To salvage material left on the battlefield such as guns, wire and grenades.
Sap	Forward listening post.
SSM	Squadron Sergeant Major.
Sub/Subaltern	A junior officer - lieutenant or second lieutenant.
TMB	Trench Mortar Battery.
Trench foot	A condition similar to frostbite, caused by prolonged exposure to cold and damp.
Trench fever	A bacterial infection transmitted by body lice.
Trooper	A cavalry rank equivalent to private. Men serving in the North Irish Horse were often referred to as 'Trooper'. However this was incorrect, as the rank did not apply to the reserve regiments such as the North Irish Horse.
Uhlan	German light cavalry lancer, a term used by British troops to describe any German cavalryman carrying a lance.
Ulster	In this volume the term 'Ulster' refers to the most northern of the four Irish provinces, comprising the nine counties - Antrim, Armagh, Cavan, Donegal, Down, Fermanagh, Londonderry, Monaghan, Tyrone - and the city and county boroughs of Belfast and Londonderry.
UVF	Ulster Volunteer Force.
WO	Warrant Officer - a rank between commissioned officer and NCO.

Sands, Private David : 112, 165

Sands Private Patrick : 112

Scott, Captain Victor Harry : 27, 161

Scott, Major Robert Hamilton : 24, 26, 27, 161,165, 229

Scott, John Mr : 93

Scott, Lieutenant William G. : 93

Scott, Rev. Gordon : 114

Seawright, Lance Corporal Thomas : 110,

Sheridan, Mr James : 174

Sheridan, Mrs Mary : 174

Sheridan, Private James : 174

Sheridan, Private Thomas Joseph : 174

Simmons, John Mr : 92

Simmons, Lieutenant Richard : 92

Simpson, Private William : 132

Simons, Private John : 197

Simons, Mr Thomas : 197

Simpson, Private Samuel : 227

Skiffington, Private Alexander : 243

Slater, Private Thomas : 223

Sloan, Private Thomas : 173

Sloan, Robert : 71,173

Sloan, Staff Sergeant Major Robert : 172, 173

Sloan, Trooper William : 71, 173

Smith, Lance Corporal Samuel : 243

Smith, Private William : 150, 195

Smith, Mr Samuel : 195

Smyth, Captain C. B. F. : 203

Smyth, Captain E. F. : 203

Smyth, Major Robertson Stewart : 203

Smyth, Mr Wm. : 203

Somerville, Private Robert : 152, 243, 244

Stephenson, Private Joseph : 227

Stevenson, Captain Robert : 17, 26, 27, 104, 144,159, 199

Stevenson, Private Albert : 227

Stewart, Private James : 76, 244

Stothers, Private Nathaniel : 224

Strain, Private Henry : 244

Stratton, Private William : 244

Stratton, Private William James : 244

Sugars, Lieutenant Harold Saunderson : 191

Sullivan, Nurse : 52

T

Taylor, Private Robert Thomas : 105, 128, 181, 245

Teague, Mrs Maria : 112

Telford, Private William John : 119

Tohall, Mr Henry : 161

Tohall, Private Patrick : 161

Tolerton, Lieutenant Lee : 171

Toner, Private John : 120

Tottenham, 2nd Lieutenant Arthur Henry : 207, 208

Tottenham, Mr Lowry Cliffe Loftus : 207

Travers, Lieutenant Arthur Stewart : 167

Travers, Colonel Henry : 166

Travers, Major Hugh Price : 166

Troughton, E. Mr: 93

Troughton, Second Lieutenant John Herbert Watson : 93

V

Vallely, Private Joseph : 109

Venables, Nurse Miss : 182

W

Waterworth, Rev. W. : 82

Watson, Mrs : 93

Watson, Rev. John : 167

Watt, Mr Joseph : 195

Watt, Mrs James : 192

Watt, Nurse Sarah : 195, 245

Watt, Private Joseph : 195, 245, 246

Watt, Trooper Alexander : 245

Watt, Trooper William : 195

Weir, Mr John : 204

Weir, Mrs Margaret : 204

Weir, Private Armour : 66

Weir, Private John : 204

White, Private Thomas : 111

Whitley, Mr Eugene : 156

Whitley, Private John : 156

Whittle, Corporal William : 198

Whittle, Mr Robert : 198

Wigton, Private Robert : 196

Wigton, Mr William : 196

Williamson, Mr Andrew : 195

Williamson, David : 17

Williamson, J. Moore : 72, 188

Williamson, Lance Corporal John : 180

Williamson, Lieutenant Davis : 72, 188

Williamson, Private Gervais : 225

Williamson, Private Guy : 227

Williamson, Private Jack : 195, 196

Williamson, Private Thomas : 246

Wilson, Dr T. F. : 92

Wilson, Private Michael : 110

Wilson, Private Robert John : 246, 247

Wilson, Private William J. : 111, 112

Wilson, Rev. George : 93

Wilson, Second Lieutenant Thomas Aiken : 136

Woods, Private James : 205

Wright, Second Lieutenant Matthew John : 247

Y

Young, Private Joseph : 225

Notes

Notes